THE HARLEM RENAISSANCE REMEMBERED

Selected List of Other Books by Arna Bontemps

STORY OF THE NEGRO
WE HAVE TOMORROW
CHARIOT IN THE SKY
GOLDEN SLIPPERS (*Anthology*)
BLACK THUNDER
GOD SENDS SUNDAY
100 YEARS OF NEGRO FREEDOM
AMERICAN NEGRO POETRY (*Anthology*)
FAMOUS NEGRO ATHLETES
HOLD FAST TO DREAMS (*Anthology*)
GREAT SLAVE NARRATIVES (*Anthology*)
FREE AT LAST: *The Life of Frederick Douglass*
YOUNG BOOKER: *Booker T. Washington's Early Days*

With Jack Conroy

THE FAST SOONER HOUND
THEY SEEK A CITY

Edited by Langston Hughes and Arna Bontemps

THE BOOK OF NEGRO FOLKLORE
THE POETRY OF THE NEGRO (1746-1970)

THE HARLEM RENAISSANCE REMEMBERED

ESSAYS EDITED WITH A MEMOIR

BY *Arna Bontemps*

ILLUSTRATED WITH PHOTOGRAPHS

DODD, MEAD & COMPANY : *NEW YORK*

Photographs courtesy of the Yale University Library

Thanks are due to the following for permission to reprint the material indicated: Arno Press for excerpts from *A Long Way From Home,* Arno Press 1969. Harper & Row, Publishers, Inc. for lines of poetry from the following works by Countee Cullen: *Color,* Copyright, 1925 by Harper & Row, Publishers, Inc., renewed, 1953 by Ida M. Cullen; *Copper Sun,* Copyright, 1927 by Harper & Row, Publishers, Inc., renewed, 1955 by Ida M. Cullen; *The Black Christ,* Copyright, 1929 by Harper & Row, Publishers, Inc., renewed, 1957 by Ida M. Cullen; *The Medea,* Copyright, 1935 by Harper & Row, Publishers, Inc., renewed, 1963 by Ida M. Cullen; for excerpts from "Banana Bottom" by Claude McKay, Copyright, 1933 by Harper & Row, Publishers, Inc., renewed, 1961 by Hope McKay Virtue; for excerpts from "Banjo" by Claude McKay, Copyright, 1929 by Harper & Row, Publishers, Inc., renewed, 1957 by Hope McKay Virtue. Frank Horne for excerpts from his poetry. Third World Press for "The Patterns of the Harlem Renaissance," Copyright © 1972 by George E. Kent, reprinted from George E. Kent, *Blackness and the Adventure of Western Culture,* Chicago, 1972. Twayne Publishers, Inc. for excerpts from "Flame-Heart," "The Negro Dance," and "North and South" from *Selected Poems of Claude McKay,* Copyright © 1953 by Bookman Associates. Hope McKay Virtue for excerpts from letters of Claude McKay in the Claude McKay Folder, James Weldon Johnson Memorial Collection, Yale University and excerpts from *My Green Hills of Jamaica* to appear in the forthcoming edition of *The Unpublished Works of Claude McKay.*

ISBN: 0-396-06517-1
Library of Congress Catalog Card Number: 72-723
Printed in the United States of America
by The Cornwall Press, Inc., Cornwall, N. Y.

To Charles S. Johnson and Alain Locke

Contents

Illustrations

CHAPTER 1

The Awakening: A Memoir

ARNA BONTEMPS

The Harlem Renaissance, so called, was publicly recognized in March of 1924. Much that had gone before can now be seen as part of the Awakening, but still another year was to pass before those personally involved could make themselves believe that they were, or had been, a part of something memorable.

What made their decade memorable, of course, was not simply an influx of black migrants from the South and the West Indies in that post-World War I era, as some have concluded. If that had been true, the sociologist Charles S. Johnson, who seemed more profoundly aware of the ferment than anyone else at the time, might better have remained in Chicago or gone to Detroit to put up his antennae. But an upsurge of Negro creativity, such as New York's Harlem was beginning to detect, to produce, and to foster, required more than a single source. It demanded an array of factors, a favorable conjunction.

Nor can the Southern region, that vast everglade of black life and vitality, be credited too much or too directly for the impulse. Neither Countee Cullen nor Langston Hughes, Jean

Toomer nor Claude McKay was born or raised there. Nor were the fiction writers or the second echelon of black poets its products in most cases. But there can be no doubt that there was a happening in black America in those days and that suddenly stars began to fall on a part of Manhattan that white residents had begun abandoning to black newcomers.

It would not be far-fetched to say that a poem by a ghetto boy, appearing in the DeWitt Clinton High School literary magazine in January 1921, was the first clear signal. *The Magpie* had discovered and opened its pages so cordially to young Countee Cullen that he had become its associate editor, as well as a frequent contributor, and the poem he offered in this issue was titled "I Have a Rendezvous with Life (with apologies to Alan Seeger)." Cullen was a senior at DeWitt when this was published and by then actually a more sophisticated poet than these lines indicated, but he was obliged to bow graciously when he detected the tenor of responses that greeted his verse. In fact, he decided to enter it in a contest for high school writers sponsored by a woman's organization. Again the responses fairly took his breath. Here was a brown boy from the depths of black Harlem giving an affirmative answer to the melancholy acceptance of death by a disenchanted American expatriate fighting in a French regiment. The irony of Seeger's being killed in action was no greater than the irony of Cullen's optimism, everything considered, and the latter caught the attention of the daily newspapers, as the former had done earlier. People began quoting Cullen's poem. Teachers read it to their classes. Ministers read it to fashionable congregations. Indeed, everybody except Countee Cullen himself seemed moved by the thought of a black boy, less than prepossessing in personal appearance perhaps, insisting that putting meaning into his life, such as it was, was more urgent than contemplating death.

Cullen's brave, if boyish, proclamation was followed just six months later by the publication in *The Crisis,* the influential and widely read organ of the National Association for the Advancement of Colored People, of a free-verse poem, by another black youth, titled "The Negro Speaks of Rivers." Langston Hughes, its author, had graduated from high school in Cleveland, Ohio, a year earlier, and Hughes later indicated that "Rivers" had been written directly after that event. "Rendezvous" struck New York like a lonesome meteor, burned brightly for a short time, then faded. "Rivers" touched down more like twilight itself. That both were harbingers is now evident, and it is no surprise that when the literary and cultural Awakening won attention three years later, these two poets, though still unpublished in book form, were the new stars that caused the eyes of both black and white intellectuals to blink.

If "one clover and a bee/ and reverie" is all it takes to make a prairie, an observer with the second sight of an Emily Dickinson might similarly surmise that two such teen-agers as Countee and Langston could at least wake up a *renaissance,* given the time and the place.

The two had not known each other before they began to be noticed, but it is interesting that only a few blocks separated them during Hughes's freshman year at Columbia University. In their personalities and backgrounds, as in their attitudes toward life, there was little to suggest the twin roles in which they were about to be cast.

It was well known around the Salem Methodist Episcopal Church in Harlem—"Mother Salem," as it was sometimes called—that the childless pastor and his wife had adopted Countee and given him their name and a home in the fourteen-room parsonage of the church when the boy was about eleven years old. Countee's gratitude to his foster parents never ceased to be a part of his adult personality. His poetry reflected it, even when he became mildly critical of the elder Cullen's fundamentalism. Not even sad or tragic themes deprived his lyrics of thankful overtones.

In contrast to the melancholy beginnings that brightened so abruptly for young Countee, dilemmas clouded Langston Hughes's early years, dilemmas that became more and more difficult as he reached manhood. Blessed with charisma and an instinct for tolerance, he was thwarted by parents who could not bear each other. Loved jealously and possessively by each, his childhood and adolescence, which could otherwise have been enjoyed if not romanticized, were marred by shuttling between an unhappy father prospering in Mexico and an unhappy mother working as a waitress in Ohio. But out of the ordeal had come the pensive interludes in which he conceived "The Negro Speaks of Rivers," as well as another poem, shortly afterward, in which he wrote, "Caesar told me to keep his doorsteps clean. They lynch me today in Texas."

Needless to say, it took longer for ripples from such poems, dropped like pebbles in a sullen pond, to reach the outer edges of black consciousness than for those registered by "I Have a Rendezvous with Life," but this did not yet matter. What mattered was that between the astonished attention drawn to Cullen and Hughes by early writings in 1921 and the occasion at which both were presented (one in absentia) to a cross section of literary opinion in New York in the spring of 1924, other things occurred.

I have the chronology in order because 1921 was the year when, half-hidden near the back of a large freshman English class at a small college in northern California, I peeped over the shoulder of the student in front of me and saw an approving smile on the face of the teacher as he read a paper

I had submitted in response to the current assignment. I was more embarrassed than flattered by the attention it drew, but the teacher's smile lingered, and I came to regard that expression as the semaphore that flagged me toward New York City three years later.

Meanwhile, *Shuffle Along,* an all-black musical comedy, became a smash on Broadway at about the same time Cullen and Hughes were making their initial bows. A happier conjunction could scarcely have been imagined, and the impact of this production, the wide popularity of its songs, the dazzling talent of its performers almost lifted the boy poets off their feet. Both began composing lyrics such as "Shake your brown feet, Liza,/ shake 'em Liza chile," or "To do a naked tribal dance/ each time he hears the rain." Both became stagestruck at this tenderly impressionable time, and neither ever completely recovered. They met and made friends of actors, and many of the musicians, composers, and dancers in the company.

The exuberant music of *Shuffle Along,* including songs such as "I'm Just Wild About Harry," "Love Will Find a Way," and "In Honeysuckle Time," is thought of with more than nostalgia, however, when one remembers the seething American cities torn by race riots in the post-World-War-I years in which it was produced.

Spared these racial convulsions, New York became a locus for what I would regard as a more exciting and perhaps more telling assault on oppression than the dreary blood-in-the-streets strategy of preceding years. *Shuffle Along* was an announcement, an overture to an era of hope. It was running triumphantly near Columbus Circle when Marcus Garvey, in a completely different mood, called an international convention of his Universal Negro Improvement Association to meet in Harlem in August 1921.

Short, squat, beaming with visions, regally attired, the visitor from Jamaica, in a spellbinding West Indian cadence, gave voice to dreams that literally blew the minds of a large segment of his impoverished generation of black humanity in the New World. In all seriousness he "declared" the republic of Africa and designated himself provisional president, while visitors from the West Indies, Africa, Europe, Central America, and Canada jammed Liberty Hall, as his large barnlike building in Harlem was called, and listened with a kind of awe. It had taken him five years to bring this moment about, but the audacity of his effort and this demonstration of power to captivate astonished and almost stunned many intellectuals. Nothing quite comparable had ever occurred before in the New World experience of black people.

If one were looking seriously for a contretemps in New York sufficient to ignite the incandescence of the ensuing years in Harlem, perhaps it could be found somewhere between these events. Both Cullen and Hughes were aroused by the two happenings, but apparently with different results. Happy in his new home and pleased with the personal attention he had received thus far, Cullen determined to make his last semester at DeWitt Clinton his best. Langston Hughes, on the other hand, still troubled by dilemmas, decided at this time to drop out of Columbia University.

The three years which followed, one can now see, were crucial to the careers of each as well as to the afflatus of the Harlem twenties, but neither poet was conspicuous during this interlude. Cullen wrote nothing as arresting as "I Have a Rendezvous with Life," and Hughes sent to *The Crisis* nothing comparable to "The Negro Speaks of Rivers." While these two were temporarily out of sight, however, other relevant events occurred, other poets appeared.

The following year (1922) marked the publication by Harcourt, Brace & Company of Claude McKay's *Harlem Shadows.* This was the first time in about a decade (since Dodd, Mead's publication of Paul Laurence Dunbar's posthumous *Complete Poems*) that a major American publisher had brought out a collection of poems by a Negro. It was the first time in nearly two decades that any such publisher had ventured to offer a book of poems by a living black poet.

I remember it well. I had been a summer school student at UCLA and picked up a copy of the McKay poems in the main public library on the way home. I had not seen a review or heard any mention of the book, but the first sentence of the Introduction made any such announcement unnecessary. "These poems have a special interest for all the races of man," it said, "because they are sung by a pure blooded Negro." Naturally I had to borrow the book that very minute, read it on the yellow Pacific Electric streetcar that day and a second time that night, then begin telling everybody I knew about it.

The responses of black friends were surprising. Nearly all of them stopped to listen. There was no doubt that their blood came to a boil when they heard "If We Must Die." "Harlem Dancer" brought worldly-wise looks from their eyes. McKay's poems of longing for his home island melted them visibly, and I think these responses told me something about black people and poetry that remains true. Certainly it was in my consciousness when I headed for New York two years later.

The year of *Harlem Shadows,* as it happened, was also the year that Jelly Roll Morton was playing in Los Angeles at a public dancehall on North Main Street and then, following the midnight closing hour, bringing his group to Leak's Lake on what is now Imperial Highway but was then Linnwood Road, just beyond the city limits and not covered by the closing ordinance. I saw this arrangement from close up because my cousin, with whom I often stayed when home from college, played with the band at Leak's Lake, and I would go with him and listen closely to the haunting music throughout the night.

I made no immediate association between this provocative new sound and the cadences of Garvey's dream or Claude McKay's nostalgia for his West Indian homeland and the kinship he felt for the blacks he met in Harlem. That was to come later when jazz began to gain respectable acceptance in the so-called temples of entertainment. It had not happened then.

Near that time, possibly in the same year, Garvey came to Los Angeles, still refulgent with éclat from his pontifical declaration of the republic of Africa and the amazed attention it had earned him. I went with my trumpet-playing cousin to Trinity Auditorium in midtown Los Angeles to hear him. He looked just as he had been described and pictured, but I was not prepared for his oddly lyrical style. The audience swayed and was transported. So I was not surprised when it was rumored a few days later that among the believers he had made on this visit was one of the foremost Baptist preachers in the city, whose church was on Naomi Street near Twelfth, the church which certain friends of ours attended, including the father of the boy who was soon to become my brother-in-law. This minister promptly dropped his charge and joined the Garvey entourage. The harvest was ripe, I heard another believer say, and the pudgy spellbinder had come with his sickle to reap.

For my own part, and I think this was the attitude of my associates, I never took Garvey literally. His bleating voice, calling to the "beloved and scattered millions," was to me a far-off poetry, like the lyrics of some spirituals—"Bright

Sparkles in a Church Yard," for example, or "Walk in Jerusalem Just Like John," or "I Looked Over Jordan and What Did I See,/ a Band of Angels Coming After Me," or "Swing Low, Sweet Chariot."

Conjunctions such as these, one might say, began to make a clearer pattern in 1923. In January of that year a young veteran of World War I became the editor of *Opportunity: A Journal of Negro Life,* the expanded organ of the National Urban League. He was Charles S. Johnson, who had won his spurs in the riot-torn Chicago branch of that organization and at the University of Chicago. Most significantly, however, Johnson was a fledgling sociologist with a roving eye.

Which is to say, he promptly detected a relationship between artistic labors and the doctrine of useful, and gainful, employment as built into the aims of the Urban League. While he pondered this notion, two further advances in black self-expression in the United States occurred, and both supported his thesis. One was the publication of the book *Cane* by Jean Toomer, of which Johnson was to say in retrospect:

> Here was triumphantly the Negro artist, detached from propaganda, sensitive only to beauty. Where [Paul Laurence] Dunbar gave to the unnamed Negro peasant a reassuring touch of humanity, Toomer gave to the peasant a passionate charm.

The emergence of so complete a literary talent among Negro youth struck him as "an elaboration of [Booker T.] Washington's principles of stressing work rather than the rewards of work." And this was certainly a fresh interpretation of the aims and purposes of the League.

As if *Cane* were not itself confirmation enough of Johnson's feelings about artistic endeavors and achievements, his first year as editor of *Opportunity* made him a close-up witness to a far more tumultuous one. For 1923 was the year of Roland Hayes's concert debut in the United States. He had sung as a student at Fisk University and in small churches around the country for years before the opportunity to study seriously in Boston presented itself, and this had led to Europe as early as 1920. His sojourn in England and on the Continent for the next three years remained a mystery to those who had heard him earlier when he was barnstorming in the American hinterlands, but by the spring of 1923 surprising tidings began to reach the small sequestered college at which I was a senior. The burden of the report was that the eager young singer some of us had heard in Los Angeles so long ago was doing uncommonly well abroad.

When Roland Hayes appeared first as soloist with the Boston Symphony Orchestra under the direction of Pierre Monteux and soon followed it with the Town Hall concert debut, the popular columnist Heywood Broun was prompted to write, almost breathlessly: "I saw a miracle in Town Hall. Half of the people were black and half were white and while the mood of the song held, they were all the same. They shared together the close silence. One emotion wrapped them. And at the end it was a single sob."

Johnson's magazine took note, but I remained unaware. *Opportunity* was not seen in any of the places where I read in those days. This did not matter. Hayes promptly became a national symbol, if not a legend, the first of his color ever to invade the closed precincts of top-level concert music in this nation. His cross-country tour that year was a succession of triumphs. Charles S. Johnson did not fail to put it all in context. By the following March, 1924, he was ready to make a pragmatic response.

The upsurge of creativity he proposed to celebrate in the pages of *Opportunity* in its second year is indicated in one of his letters. Eagerly awaiting the arrival of a young woman from Minnesota, whose employment as secretary in his office he had been able to arrange, he wrote her a confirming letter on March 24, 1924, in which he observed:

> You could have been of enormous assistance to me this past week when I was arranging for the "debut" of the younger Negro writers. It was a most unusual affair—a dinner meeting at the Civic Club at which all of the younger Negro writers—Cullen, Walter White, Walrond, Jessie Fauset, Gwendolyn Bennett, Alain Locke, M. Gregory, met and chatted with the passing generation—Du Bois, Jas. Weldon Johnson, Georgia Douglas Johnson, etc. and with the literary personages of the city: Carl Van Doren, editor of the *Century,* Frederick Allen of *Harper's,* Walter Bartlett of *Scribner's,* Devere Allen of the *World Tomorrow,* Freda Kirchwey of the *Nation,* Paul Kellogg of the *Survey,* Horace Liveright of Boni, Liveright Publishers etc.—about 100 guests and tremendously impressive speaking. I'll have an account of it in the magazine. It would have given you a first hand introduction to the "last worders" in literature. But principally it served to stimulate a market for the new stuff which these young writers are turning out. The first definite reaction came in the form of an offer of one magazine to devote an entire issue to the similar subjects as treated by representatives of the group. A big plug was bitten off. Now it's a question of living up to the reputation. Yes, I should have added, a stream of manuscripts has started into my office from other aspirants.

It was not until the May issue that Johnson's report of the occasion appeared in *Opportunity,* and in it he added the names of Langston Hughes and Jean Toomer, both of whom were known to some of the dinner guests, and both of whom were out of the country on March 21, the date of the affair at the Civic Club. Johnson was pleased to call the dinner a "coming out party" for an informal group designated as the "Writers' Guild." The roster of its members did not include Toomer, though Horace Liveright, publisher of *Cane,* was there to praise the book and to lament its disappointing sales. Appearing instead among the members of the Writers' Guild were the names of a young library assistant and a college student employed as a page, both associated with the 135th Street Branch of the New York Public Library. Regina Anderson and Harold Jackman are nowhere later referred to as writers in annals of the Harlem Renaissance, but their places among the Harlem group were never questioned. Miss Anderson shared an apartment with Ethel Ray (the secretary to whom Johnson wrote with such ebullience on March 24) after Miss Ray's arrival in New York. And the two young women, both contributing positively to the charm of the era, became involved in still other ways.

Harold Jackman became Countee Cullen's closest friend. They were the David and Jonathan of the Harlem twenties. Cullen dedicated his poem "Heritage" to Jackman and, knowing the two, one imagines that a number of the other Cullen poems might well have carried the same dedication. Moreover, it is the painting of Jackman by Winold Reiss that the famous artist used as the *beau idéal* of the Negro college student in New York at the time of the "upsurge." A reproduction of it in black and white appeared a year later in the special issue of the *Survey Graphic* mentioned by Johnson. A picture of Regina Anderson had already appeared on the cover of an issue of *The Messenger.* The beauty of Ethel Ray was too fair to reveal her true identity in that black-is-beautiful environment.

In the same issue of *Opportunity* in which he reported the Civic Club gathering, the editor printed Carl Van Doren's after-dinner remarks under the caption, "The Younger Generation of Negro Writers."

> I have a genuine faith in the future of imaginative writing among Negroes in the United States. This is not due to any

mere personal interest in the writers of the race whom I happen to know. It is due to a feeling that the Negroes of the country are in a remarkable strategic position with reference to the new literary age which seems to be impending.

Long oppressed and handicapped, they have gathered stores of emotion and are ready to burst forth with a new eloquence once they discover adequate mediums. Being, however, as a race not given to self-destroying bitterness, they will, I think, strike a happy balance between rage and complacency—that balance in which passion and humor are somehow united in the best of all possible amalgams for the creative artist.

The Negroes, it must be remembered, are our oldest American minority. First slavery and then neglect have forced them into a limited channel of existence. Once they find a voice, they will bring a fresh and fierce sense of reality to their vision of human life on this continent, a vision seen from a novel angle by a part of the population which cannot be duped by the bland optimism of the majority.

Nor will their vision, I think, be that solely of drastic censure and dissent, such as might be expected of them in view of all they have endured from majority rule. Richly gifted by nature with distinctive traits, they will be artists while they are being critics. They will look at the same world that the white poets and novelists and dramatists look at, yet, arranging or enjoying it, will keep in their modes of utterance and sympathies, the memories, the rhythms of their ancient stock.

That Negro writers must long continue to be propagandists, I do not deny. The wrongs of their people are too close to them to be overlooked. But it happens that in this case the vulgar forms of propaganda are all unnecessary. The facts about Negroes in the United States are themselves propaganda—devastating and unanswerable. A Negro novelist who tells the simple story of any aspiring colored man or woman will call as with a bugle the minds of all just persons, white or black, to listen to him.

But if the reality of Negro life is itself dramatic, there are of

> course still other elements, particularly the emotional power with which Negroes live—or at least to me seem to live. What American literature decidedly needs at the moment is color, music, gusto, the free expression of gay or desperate moods. If the Negroes are not in a position to contribute these items, I do not know what Americans are.

I have sometimes wished that I had been present to hear his remarks on that occasion, but I didn't arrive till three months after they were reported. In the months following college, not able to find a job in Los Angeles, though I imagined myself modestly prepared, I took the civil service examination and was employed as an extra during the Christmas holidays in 1923. This brief experience became memorable to me in several ways, the most important of which was forcing a close look at my situation as a black college graduate, now twenty-one, in such a place as Los Angeles. After the holidays I found myself included among a small number of the extras retained by the post office. With the work settling down to a slower pace, I began to talk more to the other clerks and to form opinions of the personalities of those around me and the ways in which they had been affected by the situation, particularly the younger blacks like myself. This was their life, their present and their future. In the weeks of learning the *scheme,* as the distribution chart was called, I secretly decided that it could not be mine.

Unable to sleep well in the daytime after working at night, I began reading with a kind of frenzy. When I had worked my way through the neighborhood public library, I took on the main library—novels, poems, dramas, histories, biographies, whatever.

I also wrote, and before long I was venturing to send poems I had written to a few magazines. No results followed, of course, which I can well understand now as I look at what I showed them, but then I noticed something in *The Crisis* which seemed to invite contributions by young blacks. So I promptly picked out one of the rejected poems and mailed it. When Jessie Fauset answered, saying they were pleased and would use it, I couldn't hide my delight and mentioned it to my cousin, who was working beside me, and he couldn't keep it secret either. The word went around the post office.

This proved to be enough to bring out another revelation among the night clerks: I was not the only Negro in the office who was writing, keeping it to himself, and who had received encouraging news from New York. Nor was it long before someone put the two reports together and arranged to introduce to each other the two new employees who had caused all the gossip.

Wallace Thurman was not as new in the post office as I was. Moreover, like nearly everybody else I knew in those days, he seemed somewhat older than I. He was certainly more knowledgeable about current writing and more "worldly wise," as the adult generation of that time might have put it. His letter from *American* magazine, as he explained it, and mine from the vastly less prestigious *The Crisis* gave us something to talk about, but soon thereafter he disclosed that his had been a false alarm. The editors, he said, had expressed "interest" and asked for changes in his story. He had allowed his hopes to rise like rockets. Now the editors were saying that whatever it was that interested them on first reading had been lost in his rewriting. The black publication, however, the organ of the NAACP, made good on its promise to me, and by July I had (a) received a copy of the August issue, which carried my poem, (b) resigned my job in the post office, and (c) packed my suitcase and bought a ticket to New York City.

En route I spent a day in Chicago and tried to find some

cousins said to have been with the jazz vanguard from New Orleans. My father had lost track of these children of his older brothers, and I was unsuccessful in my efforts to find the young woman married to the jazzman known as Kid Ory or the string man named Willie who had played with first one then another of the bands down home. The part of Chicago I saw on my layover that day included the apartment complex now remembered as "The Mecca" and the area around 35th and State Streets and Wabash and Prairie Avenues.

Stopping in Washington, D.C., the next day, my luck improved. A girl in Los Angeles had made me promise to call her former classmate there, and the result was an afternoon in which I saw the government buildings with a pretty girl guide, climbed the Washington Monument with her, and recognized a young man with a horn on a decorated truck with other musicians. A few years earlier the young man with the horn had lived with his parents in our neighborhood in California and was remembered mainly for the shrillness of the trumpet on which he practiced. The next time I was to see him he had become a member of young Duke Ellington's first band. After this pleasant day in Washington I felt ready for whatever lay ahead in Harlem.

I came up out of the subway at 125th Street and Lenox Avenue and stood blinking in the sun. I didn't know anyone in New York, and the person to whom I had a letter of introduction had moved, or at least was not home. But I was in a mood to expect kindness from strangers, especially middle-aged black preachers and their high-styled dowager-type wives; and in the case of the newly arrived couple who rented me a room I was not disappointed. They offered to adopt me. Obviously that was long before the dread depression of the 1930s changed the hearts of gentle people. Before the day was over, I was back on the street, exploring the scene and trying to find the public library.

When I located it and applied for a borrower's card, the girl at the desk looked at my name and showed surprise. Then she went to a shelf, got the current issue of *The Crisis,* and asked me if I was the person responsible for the poem she had just read. Her surprise, she said, was that she had assumed that all names ending with *a* are women's names. I told her that I didn't choose mine, and I hoped she wouldn't hold it against me. Apparently she didn't. A few weeks later I took her to a party. I might have forgotten about it had I not seen the incident recalled in the biography of Countee Cullen. The girl didn't tell me she was Countee's cousin, but I now understand why she saw to it that I promptly became acquainted with his poetry.

Two poems by him accomplished this and at the same time made me acquainted with *Opportunity: A Journal of Negro Life* in which they appeared, and which I was seeing for the first time. "Brown Boy to Brown Girl" sounded to me like the voice of my own experience. I was enchanted. On second thought, however, I was deeply humiliated to realize how far behind I was in the kind of self-expression which in the past had given me courage and solace when I needed them. Nevertheless I went to my room and wrote something and sent it to the same magazine. Soon it was published. So I tried again and sent them

> We are not come to wage a strife
> With swords upon this hill.
> It is not wise to waste the life
> Against a stubborn will.
> Yet would we die as some have done:
> Beating a way for the rising sun.

A young man who said he read *Opportunity* regularly told me he had been a classmate of Cullen's at DeWitt Clinton High School and asked if I would let him take me over to meet his former classmate. So we walked to the parsonage and rang the bell. When the door opened, a natty middle-aged man paused a second, then threw up his hands in surprise and shouted up the stairs, "Countee! Countee! Come down. Mr. Hughes is here."

When the younger Cullen appeared, the fellow who had brought me found it necessary to explain first who *he* was, for fear Countee would not remember. Countee did, but vaguely, I thought, and so did the young man, because after introducing me he politely excused himself, saying he was on his way to work.

Reverend Cullen was still standing by when Countee cleared up the basic confusion. They had heard that Langston Hughes was back in town after seafaring and sojourning abroad, and the foster father had mistaken me for him. Hughes and I did look somewhat alike at that time, Countee thought, but the Cullens had not expected him, in any case, and they remained as cordial as if I had been the romantic wanderer.

Presently Countee was telling me that John Keats was his god and Edna St. Vincent Millay his goddess. Having entered his house under mistaken identity, I felt, I hurried away and returned to the library. That evening I began reading poets scarcely mentioned in my own college years. A few days later Cullen called to say he had been invited and asked to extend the invitation to me to attend a small gathering at which the authentic Langston Hughes was expected. By this time the weather had changed, and I remember shivering as we walked to an apartment building on Edgecombe Avenue a few blocks above 135th Street. The charming hostesses turned out to be the not entirely unfamiliar Regina Anderson and Ethel Ray. Nor were all of the guests unfamiliar. Jessie Fauset remembered writing to me in California and using the poem in August. Charles S. Johnson complimented "The Daybreakers" and introduced his wife, Marie. Alain Locke overheard and added that he wished to use it in his *The New Negro,* then on the press—if and when there should be a second printing. Countee Cullen then introduced me to Eric Walrond, a young West Indian short-story writer from whom much was expected. To a hopeful newcomer, just beginning to feel comfortable in Harlem, the atmosphere was already heady, but the appearance of Langston Hughes, wearing a plaid mackinaw, smiling shyly, galvanized it. He was the honored guest, and indications were that his fan club was already forming. Some of the most enduring of his poems had been printed in *The Crisis* in his absence, but clearly he had little knowledge of their impact. Disposing of the amenities with ease and apparent pleasure, he was drawn into a chair and asked what he had been doing and writing while away. He mentioned the agonies of beachcombing in Italy but spoke more cheerfully of his employment as a dishwasher in the Grand Duc nightclub in Paris, and began reading from his notebook the sea pieces of his voyages and the jazz poems he had written, inspired by the black American musicians who entertained in Paris. He concluded with "The Weary Blues."

Thinking about that evening from this distance, I can't help contrasting it with the fictional highjinks contrived by Wallace Thurman, for example, a decade later and attributed to the Harlem literary youth of the "New Negro" enclave. Thurman had arrived a year afterward but never became closely associated with those who gathered at this time to welcome the wandering poet who had caught their fancy.

The Johnsons left early, as I recall, because they lived in Flushing and may have had babies at home, but before they left Johnson spoke of his aim to conduct a literary contest through *Opportunity*. He had found a donor, and substantial prizes would be awarded in the fields of poetry, short stories, essays, and one-act plays. The contest would be open to Negroes anywhere in the nation and would be judged by panels of the most respected pundits. He was terribly excited about the plan, and meeting Langston and listening to some of his most recent poems only intensified his feeling.

Among those who lingered were a couple of young men who clearly had eyes for the hostesses and may have intended to help with the dishes. Some of us left with Langston and walked him to the 135th Street YMCA, where he was stopping. His mackinaw was not warm enough for nights like that, he observed, but we forgot the cold when first one and then another recalled the poem by him that they liked best. Cullen named the "Song for a Suicide's Note," which I had missed, and Langston promised to send me a copy when he reached his mother's new home in Washington, D.C. He did not forget to keep the promise, and this initiated early in 1925 a correspondence that continued uninterrupted until the week he went to the hospital for the last time in 1967.

Something also came, where I was concerned, of Charles S. Johnson's projected literary contests. I knew I had nothing in my own small collection that could have been competitive, so I didn't enter that year. When the contest was repeated a second and a third and a fourth time, however, I took my courage in my hands, and my life has never been the same since. The *Opportunity* contests, with their Awards dinners, their distinguished guests, their renowned judges, and the news coverage marked milestones in the careers of Langston Hughes, Zora Neale Hurston, Dorothy West, John P. Davis,

Loren Miller, Allison Davis, Arthur Huff Fauset, and ever so many others. Seeing the attention these contests drew, no doubt, *The Crisis* decided to revive the similar contests they had previously conducted with much less significant responses. This time some of us who had been *Opportunity* winners were personally urged to compete, and not all of us were disappointed.

Hughes's "The Weary Blues" caught many eyes when it won and promptly became the title poem for his first book of poetry, and he was launched on a professional writing career that neither dismal times, witch hunts, nor ordinary adversities were able to stymie. Cullen's first book, *Color,* had preceded *The Weary Blues* by a few months, thanks largely, no doubt, to the impression he made at the March dinner at the Civic Club and to the publication of his poems in major American magazines in the following months. Together the two poets became twin stars of the black Awakening in literature.

Among those who attended the Awards banquets and were properly impressed was one who had the prophetic insight to make himself an unofficial keeper of the records for the "New Negro" phenomenon. Fortunately, in his case, he was white and had the means to make sure the documentation did not get scattered. Moreover he had an ulterior purpose, which sometimes helps when one is pursuing a labor of love. Carl Van Vechten, as he once confessed to me, had always liked Negroes. He was already deeply fond of James Weldon Johnson, and he became enchanted by Langston Hughes and Zora Neale Hurston when he met them at the first *Opportunity* dinner (banquet), and his friendship for all three (as well as for a good many other blacks) became lifelong. His immediate as well as ulterior reason for keeping every scrap of their works he could put his hands on was that he had conceived the revolutionary idea of writing a novel about the ferment in the arts he now saw bubbling out of Harlem.

He was in no sense a novice carried away by a sudden brainstorm. Van Vechten's *Peter Whiffle* and his *Blind Bow Boy* had both been uncommonly successful. *The Tattooed Countess* was the latest. His place among America's smartest, naughtiest, and most skillful novelists and essayists was already secure. In the wake of these sophisticated writings his well-announced purpose was to treat the meanderings of an aspiring black writer in what might be described as the underworld of the arts. In the same year in which Langston Hughes's *The Weary Blues* was published (with an introduction by Carl Van Vechten), Van Vechten's own *Nigger Heaven* came out like a thunderclap.

Obviously neither author had been influenced by the other. Hughes had not read either of Van Vechten's earlier novels at the time his own early poems were written or submitted. Van Vechten's hero in *Nigger Heaven* might have been, as some thought, a reflection of Eric Walrond's literary questing, but in appearance the fictional black writer had been given the spit-and-image of Harold Jackman. Black readers in Harlem sometimes felt they could identify prototypes of the secondary figures in the story, but this was only the beginning of discomfiture. Benjamin Brawley, author of *The Negro Genius,* spoke for a rising tide of resentment when he wrote that *Nigger Heaven* was "the perfect illustration of a book that gives the facts but that does not tell the truth."

The question had to do with the proper way in which to present black people and the black experience in literature. The debate that ensued was intense, sometimes almost acrimonious. It divided the tight ranks of black leadership by putting W. E. B. Du Bois and Charles W. Chesnutt on the side with Brawley, and James Weldon Johnson and Charles

S. Johnson with the opposition. Meanwhile, in 1926, Langston Hughes made this statement on behalf of the writers in Harlem with whom he had begun to rub elbows:

> We younger Negro artists who create now intend to express our individual dark skinned selves without fear or shame. If white people are pleased we are glad. If they are not, it doesn't matter. We know we are beautiful. And ugly too. The tom-tom cries and the tom-tom laughs. If colored people are pleased we are glad. If they are not, their displeasure doesn't matter either. We build our temples for tomorrow, strong as we know how, and we stand on the top of the mountain free from within ourselves.

He had himself received some patronage from a benefactor who identified herself as "godmother" when she wrote, but he knew very little about her except that she seemed gracious and gentle and had a history of assisting budding artists, especially when they happen to be American Indians, Mexicans, and now Negroes. He terminated the "godmother-protégé" relationship abruptly, however, when she made it clear that she expected him to be guided in his writing by her philosophy.

Not all the younger artists who had been offered encouragement in the form of financial aid as the Renaissance reached this point renounced it immediately, but I felt the Hughes statement represented a consensus.

In addition to being the year of *Nigger Heaven, The Weary Blues,* and the Langston Hughes "manifesto"—and the agonizing debate among blacks as to the image they would accept of themselves in literature—1926 was also the year in which I received a personal letter from Dr. W. E. B. Du Bois and answered it in this way on October 23:

> Of course I am overjoyed and very much excited over the good news of your letter. This is my second prize this year. But

this is the only one I had courage enough to hope for. The reason was that I sort of liked the Nocturne myself—as compared with my other attempts. Indeed I shall be at the International House Monday night. Could I know the time? I shall try to find the place—I have never been there.

Many, many thanks to you and to the "perfect" judges.

Very sincerely yours,

In a postscript I enclosed the following:

You ask for a photograph and biographical facts. Here are the facts. . . . I am a Californian, born in Louisiana and living in New York City. I went to the California schools until I had earned a B.A., stayed at home a year waiting for my twenty-first birthday, then came East. In New York I have been teaching and studying a bit on the side.

My first published poem appeared in *The Crisis* of August, 1924. This year has been a rather good one for me: two poetry prizes and a wife.

This is all I can think of. I have decided not to attempt an autobiography soon.

Nigger Heaven remained for months on best-seller lists, and while this continued Harlem was discovered by the local, national, and international smart set. They came in droves, as we sometimes say, from Park Avenue as well as from abroad, and from remote parts of this country. And, significantly, this influx brought on phase two of the Harlem Renaissance, the phase in which the travail of the young black artists caught the attention of more mature, more "professional" whites and became an exotic vogue with the cognoscenti. Witness the effects of jazz on American popular music and dance, the national rage of the Charleston (first introduced by blacks in *Runnin' Wild* in 1924), and a growing stream of highly popular books about blacks by white authors, books not always appreciated or regarded by the blacks as "telling the truth," now updated by them to "telling it like it is," but clearly telling it like throngs of readers wanted to hear it.

The dramatization of DuBose Heyward's *Porgy* in 1927 was representative of this phase, while the impulse that Charles S. Johnson had sought to promote in 1924 held steady. The *Opportunity* contest and Awards banquet was still an inspiring event, and again I attended with pleasure. In 1927, too, the "passing generation," which Johnson appeared to have regarded as passé in 1924, asserted its continued vitality. This was the year of James Weldon Johnson's *God's Trombones* and of the reissuing of the same author's *Autobiography of an Ex-Coloured Man,* this time by a major New York publisher. The Awakening, in short, had begun to look back and discover its own deeper roots, to see itself in a widening context.

When Claude McKay's first novel, *Home to Harlem,* was published with considerable fanfare in 1928, the *Nigger Heaven* audience was ready to receive it with joy, but the Brawley–Du Bois supporters became even more vituperative. As a black author, as a sensitive poet who knew as much about oppression as anyone could, they felt, he should not have done it. McKay returned to the United States after the Renaissance was over and replied to this chastisement.

By the time of the *Home to Harlem* outburst, I was writing a novel of my own, and in the year of the stock market crash I discovered that publishers were not ready or were in no mood for a first novel with autobiographical overtones about a sensitive black boy in a nostalgic setting. At least three of the editors who turned it down, however, went out of their way to praise one of the minor characters in the story and to hint that more about him might be what they would like. Pondering their leads only as long as it took to get my hands on a typewriter, I responded with *God Sends Sunday.*

Du Bois did not fail to express pained displeasure—in much the same terms as my own upright father used when he read it—and I, in my exhilaration, was convinced that neither quite understood. When the Writers' Guild, the same group that had itself been honored by Charles S. Johnson and his Urban League staff at the Civic Club, gave me a glittering reception in Harlem on the publication of *God Sends Sunday,* I couldn't help thinking of legendary people of antiquity pleasuring themselves and celebrating as their cities were about to be destroyed. Within another year I was far away and writing short stories such as "A Summer Tragedy," most of them never published, and brooding over a subject matter so depressing that I could find no relief until it resolved itself as *Black Thunder.*

The golden days were gone. Or was it just the bloom of youth that had been lost?

CHAPTER 2

Patterns of the Harlem Renaissance

GEORGE E. KENT

The single unifying concept which places the achievement of the Harlem Renaissance in focus is that it moved to gain authority in its portrayal of black life by the attempt to assert, with varying degrees of radicality, a dissociation of sensibility from that enforced by American culture and its institutions. As will be seen, the achievement of the writers was the breaking of ground, which left the soil in a much more receptive condition for future tillers. It did not, however, achieve the radical dissociation of sensibility (a dissociation at the roots) which many of today's black writers are attempting to assert.

By the term sensibility I mean the writer's means of sensing, apprehending, his characteristic emotional, psychic, and intellectual response to existence. We may say, for example, that Paul Laurence Dunbar, writing at the turn of the century, retained in his sensibility too much of the nostalgic glow for the lost plantation days, exploited and conferred by such white writers as Thomas Nelson Page and Joel Chandler Harris, to get at the deeper levels of the complexity, density, and variety of the black life of his time. There were, of course, practical problems which reinforced the exercise of such a sensibility: the expectations of a white audience, who largely provided the cash (although Dunbar's celebrations of the simple delights of black life were enjoyed by a rather sizable black audience); and the expectations of publishers of magazines and books.

On the positive side, Dunbar, while narrowing the black folk tradition to largely the idyllic, infused his poetry with a flowing music and a humanity not available from the white writers. Since blacks are so often portrayed as conferring hatred upon each other, it should also be mentioned that Dunbar is not often surpassed in reflecting the joy that blacks frequently experience in being with each other.

For the Harlem Renaissance, a Dunbar is thus both a precursor, a fact seldom mentioned, and a sensibility against which to revolt. His poetry influenced the early Langston Hughes, and his single novel to focus upon blacks, *The Sport of the Gods,* a novel with settings both on the plantation and in New York City, influenced the portrayal of city life during the Renaissance.

There are other important precursors, whose sensibilities and works mark out, sometimes by contrast and sometimes by certain similarities, the paths of revolt and engagement that Harlem Renaissance writers reflect. Charles Waddell Chesnutt had strongly reflected definitions from black folk traditions, one of the important resources of the Renaissance, in such works as *The Conjure Woman* (1899), and certain stories in the collection *The Wife of His Youth and Other Stories* (1899). To a lesser degree of effectiveness, Chesnutt handles sharp insights from folk tradition in his novels—the most memorable gestures and characters have it as their source, despite the rituals warmly endorsing the whiteness of several mulatto characters. I would simply point out here that he worked in a tight framework that allowed his racial identity to go, for a while, unnoticed. Within this framework he was able to do several things: produce "Baxter's Procrustes," a short story that shows complete mastery of the form; make more use of the folk's supernaturalist and conjure tradition in *The Conjure Woman* than has since been made of it; and make an effective use of "fooling massa" folk tradition in such a hilarious short story as "The Passing of Grandison."

The area which Chesnutt presents for revolt is the devices of his framework, which for a brief period were myths of whiteness that appeared in his novels, the exalted position that he gave to the white narrator and his wife in *The Conjure Woman,* and his tendency to associate culture mainly with his light-skinned characters.

Because of its concentration upon the working out of the principle that character is fate, its low-key presentation of racial propaganda, and its varied portraits of black life, James Weldon Johnson's *The Autobiography of an Ex-Coloured Man* is usually greatly emphasized as a precursor of the Renaissance. It also gives a more penetrating rendering of the psychology of the mulatto who decides to pass than Chesnutt usually afforded. On the negative side, what students quickly notice is that the hero, who is not forced into a knowledge of racial identity until late in childhood, never becomes black in any psychological or inescapable sense, and the title, *Ex-Coloured Man,* is therefore misleading.

Seldom mentioned as a precursor to the Renaissance is W. E. B. Du Bois's *The Souls of Black Folks* (1903), although the book had more impact upon aspiring young blacks than any other single work. Langston Hughes mentions its inspiration—as does Claude McKay. Several of its essays represent a concern with folk, folk music, and the grim struggle of soul that usually turned out to be its own and only reward.

Du Bois was later to define the limits of its sensibility—one which asserted confidence in moral suasion, reason, the individual's triumph in mastering culture, the possibility of insuring a nobler American racial life through the joint efforts of a black and white aristocracy. His grim, intractable facts often contradict the viability of his sensibility in *The Souls of Black Folks,* and he was later to feel that the book would have profited by absorption of Marx's description of the impact of economic motive upon the lives of men, and Freud's understanding of the unconscious and the operation of sex within the psyche.

It will be seen so far that powerful personalities and areas of distinctive achievement were preparing the way for a Renaissance in which blacks would attempt to move with a more secure possession of self. It is necessary now to record some nonliterary events whose ferment helped to produce a black consciousness of sufficient magnitude to support the turn in the road which Harlem Renaissance writers were engaged in making.

By 1910 the NAACP had been established, with Du Bois as director of publicity and editor of *The Crisis,* a magazine which was to provide a conservative, but fighting, nationalism and a mass-circulation forum for black writers of the 1920s. In the following year the National Urban League came into being, and in 1923 its organ, *Opportunity,* was established to provide an outlet for black writers. Besides representing organizational growth, these groups thus afforded what earlier black writers could not depend upon: outlets sympathetic to their bent and aims.

From 1916 to 1919 the great migration of Southern blacks to Northern urban areas was in progress. By 1918, one million blacks were estimated to have left the South, although the North and West in public census showed a net gain of only

333,000. World War I, of course, and the country's closing of the doors to immigrants, made for a labor demand which Northern industry attempted to fill by persuading and encouraging black Southerners to emigrate, an act made easier of fulfillment because of injustice in Southern courts, lynchings, discrimination, a severe labor depression in 1914 and 1915, which brought wages down to seventy-five cents per day and less, and 1915 floods, which left thousands homeless.

The Pennsylvania Railroad alone brought 12,000 to work on its tracks—all but 2000 from Georgia and Florida. Nearly 27,000 blacks found jobs in shipbuilding, 75,000 in coal mines, 300,000 on railroads. Other industries represent large figures. One additional dramatic change is represented in the fact that 21,547 black women were employed in 75 different tasks in typical industrial plants.

Then World War I provided a large number of black men with an experience abroad in which they seemed, for the first time, to be respected simply as men, when white Americans weren't busy corrupting the minds of the French.

The period had its built-in devices for disillusionment. Few black workers were accepted in labor unions. The end of World War I saw extraordinary violence inflicted upon blacks, as whites became uneasy as to how blacks were going to adjust to postwar "normalcy." Thus, in what is known as the red summer of 1919, race riots occurred in twenty-five cities—North, South, East, and West. Some of the cities: Washington, D.C.; Chicago; Knoxville, Tennessee; Omaha, Nebraska; Tulsa, Oklahoma; and Elaine, Arkansas. During the first year of post-World War I, whites lynched seventy blacks—ten of the group being soldiers still in uniform. Fourteen blacks were publicly burned—eleven while still alive.

There were, of course, other discouraging matters that were helping to re-form the consciousness of a people into one against which a black writer could test his own. This formation was itself a positive thing. As Alain Locke, a chief mentor of the Renaissance, has pointed out, blacks heretofore had common problems without a common consciousness.

This consciousness was to acquire further substance through the coming forth of a West Indian nationalist, Marcus Garvey, who was to build a huge mass movement which would give to the ordinary black man greater psychological security in his sense of selfhood and a strong feeling of identity. Asserting that racial prejudice was endemic to a white man's civilization and that appeals for justice were therefore futile, advocating the establishment of a black state, pride in all things black, self-help, racial purity, separatism, and confidence in a glorious African past, Marcus Garvey claimed a black following that numbered in the millions. He also collected millions of dollars, built institutions for his programs, and posed a threat internationally before he was cut down and deported by the United States government, under dubious procedures. His impact on blacks and the Renaissance was strong, even where poets merely wrote literary versions of an African homeland.

A new assertiveness was abroad. In the riots, more than ever before, the shedding of black blood cost the shedding of white blood. The NAACP had begun to accumulate a string of landmark victories in the courts and to emerge as powerful propagandist and national lobbyist. Out of the greater freedom space provided by the North and the foregoing experiences came the tensions mingling in consciousness, which provided both disillusionment and greater hope—and the birth of the black Renaissance.

From white writers came important contributions that widened the area of public acceptance of portrayals of black life. The American public had seen black life as worthy of literary consideration mainly in terms of buffoonery, pathos, or malicious stupidity. The lens was that of minstrel tradition.

Here three white playwrights made a powerful impact. Ridgley Torrence, who felt that black life might produce some of the powerful drama in the world, gave serious treatment to it in three plays that were produced with such black actors as Opal Cooper, Blanche Deas, and Inez Clough. The landmark plays were *Granny Maumee, Simon the Cyrenian,* and *The Rider of Dreams.*

In 1919 from Eugene O'Neill came *The Dreamy Kid,* a gangster play, and *The Emperor Jones,* in which both Charles Gilpin and Paul Robeson, at different times, played the title role. O'Neill followed these two plays with a tragedy of interracial marriage, *All God's Chillun Got Wings.*

Paul Green contributed important folk plays, the most outstanding of which was *In Abraham's Bosom,* involving the tragic aspirations of a Southern mulatto and featuring such black actors as Julius Bledsoe, Rose McClendon, and Abbie Mitchell. Although the plays hardly gave satisfactory treatment to black lives, they did approach them with a new seriousness and sometimes through a tragic vision.

The playwrights helped to increase the acceptance of serious black actors, but of course had little effect in opening the stage to black playwrights, a problem which the Harlem Renaissance did not solve.

In the general American context, it should also be mentioned that the post-World War I period represented a resumption of a questioning attitude on the part of white writers, a desire for release from a constricting respectability that promoted an interest in the exotic and in primitivism, and some serious interest in social and labor problems as evinced by the studies of Frank Tannenbaum and others. Sinclair Lewis's *Main Street* appeared in 1920 and *Babbitt* in

1925. Then there was Theodore Dreiser's *An American Tragedy* in 1925, and other works representative of the Roaring Twenties and the quest of whites for the primitive, a quest which helped to unlock doors of prestigious publishing houses to black writers who had formerly found the doors locked, barred, and bolted.

The foregoing formed the setting and commingling tensions that buzzed in what is known as the Harlem Renaissance. We may now have a general look at some personalities before focusing upon specific authors and issues. As we move into the discussion it will be good to keep in mind that we are entering a period in which all the arts, not merely the literary, bloomed, although this essay is confined to a consideration of literary issues.

II

The array of personalities in the literary area is startling. Few were born in New York, although we speak of a Harlem Renaissance. Claude McKay, one of the movement's ornaments, was born in Jamaica, Eric Walrond, short-story writer, in British Guiana. Others, such as Langston Hughes and Arna Bontemps, represent Kansas and Louisiana and California.

Most bore credentials of a talented tenth, though some were able to allow the credentials to hang very loose. The older shepherds, mentors, and sometime contributors brought both formal credentials and a cosmopolitanism that few Americans could match. W. E. B. Du Bois, scholar, and editor of *The Crisis,* reflected an old-time Yankee New England upbringing, a Fisk-Harvard American education, with a Ph.D. as his terminal degree, and study in European universities. By the time of the Renaissance, he was already a scholar and intellectual leader of world stature.

Alain Locke, who was to provide brilliant criticism and interpretation: Harvard Ph.D. and Rhodes Scholar, a most cosmopolitan man.

Charles S. Johnson, editor of *Opportunity:* educational background—the University of Chicago; eventually a distinguished scholar in the social sciences and President of Fisk University.

James Weldon Johnson, product of a cultivated family and Atlanta University, a composer, novelist, poet, educator, diplomat. Again, a most cosmopolitan man.

In the younger group, there was also the evidence of considerable formal education, and cosmopolitan experience through travel and varied cultural contacts. Claude McKay derived from a very British-oriented school system and further study at Tuskegee and Kansas State University. It should be added of course that McKay had an across-the-board contact with both the masses and advanced political and literary circles, as reflected in his autobiography, *A Long Way From Home.*

Langston Hughes, who perhaps had the greatest range of contact with the masses and all manner of men, was eventually a graduate of Lincoln University. Both Hughes and McKay had lived the lives they sang of in their songs. But McKay's apartness is always clearly evident, and his role as the cultivated bohemian and radical is carried with a flourish. Hughes seems easily to exemplify a natural identification with the masses, to be a sort of born "everyman." But it is also to be noted that a reading of his autobiographies, *The Big Sea* and *I Wonder As I Wander,* does not exactly unlock the privacy of his soul.

Rudolph Fisher, B.A. and M.A., Brown University, M.D., Howard University, specialist in roentgenology, exemplified in his novels and short stories a very intimate and sophisticated contact with the range of blacks and whites of the period.

Perhaps a greater rigidity of class background is exemplified by Jean Toomer, a product of the University of Wisconsin, with further study at City College, New York; and by Jessie Fauset, the novelist devoted to the more secure group of blacks, who was a graduate of Cornell, with further study in France. However, Toomer's *Cane* reveals both the exiled narrator and a considerable grasp of a broad range of black characters. Certainly, in *Cane,* his own difference from his characters seems to provide just the right tension for insight, although it may also be a source of excessive poeticizing.

Now one can continue to run down college degrees and special cultivation with a large number of the stars of the Renaissance: Fenton Johnson, Arna Bontemps, Frank Horne, and especially Countee Cullen—Cullen because the symbols of middle-class respectability do seem awesome and controlling, from the elaborate religious background through such matters as the New York University–Harvard education and his social-register marriage to W. E. B. Du Bois's daughter. The marriage, as described by Blanche Ferguson in *Countee Cullen and the Negro Renaissance,* seems a special kind of flight from reality.

But my point is not a simple putdown of Renaissance figures as "bourgeois," lacking relevance to the people whose struggles and qualities they were to portray. I am simply trying to get into one basket the sense of variety of tensions modifiable by highly individual personalities.

On the positive side, their status gave them a certain psychological poise—a perspective from which they could not easily be overawed by definitions of black realities provided by American and Western culture. As blacks active during the 1920s their education would not automatically separate them from other blacks. Indeed, the 1920s provided still a solid racial boxing-in that required that if a black was to get away from other blacks, he would have to work at it, make a special job of it. Despite W. E. B. Du Bois's famous reticence, a study of his range of contact with backwoods blacks at certain periods of his life would probably reveal some very startling statistics.

The heavyweight middle-class symbols do have their negative side. It comes quickly into focus if a couple of the more absolute principles which Ralph Ellison was espousing in the 1940s are applied: the black writer, if he is to be effective, must move his own consciousness beyond the furthermost reach of bourgeois consciousness; and techniques must be both a reflection and instrument of consciousness. Ellison seems to mean that one must achieve a freedom from the mythologies which inform the vision of the white middle class if one is to see fully the contours of the black image, and that technique must be equal to the complexity of one's awareness.

Now I have already suggested that many Harlem Renaissance writers brought to their task a cosmopolitanism and a wide range of experience that protected them from the simplest myopia of a middle-class perspective. By looking at individuals, we can see to some extent the degree to which artistic freedom resulted, and we should add to the writers' trump cards their recourse to bohemianism.

Claude McKay, for example, struck the first powerful Renaissance notes. In 1919 he published the famous sonnet "If We Must Die" in *The Liberator,* the magazine of bohemian radicalism. The sonnet, a call to blacks to meet violence with violence, evidenced a new ease with poetic form, a newly achieved psychological freedom, and McKay's ability to bend traditional forms to his purpose. Further, he was aware of the sonnet's social and other traditions. Evident in poems in

Harlem Shadows (1922) and subsequent poetry was a sensibility freer than that of most Harlem Renaissance writers, one that could flash forth an absolute sense of manhood and celebrate or defy with tenderness or a blazing anger. In major fictional works, such as *Home to Harlem* (1928), *Banjo* (1929), and *Banana Bottom* (1933), he showed a grasp of the big picture of black life and an extensive range of contact.

Still, as with other brilliant writers of the Renaissance, one feels a potential greatness that is not quite achieved. His poetry, including "If We Must Die," which according to his autobiography, *A Long Way From Home,* moved his fellow dining-car workers to tears, remains splendid beauties in a medium-sized room. Though he deals with ordinary black life, the center of his poems is really their speaker of cultivated sensibility—a natural aristocrat. The fiction celebrates the vitality and beauty of blacks, but McKay raises questions of national significance only to resolve them by sentimental endings that do not really resolve. The form of soul is frequently bohemianism.

I would suggest that McKay was unable to achieve sufficient freedom from his early British-oriented education, that his bohemianism permeated his radicalism, and that a sense of individual apartness left him open to one of the more neutralizing forms of middle-class reaches—romantic individualism. Such handicaps were a barricade between him and ultimate realization of his potential, despite his additional armor of socialism and radical politics.

Jean Toomer, whose *Cane* (1923) is a group of narratives and poetry that continues to amaze people, allows us to say little more than that the book itself bears the mark of greatness. But following it, Toomer abandoned blacks as a literary subject. From biographical reports and his own autobiographical comment, it is clear that he was very much moved by the range of philosophical possibility in the idea of identity. In *Cane* his Southern rural characters retain a kind of wholeness and richness of soul, although there is no viable avenue for the soul's fulfillment. His more northward-situated characters suffer from attenuation of soul under the impact of modern industrialism and respectability. His subject is the thwarted fulfillment of the soul.

Toomer may have represented the kind of racial consciousness that for a brief interval is most intense precisely because it is about to disappear. We should perhaps be thankful that he rendered this intensity with such great artistic power before he gave up his racial identity—or merged it, as he would have seen the situation.

Cane is a storehouse of contemporary techniques. Perhaps one vestige of Toomer's middle-classness, however, is the distance of the narrator from several of the characters. But it can hardly be said to block him from a sense of their beauty.

Langston Hughes, whose poetry in *The Weary Blues* (1926) and *Fine Clothes to the Jew* (1927) displays a talent that had great impact, reflects in his autobiographies, *The Big Sea* and *I Wonder As I Wander,* a well-worked-out grasp of his task and times. In 1926, in the famous manifesto "The Negro Artist and the Racial Mountain" he attacked the tendency of middle-class blacks to suppress their black selves and heritage in an uncritical embrace of whiteness, and announced his commitment to the low-down blacks in whom the richness of the black soul remained uncorrupted.

His images of the low-down blacks in his manifesto are oversaturated with romantic bohemianism and do not really get at the workaday world in which most blacks were embattled. But they do show a move away from middle-class consciousness. It was a good first step, and Hughes was to continue to grow. Arthur P. Davis, in his essay "The Harlem of Langston Hughes' Poetry," included in Gross and Hardy's *Images of the Negro in American Literature,* has traced a shift of focus from uncritical celebrations of black vitality and joy to confrontations with the grimmer aspects of black life, from which a deep spiritual beauty emerges.

Hughes backed up his revolt by considerable experimentation with forms derived from black folk culture and adapted in the modern city. The forms themselves contain stances toward existence, and their value for the self-conscious writer is not in their quaintness but in their *forms of response to existence* and their spiritual beauty and other implications. Thus he invested his poetry with the inner spirit of the blues, spirituals, folk ballads, and gospel songs. From a deceptive simplicity arise powerful suggestions concerning the variety and complexity of the black experience. He, of course, did extraordinary work in other forms.

But what I'm trying to suggest is that he was sufficiently involved through the folk forms in an alternative to white- or black-middle-class consciousness to gain an elaborate sense of black life.

Hughes is one of the lasting fruits of the Renaissance, and we forget that a movement is finally measured by a few men who persist and realize its potentialities. Hughes's complexity is even more difficult to suggest in a few lines than that of Claude McKay. He gave folk and cultural tradition a greater rendering power than it had had before in self-conscious literature. His use of blues form and jazz rhythms was the major innovation in black poetry of the Harlem Renaissance, and his alliance with free verse provided him with the benefit of a form known for flexibility and freedom from rigid implications and limitations of the more restricted verse. Hughes has cumulative impact, and if read with a sure sense of the implications of folk culture in mind, reveals discoveries not yet domesticated by the public. To illustrate: his novel *Not Without Laughter,* though flawed, attempts to embody, separately and then combined, the blues and spirituals traditions; and his short play *Soul Gone Home* reaches into religious and supernaturalist sources.

Hughes's main limitation is that, for whatever reason, he remained too close to the folk forms and did not take the liberty to force upon them as much signification as they could be made to bear.

Countee Cullen's lyric gift is well recognized, and the prevailing dictum is that his poems involved with race are probably his best, although he did not want to be judged as a Negro poet. Although one seldom feels that Cullen has arrived at a point of unfamiliar ground in the official black middle-class perspective by which he was surrounded, his gift was that he could say things in a music that was beyond pre-1920s achievement. He suffers, of course, by placing himself within the shadow of Keats. But one has conveyed from his first volume of poetry, *Color* (1925), a skill with traditional forms that he did not lose, even if he did not seem to attain much of the continued growth that was expected. On the negative side, Cullen's cultivated speaker in his poems seems to provide too little variation in modulations for the situations he described.

"Heritage," his most famous poem, for example, asks "What is Africa to me?" and gives a run-down of standard public images of Africa and finally a criticism of the necessity to worship a white god; but the speaker's highly cultivated tones, as beautiful as they are, do *not* convey a sense of the grittiness of the situation. One must locate the poem's conflict in a cultivated speaker's feeling of alienation, and not with any specifics concerning a real Africa. As Stephen Bronz points out in *The Roots of Negro Racial Conscious-*

ness, Cullen's preoccupation with beauty is rendered largely through sound and color.

For the rest of the Renaissance, Cullen was to continue publishing poems that represent fine expression, without going beyond his earlier work and without meeting sterner tests provided by his master, John Keats: concreteness and economy deeply communicating the tension of a tragic vision.

In the novel *One Way to Heaven* (1932) Cullen provides delightful satire on religion and black-upper-class pretensions, although it is apparent today that he knew some of his key characters only well enough to provide a middle level of seriousness. He had the possibilities of a great novel developing through the characters of Sam, his wife, Mattie, and his wife's mother. They are powerful figures of black tradition: Sam, as the religious trickster and rounder; his wife as an uneasy container of black religious tensions; the mother as one who is able to combine them with a direct confrontation with the vitality of life.

However, Cullen needed to be able to analyze both Sam and his wife at great depths; instead he gives us types, a procedure that works well with his upper-class characters, toward whom his attitude is consistently satirical. But he invites the reader to a journey of discovery, in the case of the lower-class characters, and then cuts short the journey.

Bronz and others have seen Cullen as violating his principle of showing only the more pleasant and respectable sides of black life. But the unsavory aspects are so well distanced and the respectable, though satirized, so much at the foreground, that such a judgment does not seem serious.

Cullen thus represents the triumph of the middle-class consciousness. And his fineness must be enjoyed within it. He brings us to other writers usually immediately placed within the ultrarespectable group: Jessie Fauset, Nella Larsen, and

Georgia Douglas Johnson, along with such older persisting writers as Du Bois and James Weldon Johnson and Walter White.

Ironically, they suggest, as Cullen does not, that very significant distinctions and certain revisions of judgment may occur as we restudy them. Fauset, Larsen, and Walter White, the famous head (at the time of his death) of the NAACP, are frequently placed in a category labeled "themes of upper-class respectability and passing across the color line," with "propaganda" further defining Walter White's *The Fire in the Flint.* However, Fauset deserves restudy for her concern with character and reflection of a class. A rereading of Nella Larsen today suggests, despite the fact that her novels *Quicksand* and *Passing* deal with some light-skinned characters who pass for white, that the author's real interest was to test the characters of blacks whose cultural circumstances provided a high level of choices. Larsen also, in *Quicksand,* used, effectively and unsentimentally, sharp contrasting pictures from folk tradition.

I am not sure that under restudy her stature would increase beyond that given to her by Robert Bone in *The Negro Novel in America,* but some valuable light on the Renaissance may be shed by a more accurate adequate critical description of her intentions. Certainly one regrets that she did not write more novels and senses that she had a complexity of awareness that might have produced great works. Her work suggests that she had taken more than passing notice of Henry James and Edith Wharton.

As to Walter White, one might refer to the description of his handling the passing-for-white theme given in Sterling Brown *et al., The Negro Caravan,* which suggests White's intimate rendering of the subject and the variety of his portraiture. Georgia Douglas Johnson, who wrote mainly conventional but competent lyrics about a woman's life, could be more concretely engaged and described. W. E. B. Du Bois, who in *The Silver Fleece* (1910) wrote with a rather challenging depth of social reference, labors as a creative writer under the shadow of himself as scholar and propagandist. His criticism in *The Crisis* of the 1920s does give evidence of viewing literature as uplift instrument, but other critical comments by him would hardly seem so easily categorized. Du Bois does not hesitate to be propagandistic as evidenced by his Renaissance novel *Dark Princess.* But a study which carefully sorted out his varied tensions and took into consideration imaginative works that do not fall within simple genre categories would give us a more confident estimate of his literary stature. He was hardly a man to be contained by simple categories.

James Weldon Johnson's brilliant creative achievement for the Renaissance resides in the volume of seven folk sermons rendered in poetry without heavy reliance upon dialect, and in the reissuance of his pre-Renaissance novel, *The Autobiography of an Ex-Coloured Man,* which gained more attention during the Renaissance than it had attracted before. Johnson's cosmopolitanism always extended his reach and his grasp. The sermons are beautiful still. We would do well however to study the sermons in comparison with actual folk sermons, in order to give stronger authority to our critical judgment, since the obligation of the self-conscious writer is to carry us to a different sort of awareness than that provided by the folk. The folk form, that is, should increase the distinction of the new thing that the self-conscious writer makes out of it. An outstanding example of its potentiality is Ellison's use of the True Blood narrative in *Invisible Man.*

We will have to return briefly to James Weldon Johnson as critic, after looking at a few individuals who are not easily attachable to preceding groups. Eric Walrond in *Tropic Death* (1926), a series of short stories on Caribbean life, reveals an ability to get inside black life and render it through sharply etched images and a dialect that carries voice tones.

Rudolph Fisher, who had the lightest touch of all the Renaissance writers, managed an intermingling of kindly satire and bittersweet tensions in his fiction. Although he is well known for his novels, *The Walls of Jericho* (1928), which presents a cross section of black life, and *The Conjure Man Dies* (1932), in which he begins a black tradition of the detective story, it is in such short stories as "Miss Cynthie," "The City of Refuge," and "High Yaller" that he achieves a tight form that renders some of the plight of the newly arrived Southern migrant and the tensions of color caste. In such a novel as *The Walls of Jericho* we have good fun and pictures of life that grow serious, but are held in check by a middle-class sense of hearty good will, exemplified by an author expert at pulling strings.

The short stories approach the stark threats of life in the destruction of the idealistic Southern migrant in "The City of Refuge" and the hard choices forced by the tensions of color caste in "High Yaller." Once again one feels onself in the presence of a writer of potential greatness. Unfortunately, Fisher died at the age of thirty-seven, so it cannot fairly be said where his talents would have led him. During his brief life, he gave us pictures of the ordinary workaday black who was largely neglected by other Renaissance writers.

Wallace Thurman, who is perhaps most famous for his bitter satire of the Renaissance in the novel *Infants of the Spring* (1932), deserves some reexamination for potentiality of his novel *The Blacker the Berry,* whose heroine, Emma Lou, fights the battle of intraracial color prejudice. Although his novel halts, rather than ends, it deserves greater credit for character analysis than it has been given. His play *Harlem* and his short story "Cordelia the Crude," which appeared in the brief-lived magazine *Fire,* also give some pictures of Harlem which other writers usually ignored. In the November 1970 issue of *Black World,* Dorothy West in her memoir "Elephant's Dance" portrays him as a gifted person whose unresolved personal tensions fed a fatal bohemianism. Thurman died of tuberculosis and dissipation at the age of thirty-two.

The above writers, with perhaps the addition of George S. Schuyler, the Menckenite satirist in his novel *Black No More,* will represent main patterns of the Renaissance. A fuller picture is gained by recognition of authors who established their rights to ground during the Renaissance, but reached the highest point of their careers afterward. This achievement usually meant that they were adaptable to tensions of succeeding periods, such as the Great Depression and its aftermath.

Thus Arna Bontemps, whose published work during the Renaissance included a substantial group of poems in Countee Cullen's *Caroling Dusk* and elsewhere, went on to produce more poetry, outstanding novels, including pioneer work in the historical novel, and to become the distinguished man of letters whom we are aware of today.

Zora Neale Hurston published short stories that reflected a close engagement with folk tradition, but her distinguished novels and brilliant book-length folklore studies were to come later. She still awaits the thoroughgoing critical analysis that will properly place her in the pattern of American fiction.

Sterling Brown was to demonstrate his sophisticated grasp of folk tradition, as well as other traditions, in *Southern Road* (1932), and was to make his mark as a distinguished critic. Like Zora Neale Hurston, he is yet to receive the critical attention that he deserves. It is also shocking that *Southern Road,* which goes beyond Renaissance preoccupations to concern itself with tensions of the 1930s and deeper notes of black life, has not yet been reprinted.

The Harlem Renaissance was particularly fortunate in two powerful critics, who also have not yet been systematically assessed: James Weldon Johnson and Alain Locke. Both possessed something much beyond a parochial enthusiasm and cosmopolitan sensitivity, and were able to make incisive judgment.

Johnson's contributions are particularly noteworthy in the prefaces to his two-volume collection of spirituals, *The Book of American Negro Spirituals* (1925) and *The Second Book of Negro Spirituals* (1926). His brilliant anthology, *The Book of American Negro Poetry,* also contains in its preface and headnotes extremely important criticism concerning the limitations of dialect poetry (1921, revised 1931), and his *Black Manhattan* (1930) is a very important source book for the study of black drama.

Alain Locke, best known for the brilliant anthology *The New Negro* (1925), despite his essentially middle-class sensibility and somewhat simplistic integrationist orientation, reflected a critical and cultural sensitivity that has not been surpassed. It is difficult to imagine the Renaissance without his services, critical and otherwise. Perhaps it should be said that he, in a stream of books and articles, expressed the most rounded view of black culture.

Both men tended to express an excessive optimism, but neither lacked the sharp, incisive phrase.

What, finally, does the Harlem Renaissance add up to in terms of achievement?

We must, in order to weigh its outcomes properly, acknowledge two facts: today it bears the burden of heavy critical strictures; and these strictures are, to some degree, an acknowledgment of its role as the father of many children whose features are likely to be looked upon suspiciously by the offspring.

But its negative criticism arose during its own time and included participants in the movement. Alain Locke, its chief mentor, was eventually to see it as insufficiently socially conscious. Claude McKay was to repudiate his earlier fiction as he turned to Catholicism, and to describe the Renaissance as concerned more with racial uplift, superficial white acceptance, superficial values, than representing its own people or becoming something for them.

Langston Hughes, in *The Big Sea,* was to see the movement as a time when fun was to be had by all, but also as a rebirth whose good news the ordinary black never heard of—and would not have had much time for anyway.

Then there was the bitter satire of its bohemianism, hustling, and confusion by Wallace Thurman in *Infants of the Spring.*

Allison Davis, today a famous sociologist, and Sterling Brown saw as serious limitations of the movement its failure to dramatize the deeper qualities recognizable in ordinary black people: fortitude, courage, and endurance.

Ralph Ellison has pointed out that it represented an ironic picture: a literature that was still a bawling infant choosing decadence as its model for expression—a judgment that is part of the charge that it swung open all doors to entry by whites questing for the exotic and the primitive. In this ritual white Carl Van Vechten, through his novel *Nigger Heaven,* frequently is seen as a subverter of the fiction into the paths of blatant sexuality and sensationalism.

Harold Cruse, in *Crisis of the Negro Intellectual,* saw it as lacking a true forum for hammering out a common platform or a salon for promoting intellectual excitement. In place of the cultivated and devoted woman of the arts, such as Mabel Dodge could be for whites in Greenwich Village, the Renaissance had A'Lelia Walker, a vital black woman who inherited a fortune from the hair-straightening enterprises of her mother. In her great parties, good eating, good drinking, and good publishing contacts in an area too tightly packed with people to provide overall group communion seem to have been the main advantages.

And today's young writers, while conceding that the Renaissance left them a foundation, look askance at its failure to build lasting institutions and truly to address itself to a black audience.

Certainly a good deal of the movement is placed in perspective when we realize that while the Marcus Garvey nationalist movement and the blues were allowed to make injections, they seemed to remain for most Renaissance writers superficial diversions, bastard brothers and sisters, lovable even in certain ways, but not eligible for Sunday company or a real dining-room kind of intimacy.

It must be admitted that all charges are supportable, in varying degrees, but that some seem more applicable to a part of the Renaissance than to the whole. As a single example, Ellison's charge of decadence is more applicable to certain novels and stories than to poetry. What is needed is a very exhaustive study of all forces operating within the period, so that properly weighted judgment and completely accurate descriptions can be provided.

Meanwhile, we must acknowledge several accomplishments that were fundamental.

Certainly no genre of literature went without substantial development. The short story in the hands of Toomer, Eric Walrond, and Langston Hughes became a much more flexible form for that moment of illumination of black life. The novel, while not freed from the episodic structure or audible spasms in plot movement, provided memorable analyses that occasionally stopped just short of greatness. And the drama, while sneaking only occasionally through barricades to Broadway prominence, as in the cases of Hall Johnson's *Run Little Children* and Wallace Thurman's *Harlem,* made progress in little-theater and folk drama not known before, and the minstrel tradition was mortally wounded.

Although the loss of white patronage resulting from the stock market crash critically wounded the movement, it produced writers who were to persist and whose consciousness was to become an essential metaphor for black realities of subsequent periods as they remained open to new tensions.

What we can see today, after all charges have been recorded, is that the Renaissance made paths through what had been stubborn thickets. It put muscles on nonliterary institutions, such as newspapers, the Urban League, the NAACP, labor leadership, which, however we may now categorize them idealogically, were to become powerful weightlifters. From a literary point of view, it made a strategic turn at the forks of the road.

As I said at the begining, its dissociation of sensibility from constraining definitions enforced by white-middle-class culture, though not radical, was essential, was a stronger grasp of the black selfhood which W. E. B. Du Bois had described as under threat from the black's double consciousness: the consciousness enforcing white definitions upon him; and the part that desired a full embrace of the universe.

If today we can sometimes jog, rather than puff, down the road toward self-definition, it would seem that the Harlem Renaissance was a father who should not go without thanks or reverence.

CHAPTER 3

Jean Toomer: As Modern Man

LARRY E. THOMPSON

Jean Toomer was born on December 26, 1894, in Washington, D.C., of old New Orleans Creole stock. His maternal grandfather, P. B. S. Pinchback, had been acting governor of Louisiana during Reconstruction. Toomer attended Paul Laurence Dunbar High School in Washington, then studied law at the University of Wisconsin and later at City College of New York. There he abandoned law for literature and soon became an avant-garde poet and short-story writer, contributing to such magazines as *Broom, Secession, Double Dealer, Dial,* and *Little Review.*

In 1923 he published his only novel, *Cane,* a book that was lauded in reviews but received little attention from the general public. And in that same year, Toomer came under the influence of the mystic Georges Ivanovitch Gurdjieff, who advocated "a system . . . by which one sought to attain through instruction and discipline new levels of experience, beginning with the difficult first step to self-consciousness and progressing to world and possibly cosmic-consciousness." Gurdjieff had such an impact on Toomer that a year later he went to Fontainebleau, France, to study under the mystic. When he returned to the United States he set up schools in a number of cities, including New York and Chicago.

His fascination with this psychology of self and mankind led him to conduct an experiment with eight unmarried friends (male and female) in group living in Portage, Wisconsin, in 1931. This experiment led directly to his marriage a year later to one of the participants, Marjory Latimer. She died, a year later, bearing their only child. Soon afterward Toomer was married again, to Marjorie Content, and disappeared from the literary scene to Quaker Country in Bucks County, Pennsylvania. He died in 1967, a broken man, whose talents as a writer were never fully developed.

Why did a writer of Toomer's ability suddenly up and leave, tossing into the wind the possibility of a great writing career? Here is a man who was described by Langston Hughes as "one of the most talented of the Negro writers," during the early twenties and as "a poet" by Waldo Frank. Saunders Redding, speaking of *Cane,* said in his book, *To Make A Poet Black:*

> . . . his (Toomer's) moods are hot, colorful, primitive, but more akin to the naive hysteria of the spirituals than to the sophisticated savagery of jazz and the blues.

In *Men Seen,* Paul Rosenfeld, also referring to *Cane,* said:

> Toomer's free gift has given him the vision of a parting soul, and lifted his voice in salutation to the folk-spirit of the Negro South. He comes like a son returned in bare time to take a living farewell of a dying parent.

Clifford Mason tries to deal with this problem by speaking of Toomer's alleged duality: ". . . there was the Jean Toomer of legend who went around turbaned, bouncing from Russian mystic encampments to Quaker retreats, from one white wife to a second. And then there was the inner man who denounced in early youth his 'no darker than a paper bag,' Washington, D.C., high-yaller pedigree . . ." I disagree with this idea of duality in Toomer, and in his own words this idea of black and white clashing in his inner soul is laid to rest:

> My position in America has been a curious one. I have lived equally amid the two race groups. Now white, now colored. From my point of view I am naturally and inevitably an American.

No, the answer does not lie in Toomer's duality, it lies in his quest for singularity—in his concept of himself and man in the universe. In a book titled *Essentials,* published in a private edition in 1931, Toomer put forth his philosophy of life in a series of aphorisms and maxims that dealt with the whole spectrum of human relationships, from sex and education to religion and individualism. Toomer argues that we are beings of "actualities and potentialities" which make us one in a general sense but individual also since the "actualities and potentialities" are different for everyone. But he goes on to say that modern man is losing his perception of himself:

> Modern man is losing his sense of potentiality as regards himself. Hence he is losing his sense of himself and reality.

This loss of individuality has resulted in two things: 1) a loss in initiative and a desire to conform, and 2) the growth of material values. He says:

> The desire to be has become the desire to belong
> we can belong to things, not to ourselves.

and

> We apply to machines what we do not apply to ourselves.

I said earlier that Toomer's quest was for singularity in himself and in mankind—not conformity but individuality. He wanted to be free of all the restrictions of modern society, for according to Toomer "acceptance of prevailing standards often means we have no standards of our own." Therefore he rejected racial, regional, and sexual restrictions:

> I am of no particular race. I am of the human race, a man at large in the human world preparing a new race.
>
> I am of no specific region. I am of earth.
>
> I am of no special field. I am of the field of being.

To Toomer individuality meant freedom and the power to control one's destiny. In a poem published in *Dial* in 1929, titled "White Arrow," he expresses this belief:

> Your force is greater than your use of it existing, yet you dream that breath depends on bonds I once contracted for. It is a false belief induced by sleep and fear in faith and reason you were swift and free, white arrow, as you were, awake and be.

This journey into self—this quest to find one's place in the cosmos—began to form early in Toomer. In an unpublished autobiography, *Earth-Being,* the title itself suggestive of his conception of himself, he speaks of how he first began to form opinions of himself in the universe. He says that because of his Uncle Bismarck he began to think about his position in the cosmos, "it was all wonderful. And, young though I was, I was growing a sense and forming an attitude towards my and our [all of humanity] position on earth in the universe." Toomer lucidly explains his position in that world and his function, which he claims is to be a soothsayer: "I see myself as one of countless millions of human beings. I also see some fraction of these others. I aim, then, to give a picture and critique of all life as I see it." When he talks about writing and how he perceives of himself as a writer, this image of prophet comes clearly through, "as for writing . . . I am an essentialist. Or, to put it in other words, I am a spiritualizer, a poetic realist."

This image of himself as "poet realist" or prophet helps to explain why his art is often proselytizing and why Toomer was to some degree a modern-ancient. Perhaps the best way to take a look at Toomer, the man, is to review his literature, beginning with his plays.

The fact that Jean Toomer wrote plays is a little known fact, but a very important one, for it points out a central problem in the man—the need to find different ways of communicating his ideas and beliefs to the general public. Therefore in his plays he was experimenting with forms long before anyone else. In 1922 when Toomer wrote his first play, the sound of the revolution that was to begin in the American theater was a faint whisper. O'Neill had written *The Emperor Jones* in 1920 and *The Hairy Ape* in 1922, but the plays of George Kaufman, Marc Connelly, E. E. Cummings, and John Dos Passos were still a few years in the future. Toomer was the first American playwright who was trying to do some experimentation with, as Darwin Turner says, "dramatic form and technique in order to blend social satire with lyric expression of modern man's quest for spiritual self-realization."

This can be seen clearly in Toomer's first play, *Natalie Mann*. In this play he argues passionately for the sexual and spiritual release of the middle-class black woman and by symbolic representation the sexual and spiritual freedom of all women. The core of the play is built around Nathan Merilh, a modern-day Jesus Christ, who to my mind turns out to be a voodoo priest, and his attempt to save the soul of

Natalie from the confines of middle-class values. She lives with him in New York, defying convention. She finally reaches total self-realization when he sacrifices himself and does a ritual voodoo dance which separates "individual identity from national or social origins," saving her soul.

Toomer's philosophy is built upon a feeling of the black man's natural closeness to the soil—nature (probably because he knows black folks have been prevented from entering the mainstream of society)—a theme we shall see again in the first half of *Cane.*

The black man is therefore spiritually freer and happier than the white man. In *The Sacred Factory,* he points out the mundane existence of the working class as well as the middle class with their assorted illnesses of emotional and sexual frustrations, all caused by their dependence on the machine. He again uses the ritual dance, this time having his characters dance around in circles with slow, sluggish movements, to bring home his theme—the spiritual death of a people.

There is no need to deal with Toomer's third play, *Kabnis,* at this time, since it will be dealt with in the section on *Cane.* Suffice it to say, as Turner has, "*Kabnis* is a spectacle of futility and impotence."

In all his plays Toomer uses dramatic techniques and experiments to better get across his theme. Darwin Turner, in his article "The Failure of a Playwright," speaks of Toomer's use of language, "there is an artificiality [in Toomer's use of language] that is used to reflect the dullness of superficiality of the guardians of middle-class morals." Each character in Toomer's work is representative of a human type rather than a unique individual; this shows his concern with mankind—the society rather than the person. He uses dance as "the rhythmic means by which characters release themselves from inhibiting forces," as well as to show their enslavement to society's morals.

His career as a playwright was unsuccessful probably because society was not ready for his themes and experimentations.

Cane
Oracular.
Redolent of fermenting syrup,
Purple of the dusk
Deep-rooted Cane

Her skin is like dusk on the eastern horizon
O cant you see it, O cant you see it,
Her skin is like dusk on the eastern horizon
. . . When the sun goes down.

This is the beautiful Karintha. Doomed to a fate she cannot control, she becomes pregnant because of the impatience of young and old men. "God grant us youth, secretly prayed the old men. The young fellows counted the time to pass before she would be old enough to mate with them." Bearing her fatherless child, she buries it in a sawdust pile and takes out her hate of men by selling her body: ". . . men do not know that the soul of her was a growing thing ripened too soon. They will bring their money; they will die not having found it out . . . " Karintha is doomed to a tyranny of body.

> Becky was the white woman who had two Negro sons. She's dead; they've gone away. The pines whisper to Jesus. The Bible flaps its leaves with an aimless rustle on her mound.

"Becky" is the story of a conspiracy to hide what took place under pine trees on moonless nights: miscegenation. The townspeople, black and white, try to deny Becky's existence.

"When the first was born, the white folks said they'd have no more to do with her. And black folks . . ." When the second is born, Becky is regarded as dead: "Becky has another son . . . but nothing was said . . . if there was a Becky . . . Becky now was dead." Becky is symbolically killed by the chimney on the house that the town built for her, thus easing their guilt.

"Fern," born of a Jewish father and black mother, is again a study of miscegenation. Fern is a picture of sterility and pain: ". . . if you have heard a Jewish Cantor sing, if he has touched you and made your own sorrow seen trivial when compared with his, you will know my feeling when I followed the curves of her profile, like mobile rivers, to their common delta." Fern, like Karintha, is destroyed by the greatest tyrant of all—sex. "Men were everlastingly bringing her their bodies." And like Karintha, her soul perished under the onslaught of human pleasures.

Red Nigger Moon. Sinner!
Blood-burning moon. Sinner!
Come out of that fact'ry door.

In "Blood-Burning Moon," Toomer shows another form of oppression of black people. Like the preceding stories, its driving force is sex. Louisa, the heroine, has two lovers, one black, one white, whose sexual rivalry is built upon a foundation of racial antagonism. The issue of who has the right to the black woman is not solved by the two men fighting, but by the white lynch mob. Toomer, in this story, successfully captures the essential injustice of a society which claims to be civilized, yet denies those humanistic values which make a society civilized to certain of its members.

The second part of *Cane* shifts from the rural South to the urban North, and in particular, to Washington, D.C.

Money burns the pocket, pocket hurts,
Bootleggers in silken shirts,
Ballooned, zooming Cadillacs
Whizzing, whizzing down the street-car tracks.

"Seventh Street" is the place where black people from the Southland, straight out of the cotton fields, put life into the dull life of Washington, "a crude-boned, soft-skinned wedge of nigger life breathing its leafer air, jazz songs and love, thrusting unconscious rhythms, black reddish blood into white and whitewashed wood of Washington." In Toomer's world, black folks, people used to working with their hands, people close to the soil—the cane—represent not only the "full life" but the only life. And white folks, people living in an urban environment, people out of communication with the soil, represent a monstrous farce of that life. Therefore civilization, by imposing upon us a number of meaningless bourgeois values, denies to the human soul the only thing which makes us human, the ability to empathize with one another.

"Rhobert" is therefore an attack on the value of private ownership of property—an essential Western value. The central metaphor of the story is Rhobert trying to carry a house on his head. Of course it is a losing struggle and the harder he tries the deeper he sinks into the mud of civilization:

Brother, Rhobert is sinking
Lets open our throats, brother,
Lets sing Deep River when he goes down.

"Box Seat" is the one story in which the central theme of *Cane*—the essential goodness of man being buried by houses, machines, nightclubs, newspapers, and anything else which represents modern society, that goodness being man's sense of brotherhood born out of toil with the soil and constant battle with nature—is best presented. The hero is a Christ-like figure named Dan Moore: "I am Dan Moore. I was born in a canefield. The hands of Jesus touched me. I am come to a sick world to heal it." Dan doesn't walk on water but he is from the underground, the soil, and he (the soil-canefield) will be the only saving grace for this world.

The central metaphor is the Box Seat, symbolic of the bourgeois values Muriel, the heroine of the story, carries within her soul. The seat Muriel occupies is at a vaudeville show where the main event is two dwarfs fighting for the "heavy-weight championship," again symbolic of the kind of farce of life that is called living in American civilization. The two dwarfs viciously beat each other, and at the end of the fight, the winner presents a blood-covered rose to Muriel, who recoils in horror. The dwarf pleads with her to take it, through his eyes.

Do not shrink. Do not be afraid of me
Jesus
See how my eyes look at you
the Son of God
I too was made in His image
Was once
I give you the rose.

As Muriel finally accepts the rose from the dwarf, Dan shouts: JESUS WAS ONCE A LEPER! And runs out of the theater, finally understanding the hypocrisy of civilization and the futility of trying to save it.

In *Kabnis* our journey is completed; we return again to the red soil of Georgia. Kabnis, the hero of the story, a Georgia schoolteacher from the North, is deathly afraid to confront his black Georgia tradition, preferring to hide behind his books. But like most men who try to hide, his tradition—his past—confronts him:

Night winds in Georgia are vagrant poets whispering. Kabnis, against his will, lets his book slip down, and listens to them. The warm whiteness of his bed, the lamp-light, do not protect him from the weird chill of their song:

White-man's land.
Niggers, sing.
Burn, bear black children
Till poor rivers bring
Rest, and sweet glory
In Camp Ground.

Kabnis is full of self-hatred, not only for the South but for himself as well. Moreover, he is consumed by an overwhelming fear of the land, "whose touch would resurrect him." He is contrasted with Lewis, another Christ figure, whose only function in the story is to make other characters aware of their moral deficiency. Lewis is the one who confronts Kabnis on his fear of the land: "Can't hold them, can you? Master; slave. Soil; and the overarching heavens."

Halsey, unlike Kabnis, whose manhood has been taken from him in his fear of the South, and Lewis, who has grown in his confrontation with it, has grown into Southern life and has also been destroyed by it. He belongs to the society, Kabnis doesn't, but in order to survive he has denied his manhood by not fighting the insults and indignities of black Southern life.

Father John is the symbolic connection with the ancestral past. A former slave, he lives in a basement that looks like the hole in a slave ship. Through him, Lewis and Halsey's little sister, Carrie Kate, become one with their past. But Father John cannot be the guide for Carrie Kate and the rest. Toomer himself says, "It is well to remember that the past, having meaning, cannot serve as an objective for contemporary man." Therefore, when he finally does speak, his words mean nothing. However, Kabnis in his total denial of the old man can only sink into the quicksand of self-hate.

Jean Toomer in this small book has captured the beauty and the ugliness, the power and the weakness, the "triumph and the tragedy" of life in the United States. *Cane* is a masterpiece in modern literature. It is a chronicle of Toomer's search as writer, as man, as modern man trying to find himself and consequently, peace. "I am what I am and what I may become I am trying to find out." Therefore he experimented with literary form, mixing poetry, prose, and dramatic form in his work. He used techniques such as ritualization, repetition, and understatement to give his work a poetic quality and a honey-sweet tone that pulls us into this small book to glimpse the world through the eyes of Jean Toomer.

CHAPTER 4

Under the Harlem Shadow: A Study of Jessie Fauset and Nella Larsen

HIROKO SATO

Jessie Fauset

In 1892, when the first novel by a black writer after the Civil War came out, the author, Mrs. Frances Ellen Watkins Harper, added the humble statement at the end of the novel, *Iola Leroy, or Shadows Uplifted:*

> From threads of fact and fiction I have woven a story whose mission will not be in vain if it awakens in the hearts of our countrymen a stronger sense of justice and a more Christian humanity in behalf of those whom the fortunes of war threw homeless, ignorant and poor, upon a threshold of a new era. Nor will it be in vain if it inspires the children of those upon whose brows God has poured the chrism of the new era to determine that they will embrace every opportunity, develop every faculty, and use every power God has given them to rise in the scale of character and condition, and to add their quota of good citizenship to the best welfare of the nation. There are scattered among us materials for mournful tragedies and mirth-provoking comedies, which some hand may yet bring

> into literature of the country, glowing with the fervor of the tropics and enriched by the luxuriance of the Orient, and thus add to the solution of our unsolved American problem.
>
> The race has not had very long to straighten its hand from the hoe, to grasp the pen and wield it as a power for good, and to erect above the ruined auction block and slave pen institutions of learning. . . . [1]

Thirty-five years later, young artists like Langston Hughes, Zora Neale Hurston, Gwendolyn Bennett, Aaron Douglas, and Wallace Thurman got together and published a magazine, *Fire 11*. In the "Foreword" of the magazine they wrote:

> FIRE. . .weaving vivid, hot design upon an ebon bordered loom and satisfying pagan thirst for beauty unadorned. . .the flesh is sweet and real. . .the soul and inward flush of fire. . . . Beauty? . . .flesh on fire—on fire in the furnace of life blazing. . .[2]

What had happened between the timid and humble statement of Mrs. Harper and the bold declaration of the young artists was the explosion of the black energy called the Harlem Renaissance.

It might be difficult to determine when the Harlem Renaissance really started. Langston Hughes says:

> It began with *Shuffle Along, Running Wild* and the Charleston. Perhaps some people would say even with *The Emperor Jones*, Charles Gilpin, and tom-toms at Provincetown. But certainly it was the musical review, *Shuffle Along*, that gave a scintillating send-off to that Negro vogue in Manhattan, which reached its peak just before the crash of 1929. . . .[3]

As for the literature concerned, nobody could dispute that the publication of Jean Toomer's *Cane* in 1923 marked the beginning of the new era. William Stanley Braithwaite comments on the book: "*Cane* is a book of gold and bronze, of dusk and flame, of ecstasy and pain, and Jean Toomer is a bright morning star of a new day of the Race in literature." [4] The appearance of the book was an event of national consequence. Toomer's desire to know something about himself led him to probe the significance of the South and of his being black. Perhaps Toomer's book is one of the embodiments of Alain Locke's statement that "the deep feeling of race is at present the main-spring of Negro life." [5] With Toomer, other young artists like Langston Hughes, Countee Cullen, and Claude McKay wrote poems full of wrath at the injustice toward their race, yet full of glorification of the beauty of the black people.

Of course, this flowering of the black arts did not come as suddenly as it seemed. The war and the great migration of the black people to Northern cities had something to do with it. Also "he [Negro] has seen the breaking up and melting down of old ideas and conventions and he is determined to have a hand in moulding this new thing." [6] In a way, the Harlem Renaissance and the literature of the so-called Lost Generation came from the same social situation—the breaking down of the old ideals and sense of value. Those young artists, black and white alike, widened their world into that of physical sensations. Also, while the whites exiled themselves to Europe and looked back toward their homeland and tried to find its meaning, the blacks turned their eyes to Africa and tried to find their ties to the vast continent, calling "Africa! long ages sleeping, oh my motherland, awake!" [7] With the widening of the horizon of the black world of America, it seemed to some of the black people that the boundaries of American consciousness as a whole were enlarged. W. E. B. Du Bois proudly points out:

> We black folk may help for we have within us rare new stirrings; stirrings of the beginning of a new appreciation of joy, of a new desire to create, of a new will to be; as though

> in this morning of group life we had awakened from some sleep that at once dimly mourns the past and dreams a splendid future; and there has come the conviction that the Youth that is here today, the Negro Youth, is a different kind of Youth, because in some new way it bears this mighty prophecy on its breast, with a new realization of itself, with new determination for all mankind.[8]

This movement was the restoration of "some of the things we thought culture had forever lost." [9] There was no longer the need to be "over-assertive and over-appealing." [10] The black artists felt that the American public had to acknowledge their full share in the world of art.

> Art cannot disdain the gift of a natural irony, of a transfiguring imagination, or rhapsodic Biblical speech, of dynamic musical swing, of cosmic emotion such as only the gifted pagans knew, of a return to nature, not by way of the forced and worn formula of Romanticism, but through the closeness of an imagination that has never broken kinship with nature. Art must accept such gifts, and revaluate the giver.[11]

Among those who helped this movement was Jessie Fauset, the literary editor of *The Crisis* from 1919 to 1926. Langston Hughes expresses his obligation to those people in *The Big Sea.*

> Jessie Fauset at *The Crisis,* Charles Johnson at *Opportunity,* and Alain Locke in Washington, were the three people who midwifed the so-called New Negro literature into being. Kind and critical—but not too critical for the young—they nursed us along until our books were born.[12]

Though she did "a yeoman's work for the Negro Renaissance," [13] most of her own literary activities were done during the period of the Harlem Renaissance. And the significance of the fact that her first novel, *There Is Confusion,* came out in 1924, almost simultaneously with Toomer's *Cane,* will be discussed later.

The publication of her first novel was a memorable event in the Negro literary world. W. E. B. Du Bois greeted its arrival with the following words:

> The novel that the Negro intelligentsia have been clamoring for has arrived with Jessie Fauset's first novel, *There Is Confusion.* What they have been wanting, if I interpret rightly, is not merely a race story told from the inside, but a cross section of the race life higher up the social pyramid and further from the base-line of the peasant and the soil than is usually taken.[14]

William Stanley Braithwaite comments: "Miss Fauset in her novel *There Is Confusion,* has created an entirely new milieu in the treatment of the Race in fiction. She has taken a class within the Race, given it an established social standing, tradition, culture, and shown that its predilections are very much like those of any civilized group of human beings." [15]

This statement coincides with the author's attitude expressed in the preface to her third novel, *The Chinaberry Tree.*

> I have depicted something of the home life of the colored American who is not being pressed too hard by the Furies of Prejudices, Ignorance, and Economic Injustice. . . . And behold he is not so vastly different from any other Americans.[16]

As it has become clear from these statements, Jessie Fauset's novels can be regarded as novels of manners of the Negro upper class, and her attitude is to emphasize the similarity between the blacks and the whites, rather than the difference. Yet the words in the same preface, "To be a Negro in America posits a dramatic situation," [17] cannot be ignored.

Claude McKay recalls Jessie Fauset and the world of her novel in this way:

> Miss Fauset has written many novels about the people in her circle. . . . Miss Fauset is prim and dainty as a primrose and her novels are quite as fastidious and precious. Primroses are pretty. I remember the primroses where I lived in Morocco, that lovely melancholy land of autumn and summer and mysterious veiled brown women. When primroses spread themselves across the barren hillsides before the sudden summer blazed over the hot land, I often thought of Jessie Fauset and her novels.[18]

And the best illustration of "the people in her circle" can be found in Langston Hughes's autobiography:

> At the novelist, Jessie Fauset's parties, there was always quite a different atmosphere from that at most other Harlem good-time gatherings. At Miss Fauset's, a good time was shared by talking literature and reading poetry aloud and perhaps enjoying some conversation in French. White people were seldom present there unless they were very distinguished white people, because Jessie Fauset did not feel like opening her home to mere sightseers, or faddists momentarily in love with Negro life. At her house one would usually meet editors and students, writers and social workers, and serious people who liked books and the British Museum, and had perhaps been to Florence. (Italy, not Alabama.)[19]

These two passages by McKay and Hughes illustrate very clearly the world of Jessie Fauset's novels. First of all, each of her novels is a melodrama in which a beautiful heroine and a handsome hero are finally united after overcoming innumerable obstacles. It is as dainty and pretty as a primrose. The world these heroes and heroines move about in is the world of Negro intelligentsia who believe that "Negro art . . . must be dignified and respectable like the Anglo Saxon's before it can be good."[20] Miss Fauset wants her people as good as the best of the whites. Yet in spite of her acceptance of the sense of values of the white world, her novels are full of references to racial problems and bitterness toward the injustice done by the whites to her race.

Several reasons can be given why Miss Fauset chooses the people of her circle for the characters of her novels—tales of the "non-cabareting, churchgoing Negroes, presenting in all their virtue and glory and with their human traits, their human hypocrisy and their human perversities glossed over."[21] The first one is, of course, that these are the people she knows best; secondly, according to her own words, the publication of T. S. Stribling's *Birthright* in 1922 stimulated her into fiction writing. This novel about a mulatto boy, a Harvard graduate, who, with an idealistic ambition, tried to improve his own people in a small town in Tennessee and failed, was considered as "the most significant novel on the Negro written by a white American"[22] at the time of its publication. However, the techniques are poor and ideas about the race questions are stale. In an interview Jessie Fauset tells what she thought of the book at its publication: "A number of us started writing at that time. . . . Nella Larsen and Walter White, for instance, were affected just as I was. We reasoned, 'Here is an audience waiting to hear the truth about us. Let us who are better qualified to present the truth than any white writer, try to do so.' "[23] Whether or not this kind of novel was what the audience of the time had been waiting for becomes clear if we consider the difficulties Miss Fauset encountered in her efforts to find a publisher for her first novel. Publishers rejected her manuscript because "it contains no description of Harlem dives, no race riot, no picturesque, abject poverty."[24] This shows the real attitude of the white world to the blacks.

Jessie Fauset's four novels have a similar plot—the heroine's pursuit of happiness. At the beginning of each novel the heroine has a rigid idea about the means to attain what she thinks to be happiness. The story evolves around the idea and a reader is told how her experiences in life affect and change it, or if not, what consequences the rigidity of her attitude has brought to her. In her first novel, *There Is Confusion,* the heroine, Joanna Marshall, was haunted with the idea of greatness. Even before she was five she determined that she would be someone great. She told herself: "I'll be great. . . . I'm not sure how. I can't be like these wonderful women, Harriet and Sojourner, but at least I won't be ordinary." [25] With this determination in mind Joanna tried her best to be a great singer and dancer, but in spite of her extraordinary talent, she could attain only a mild success because of her color. She forced her sweetheart, Peter Bye, who had the tendency to be easily discouraged, to be a surgeon, the hardest road to take. Joanna even interfered with her brother's marriage to Maggie because Maggie was poor and without any family connections. Finally Joanna came to realize her mistake—that greatness, fame, and material success were not happiness. The most important thing was love. She and Peter were united in marriage and the novel ends with Joanna's declaration, "My creed calls for nothing but happiness." [26]

Of course, this novel has more than this story. As Robert Bone severely says, "*There Is Confusion* is nothing if not well titled." [27] The author puts too many events in the novel to give it an artistic unity and coherence. There is the whole history of the white and black Bye family, with the story of miscegenation and exploitation, which explains Peter's subdued temperament. This story comes to its climax at Peter's encounter with his white kinsman, Merriwether Bye, on the boat to France, at Merriwether's death in the war, and with it the extinction of the Bye family on the white side, at Merriwether's grandfather's wish to acknowledge the son of Peter and Joanna as his heir, and their proud refusal. There is also a story of a short engagement of Peter and Maggie while both of them were separated from their true loves. A brief but moving tale is about Vera Manning, who could pass, and her lover, Harley, who could not, and their final separation. When William Stanley Braithwaite calls Jessie Fauset "the potential Jane Austen of Negro literature," [28] the comparison seems well taken. The subject matter is the same, and the social status of the characters is the upper middle class. But when we think of what creates the dramatic situations in the fiction of these two writers, we come to realize the vast difference between them. In Jane Austen's case, what moves the plot is a certain temperament created in each character by the manners and morals of the class he or she belongs to. In Jessie Fauset's case, though she chooses a certain class of Negro people, what really moves the story is not what is inherent to that class and hence to the character but what is imposed upon the person from outside. Miss Austen looks into the character's mind and creates humorous situations contrasting various temperaments and prejudices. In the Negro writer's novels the author's concern tends to be not psychological but social; and all the situations are serious. In a sense, Jessie Fauset's novels are those of social protest. Hugh Glouster says:

> *There Is Confusion*, while not a militantly propagandistic novel, expresses many of the racial disadvantages suffered by Negroes. The consequences of illicit relationships between master and slave are illustrated in the chronicle of the white and black Byes. . . . The operation of prejudice is revealed in schools, colleges, graduate and professional institutions, stores,

> restaurants, hospitals, theaters, and even in the world of art. Everywhere in the country the specter of discrimination is shown hovering over the Negro, limiting his sphere of activities, focusing his thinking upon his plight, and obstructing his advancement into a fuller and richer life.[29]

In her next novel, *Plum Bun,* there is a great improvement in technique: William Braithwaite calls this novel "her most perfect artistic achievement." [30] If we regard this novel as a melodramatic story of a girl who searched for a true love, fighting against adverse fate, it is the best conceived among Miss Fauset's four novels. She forms her novel around the nursery rhyme:

> To Market, to Market
> To buy a Plum Bun;
> Home again, Home again,
> Market is done.

She divides the novel into five parts, "Home," "Market," "Plum Bun," "Home Again," and "Market Is Done," to express the five stages of the heroine Angela Murrey's ambition to attain happiness through passing, acquisition of wealth, her realization of the falseness of her idea, and the final happiness with her true lover. As if to be in accord with the nursery rhyme, the story was told, at least in the beginning, in the tone of a fairy tale:

> In one of these houses dwelt a father, a mother and two daughters. Here, as often happens in a home sheltering two generations, opposite, unevenly matched emotions faced each other.[31]

Perhaps she intends to create the effect of universality using this style of writing.

To the parents, Junius and Mattie Murrey, "who had known poverty and homelessness, the little house on Opal

Street represented the *ne plus ultra* of ambition." [32] But to the elder of their two daughters, Angela, the house seemed "the dingiest, drabbest" [33] place. Angela thought that the shortest way to "the pathes which lead to broad thoroughfares, large, bright houses, delicate niceties of existence" [34] is to cross the color line and to live as a white girl. After her parents' death she cut off her family ties and even denied her only sister, Virginia, who showed color. She came to New York from Philadelphia and studied painting. The reason she chose art was not that she was interested in painting but because, through her study of art, she could meet interesting and wealthy people who would serve her purpose. She was gifted but "her gift was not for her the end of existence; rather it was an adjunct to life which was to know light, pleasure, gaiety and freedom." [35] She found out that the surest way to accomplish her ambition was to marry a rich white man. She met a very wealthy young man, Roger Fielding, and tried every means to attract him and make him love her, though she was attracted to a quaint fellow student at Cooper Union, Anthony Cross. However, the result was that Roger only made her his mistress, because he did not care to marry a poor girl, and eventually threw her away when he was tired of her.

As a subplot, Miss Fauset describes the contrasting life of Angela's younger sister, Virginia, who came to Harlem and found happiness in teaching music to black children and in her marriage to Mathew Henson. Angela thought, "Jinny had changed her life and been successful. Angela had changed hers and had found pain and unhappiness. Where did the fault lie?" [36] Miss Fauset seems to say that the fault lies in the fact that Angela used everything, her family, her friends, her profession, for the sake of her pursuit of happiness—she exploited everything, while Jinny always tried to serve others.

This preaching of Christian virtues of service and sacrifice seems a little strange, but quite acceptable, for Miss Fauset's novels are in the tradition of the eighteenth- and nineteenth-century novels in subject and technique. However, the explanation she gives for Angela's selfishness surprises a reader:

> In all her manifestations of human relationship, how selfish she had been! She had left Virginia, she had taken up with Roger to further her own interest. . . . She had been too intent always on happiness for herself. Her father, her mother and Jinny had always given and she had always taken. Why was that? Jinny had sighed: "Perhaps you have more white blood than Negro in your veins." Perhaps this selfishness was what the possession of white blood meant: the ultimate definition of Nordic Supremacy.[37]

This stereotyping of the white race as a kind of white fiend startles us when it comes from an intelligent person like Miss Fauset. Yet she never blames Angela for her most significant act—passing—for she knows the meaning of the expression "free, white and twenty-one." Also, though Harlem is gay and full of life and energy, it is "after all a city within a city." [38] The problem of crossing the color line has been treated by several black writers before her: Frances E. W. Harper and Charles Chesnutt are among them. Mrs. Harper's attitude toward this question is that the near-white people have to cast their lot with their Negro race. Miss Fauset's attitude to the race solidarity is ambivalent. As I have just pointed out, she stereotypes the two races in good and evil—beautiful and ugly. She praises the beauty of black skin:

> The girls were bright birds of paradise, the men. . .were gay fauns. In the subway beside the laughing, happy groups, white faces showed pale and bloodless, other colored faces loomed dull and hopeless.[39]

She even tries to describe the difference which the black blood made to people like Anthony and Angela—the near-white people. Yet when it comes to the question of the black intellectuals' role in the advancement of their race, her attitude becomes skeptical. She clearly shows the idea of the talented tenth, and treats the less fortunate of her race as if they were an inferior kind. Van Meier, one of the characters of *Plum Bun,* said: "Those of us who have forged forward, who have gained the front ranks in money and training, will not, are not able as yet to go our separate ways apart from the unwashed, untutored herd. We must still look back and render service to our less fortunate, weaker brethren." [40] The standard of her judgment is that of the white world. Miss Fauset fails to present a new aesthetic peculiar to her own race.

Her third novel, *The Chinaberry Tree,* is considered by many critics as the weakest among her four novels. Even William S. Braithwaite, her champion, regards the novel as "one false note" [41] among her works. Mr. Robert Bone says that "this book seems to be a novel about the first colored woman in New Jersey to wear lounging pajamas." [42] This novel deals with the narrow-mindedness of a black community in a town in New Jersey, Red Brook. The story evolves around the huge chinaberry tree that Colonel Halloway brought from the South for his lifelong lover, Aunt Sal, his mother's maid. Though he could not marry her because of her color, he did everything possible for Aunt Sal and their beautiful daughter, Laurentine. Aunt Sal was contented with her life, though she suffered a great deal from the prejudices of the white people and the moral accusation of the black people, for she knew what love meant to her. "She loved Halloway with a selfless devotion and after his death lived only in that past which he and she had found so sweet." [43] Yet the black community of Red Brook regarded her as a degenerated woman and treated her and her daughter as pariahs. They said the strange family had bad blood. The most galling experience to Laurentine happened when she was a little girl. One of her friends stopped playing with her all of a sudden. Seeing the friend playing with other girls, Laurentine went up to her and asked the reason.

> Lucy stared at her, her eyes large and strangely gray in her dark face. "I wanted to Laurentine," she answered, "but my mumma say I dasn't. She say you got bad blood in your veins." Abruptly she left her former friend, ran to the table and came back with a tiny useless knife in her hand. "Don't you want me to cut yo' arm and let it out?" [44]

Through her twenty-four years of life, Laurentine came to have an indelible complex about her birth, and every time something went wrong with her life she put the blame on it, and most of the time she was right. She wanted, above anything else, security in life. She tried in vain to make Phil Hacket, the richest Negro youth of the town, with a political ambition, marry her. Phil could not because he knew her strange parentage would be an obstacle to his career. Laurentine finally found her happiness with Dr. Denlaigh. As usual, Miss Fauset uses a subplot in this novel, describing the life of Melissa Paul, Laurentine's younger cousin. If there is anything to blame in this novel, it is this artificial subplot of incestuous love—obviously influenced by Greek tragedies—between Melissa and her half-brother, Maroly Forten.

The main point of this novel, however, is to show a reader why colored people had to be rigid with their moral code and how Laurentine and Melissa, though in different ways, had to suffer from it. Though full of descriptions of elegant lives of wealthy colored people, we cannot help feeling what a strong influence the problem of race has had in forming black people's mentality. One example of this is, when black boys started to fight at a skating carnival, the minister complained: "Now boys, boys, don't start nothin'. Too many white folks here for that. We don't want this kind thing closed to us."[45] They have to be decent and moralistic to avoid the deprecating criticism of the whites. In spite of the unfavorable criticism, this book presents a deeper and subtler problem—the impact of the racial discriminations and prejudices by the whites on the black society in the long run.

Her last novel, *Comedy: American Style,* is a curious one. So far as the techniques are concerned, this is the most elaborate of Miss Fauset's novels. Chapters are titled, "The Plot," "The Characters," "Theresa's Act," "Oliver's Act," "Phebe's Act," and "Curtain." The first two chapters show us the family background, social circumstances, and so forth, concerning the heroine, Olivia Cary, her children, and their friends. Olivia, who firmly believed that every advantage in the world can be attained only through the possession of white skin, forced her two older children, Chris and Teresa, to pass. Chris rebelled against her and, ignoring her wish, found his happiness with Phebe, a Negro girl with white skin and golden hair who remained faithful to her mother's race. But Teresa, after she was forced to denounce her handsome but brown-skinned lover, Henry Bates, came to realize that she was too much of her mother's making to rebel against her. When confronted by Henry as to whether she would choose him or her mother, she almost unconsciously said: "I was thinking, I was wondering—your Spanish, you know. Couldn't you use it most of the time and. . .and pass for a Mexican? In that way we could avoid most inconveniences. . . ."[46] This suggestion for passing hurt Henry deeply and their relationship ended. Teresa succumbed to her mother's wish and married a petty and miserly French linguist, Aristide Pailleron, in Toulouse, and led a miserable life. Oliver, the youngest and most beautiful child, had brown skin. His mother never showed him love and somehow contrived never to be seen with him on the street. When she had white women for tea at home—Olivia herself had passed into the white world—she treated the child as if he were a houseboy. When he found out that his mother thought that he was an obstacle to the happiness of other members of the family, he killed himself. Even after this tragedy Olivia was adamant in her belief. Finally, she went away to France, and the book ends with a picture of Olivia, bleak and lonely, living in a dingy Paris pension. When we finish reading the book, Olivia's coldness toward her family is unbelievable. Also, there are some unnatural situations: How could Olivia hide that she and her family were Negroes, when her husband, Dr. Cary, was practicing in the black community in Philadelphia, even though he had white skin? Yet a reader somehow is made to feel that the blame should not be placed totally on Olivia. All through this novel sufferings of the gifted and brilliant young people, like Phebe, Chris, Nicholas, and their friends—prejudices and discriminations in education, in profession, and in human relationships—are shown. You are almost convinced that you have to have white skin to enjoy living. I think the author's intention lies there, judging from the ironical title of the book.

This is the only book among her four novels with a depressing ending. Except for one slight light of Chris and Phebe's life, everything is under a dark shadow. Olivia, trying to cheat the world, cheated herself, her husband, and her family. In spite of many unnatural situations in the novel, a reader will readily accept William Braithwaite's comment on Olivia:

> She is the symbol of a force that must ultimately be acknowledged and discussed frankly by both races in America and when that discussion takes place there will be concessions and revisions on the part of white Americans which will make it possible to draw her like again as a warning.[47]

And it seems symbolic that Jessie Fauset ended her literary career with this tragic portrayal of Olivia Cary.

Jessie Fauset is not a first-rate writer. First of all she failed to attain what Alain Locke called "the buoyancy from within compensating for whatever pressure there may be of conditions from without," [48] though she was not unconscious of what was happening in the Negro world of the 1920s. Her appreciation of Negro musicals like *Shuffle Along* shows that she was aware of the new stirring of the black energy. "It is this quality of vivid and untheatrical portrayal of sheer emotions which seems likely to be the Negro's chief contribution to the stage." [49] Yet this is a far cry from the younger artists' positive affirmation of the blackness. She is unable to sing, like Claude McKay:

> But oh, they dance with poetry in their eyes
> Whose dreamy loveliness no sorrow dims,
> And parted lips and eager, gleeful cries
> And perfect rhythm in their nimble limbs,
> The gifts divine are theirs, music and laughter;
> All other things, however great, come after.[50]

In a way, she shows the tragic situation which faces many of the black intellectuals: they are making too much of the white world, so that they can never escape its influence. Even if they try to create works unique to their race, they do not possess means to express them. They are deprived of the black soul. Jessie Fauset has never known the life of the black people of the rural South, nor the ghettos of the Northern cities. She came from a well-to-do old Philadelphia family, was educated at Cornell University, where she majored in French and was elected a member of Phi Beta Kappa. She did her graduate work at the University of Pennsylvania, and had been to France three times by the time of the publication of her first novel. The only thing she could do as an artist was to produce "uniformly sophomoric, trivial and dull" [51] novels with almost painful persistency, to show the world the goodness of the black people and to ask justice for the race. In her ideas she belongs to the older school of black writers like Mrs. Harper and Mrs. Hopkins, who wrote novels to "raise the stigma of degradation from [my] race." [52] Miss Fauset never doubted the value of Western civilization. She only wanted her race to have a full share in the civilization. LeRoi Jones describes that kind of writer in "The Myth of a 'Negro Literature' ":

> The Negro artist, because of his middle-class background, carried the artificial social burden as the "best and most intelligent" of Negroes, and usually entered into the "serious" arts to exhibit his familiarity with the social graces, i.e., as a method or means of displaying his participation in the "serious" aspects of American culture. To be a writer was to be "cultivated," in the stunted bourgeois sense of the word. It had nothing to do with the investigation of the human soul. It was, and is, a social preoccupation rather than an aesthetic one.[53]

Miss Fauset does not have anything to do with "the investigation of the human soul" and her interest lies solely on the social level, yet there is one saving grace: the soundness of her judgment on racial situations in this country.

When we reflect upon the fact that her four novels came into the world between 1924 and 1934, and that the final picture she presents is the tragic product of the society of the white supremacy—Olivia Cary—we cannot deny that Miss Fauset had never drunk of the heady illusion of the Harlem Renaissance that affected many young blacks: the whites were accepting the black primitivism as a part of their civilization and hence the blacks as their equals. It was just a fad, exploited by commercialism, which came to its sudden end with the financial crash of 1929. Langston Hughes writes as follows:

> We were no longer in vogue, anyway, we Negroes. Sophisticated New Yorkers turned to Noel Coward. Colored actors began to go hungry, publishers politely rejected new manuscripts, and patrons found other uses for their money.[54]

Jessie Fauset's observation on the social scene of the United States of the time is sane and sound.

In 1950 Zora Neale Hurston, one of the representatives of the Harlem Renaissance, wrote an article, "What White Publishers Won't Print." In this article she emphasizes the necessity of novels that deal with Negro-middle-class life. She complains: "I have been amazed by the Anglo-Saxon's lack of curiosity about the internal lives and emotions of the Negroes, and for that matter, any non-Anglo-Saxon people's within our border, above the class of unskilled labor." [55] And Miss Hurston thinks that "the realistic story around a Negro insurance official, dentist, general practitioner, undertaker and the like" [56] will be a good subject for a Negro writer. When you are trying to get into a society which already has a strongly established set of ideas and standards, you cannot be accepted if you just assert your difference: you have to prove that you are capable of doing the same kind of things as the older residents of the society. At the beginning of the discussion of Jessie Fauset's novels I said that the fact that Jean Toomer's *Cane* and Jessie Fauset's *There Is Confusion* came into the world almost simultaneously was important. What I mean is that the kind of novels Jessie Fauset wrote could have been nourishment and root for the flowering of quite different kinds of works represented by *Cane,* until these two tendencies are united in one and bring about the establishment of the black culture. Unfortunately, the white world took up only one side, because it coincided, in a way, with their conception of the black people, and ignored the other. This pattern in the treatment of the black arts has been repeated again and again, and the black arts have had several false flowerings without bearing any fruit.

As I have said several times, Jessie Fauset is not a great writer. She is not even a good writer. But we cannot deny her social perspective and social sanity. She believes in the significance of the kind of novels she writes, as "Foreword" to *The Chinaberry Tree* indicates.

> . . . he has a wholesome respect for family and education and labor and the fruits of labor. He is still sufficiently conservative to lay a slightly greater stress on the first two of these four.
>
> Briefly he is a dark American who wears his joy and rue very much as does the white American. He may wear it with some differences but it is the same joy and the same rue.[57]

In this belief, she posits the problem of the black intellectuals who have been assimilated into the white world, yet her role in the advancement of the race cannot be denied.

Nella Larsen

Very few facts about Nella Larsen's life have been known. She was born in the Virgin Islands of a Danish mother and a Negro father, and married Elmer Imes, the chairman of the Physics Department of Fisk University. Their marriage was not a happy one, because Elmer fell in love with a younger woman sometime around 1929; Nella remained with him for several years after the unhappy discovery, for his position at the university required respectability. She went down to Nashville and stayed with him for several weeks each year. Lonely and unpleasant feelings had become almost unbearable to both husband and wife, which finally led to their divorce in the late thirties. The rest of her days were spent either in New York or Europe. This unusual life has much to do with Nella Larsen's novels—in subject matter and technique.

Nella Larsen published two novels in two years and ended her career as a fiction writer in 1929. Yet some critics like Mr. Robert Bone think her first novel, *Quicksand,* published in 1928, "is the best of the period, with exception of Jean Toomer's *Cane.*" [1] When it first came out, W. E. B. Du Bois reviewed the book for *The Crisis* and said:

> I think that Mrs. Imes, writing under the pen name of Nella Larsen, has done a fine, thoughtful and courageous piece of work in her novel. It is on the whole, the best piece of fiction that Negro America has produced since the heyday of Chesnutt, and stands easily with Jessie Fauset's "There Is Confusion," in its subtle comprehension of the curious cross currents that swirl about the black American.[2]

Quicksand is a very cleverly wrought novel. If you compare it with Jessie Fauset's novels, it will become evident what a gifted writer Nella Larsen is. She knows the craft of fiction: how to write effectively and economically, how to keep artistic unity, and how to maintain the proper point of view. Her interest lies mainly on the psychological and not on the social side of the matter. The title, *Quicksand,* signifies the heroine Helga Crane's sexual desire, which was hidden beneath her beautiful and intelligent surface and came up at an unexpected moment and trapped her. The novel develops stage by stage, in accord with the heroine's wandering—Naxos, Chicago, New York, Copenhagen, back to New York, and then a small town in Alabama. Helga, with a parentage quite similar to that of the author, was, at the beginning of the novel, teaching in a Southern college called Naxos. She left the school in the middle of a term because she felt restless and that she could no longer stand its philistine atmosphere. She went to Chicago, where she was rejected by her white relatives and suffered in her search for a job, because of her color. Then she came to Harlem. There she was happy for a time as a member of the sophisticated society of intelligent black people. However, the restless feeling again took hold of her and she came to know the cause of it. She went to a cabaret with her friends one night.

> They danced, ambling lazily to a crooning melody, or violently twisting their bodies, like whirling leaves, to a sudden streaming rhythm, or shaking themselves ecstatically to a thumping of unseen tom-toms. For the while, Helga was oblivious of the reek of flesh, smoke, and alcohol, oblivious of the oblivion of other gyrating pairs, oblivious of the color, the noise, and the grand distorted childishness of it all. She was drugged, lifted, sustained, by the extraordinary music, blown out, ripped out, beaten out, by the joyous, mild, murky orchestra. The essence of life seemed bodily motion. And when suddenly the music died, she dragged herself back to the present with a

> conscious effort; and a shameful certainty that not only had she been in the jungle, but that she had enjoyed it, began to taunt her. She hardened her determination to get away. She wasn't, she told herself, a jungle creature.[3]

And she felt a primitive emotion while watching Dr. Anderson, to whom she was secretly attracted, dance with a girl. "She forgot the garish crowded room. She forgot her friends. She saw only two figures, closely clinging. She felt her heart throbbing. She felt the room receding." [4] Unable to stand it any longer, she rushed out of the room. This revelation of her inner world, the world of the sensual pleasure represented by her black blood, sent her across the Atlantic to her white kinsmen, her mother's sister's family. In Denmark, living with the rich uncle and aunt, her material need was satisfied. People treated her as if she was a curious tropical creature; to be a Negro was not a handicap but an advantage to attract attention. Even a famous portrait painter, Alex Olson, fell in love with her. But when he proposed marriage to her, Helga suddenly felt that she could not marry a white man. She explained her feeling to him:

> You see, I couldn't marry a white man, I simply couldn't. It isn't just you, not just personal, you understand. It's deeper, broader than that. It's racial." [5]

She felt homesick, "not for America, but for Negroes." [6] At that moment, for the first time in her life, she forgave her father, who had run away, leaving her and her mother, and joined his people. "She understood his yearning, his intolerable need for the inexhaustible humor and the incessant hope of his own kind, his need for those things, not material, indigenous to all Negro environment." [7] This world was quite different from the one where she had lived in Denmark, the world full of "the things which money could give, leisure, attention, beautiful surroundings. Things. Things. Things." [8] Yet when she left the European country, she "already looked back with infinite regret at the two years in the country." [9] She wondered "why couldn't she have two lives, or why couldn't she be satisfied in one." [10] Once back in Harlem, she felt that she could not stay there forever. "Nor, she saw now, could she remain away. Leaving, she would have to come back. This knowledge, this certainty of the division of her life into two parts in two lands, into physical freedom in Europe and spiritual freedom in America, was unfortunate, inconvenient, expensive." [11]

In Harlem, her sensual side again awakened. Unable to resist her desire, Helga offered herself to Dr. Anderson, only to be refused. In her desperation she went out in the storm and strayed into a revival meeting. There she met Reverend Green, a fat yellow preacher from Alabama, and married him. For a time Helga was quite satisfied with her new life in a small town in Alabama, for "night came at the end of every day. Emotional, palpitating, amorous, all that was living in her sprang like rank weeds at the tingling thought of night, with a vitality so strong that it devoured all the shoot of reason." [12] She bore him four children and at the birth of the last one she almost died. While recovering from the illness, her desire for the nice things came back to her, and she realized the miserable condition into which her sexuality had trapped her. Yet the novel ends with the following passage:

> And hardly had she left her bed and become able to walk again without pain, hardly had the children returned from the homes of the neighbors, when she began to have her fifth child.[13]

This book is an interesting and curious one. The heroine is always looking for a place where she could find peace of

Arna Bontemps

Harold Jackman

Nella Larsen

Langston Hughes

Countee Cullen

Claude McKay

Zora Neale Hurston

Charles S. Johnson

Alain Locke

Rudolph Fisher

mind. It seems to me as if she is a forerunner of Joe Christmas of William Faulkner's *Light in August.* As a child of a white mother and black father, Helga could not identify herself with either race. Nella Larsen uses materialism and sensuousness to express these two worlds. In Helga these two tendencies exist together. Alex Olson expressed this as follows: "You have the warm, impulsive nature of the women of Africa, but the soul of a prostitute." [14] It is impossible to satisfy these two sides at the same time. White people were deprived of vitality and haunted with the anxiety for existence, while "everything had been taken from those dark ones, liberty, respect, even the labor of their hands." [15] It seems to me that Nella Larsen, using a very particular situation of mixed blood, expresses a tragic situation which faces us, our loss of our identity in this dehumanized and materialistic society and our need for materialistic comfort.

Mr. Robert Bone thinks that Nella Larsen gives a moral judgment on Helga:

> Helga's tragedy, in Larsen's eyes, is that she allows herself to be declassed by her own sexuality. The tone of reproach is unmistakable. It is underlying moralism which differentiates *Quicksand* from the novels of the Harlem School.[16]

He is wrong. There is no moral judgment at the end of the book. Certainly toward the end Helga longed for the niceties of the world. She dreamed "about freedom and cities, about clothes and books, about the sweet mingled smell of Houbigant and cigarettes in softly lighted rooms filled with inconsequetnial chatter and laughter and sophisticated tuneless music." [17] This is what her white blood desires. To the end, Nella Larsen watches Helga with her cool naturalist's eyes. She never says which side—white or black—

is better. There is compassion for the heroine, but no moral judgment on her.

What impresses me most is the author's almost masculine detachment and her ability to expand a small, particular situation to a larger, universal one.

Compared to this first novel, the second one, *Passing,* is a slight book. Though cleverly written, she failed to keep the thematic unity. In the middle of the novel, some curious change has happened. The question of passing has gone. This novel is a story of Clare Kendry, a beautiful girl who passed into the white world and married a wealthy man. The author's intention when she began writing it must have been to study the psychology of the people who passed—their loneliness in the white world, their desperate longing for the black world, and their terrible fear at childbirths. Yet in the middle of the book, this novel turned into a case study of a woman's jealousy. Clare met in Chicago her old friend Irene Redfield, who had married a doctor and was living in Harlem. Because of her loneliness as a person who was passing, Clare frequented Irene's house back in Harlem while her husband was away on business. She was attracted to Irene's husband, Brien, and he to her. Irene was disturbed by the situation and wished Clare would stay away or disappear. She thought: "If Clare should die! Then—oh, it was vile! To think, yes, to wish that!" [18] She felt faint and sick, but the thought stayed with her.

Then this wish came true. Clare's husband came to know his wife's black blood. He came to a party his wife was attending and confronted her. Irene was afraid, because if Clare was divorced, she would be free to be with Brien. Unconsciously, she rushed to the confronting couple: the next moment, Clare was gone through the window. When she was told that Clare died instantly, "Irene struggled against the sob of thankfulness that rose in her throat."[19] This novel is not only a story of Clare and her passing, but also a story of Irene, who jealously guarded the security of her marriage. Though the story is cleverly written and the psychology of the two women is coherently expressed, this novel fails to present the deeper meaning of the question.

Nella Larsen is not concerned with race problems in the ordinary sense, nor does she glorify blackness. She does not use the race for protest or propaganda. In that sense she is, as Mr. Robert Bone says, a rearguard of the Harlem Renaissance. Yet in her technique and treatment of her subject she is with the most advanced of the time. She is a very sophisticated writer and she is able to present her subject with wide perspective: a personal problem can be expanded to a race problem, then to a universal one. She is the first one among the black writers who has attained this artistic accomplishment. Though she has written only one good book, she can be regarded as one of the best black writers up to now.

CHAPTER 5

Langston Hughes and the Harlem Renaissance, 1921-1931: Major Events and Publications

PATRICIA E. TAYLOR

The Harlem Renaissance, or the "New Negro Movement" as it is sometimes called, coincided intimately with Hughes's literary activities. As much an influence upon as influenced by this literary and political movement, Hughes's productivity during this period occurred at about the same time in history that other significant events in the lives of black people were occurring—the Garvey movement, the start of the decline of the influence of the NAACP and its publication, *The Crisis* (begun in 1910), and other events of similar significance. Black people at the time were beginning to assert their individuality, their independence, and their originality. Hughes himself was an integral part of this emerging philosophy.

It was a time when white thinkers and writers were devoting a considerable amount of attention to the Negro. With the new-found availability of white funds to support black ventures, books by Negro authors were being published with greater frequency than ever before in history; so, too, were books about Negroes by white writers. In Hughes's own words, "It was the period (God help us!) when Ethel Barrymore appeared in blackface in *Scarlet Sister Mary!* It was the period when the Negro was in vogue. I was there."[1]

Of considerable importance to Hughes during the Renaissance period was the social life of New York's upper-class black community. It was at such parties that Hughes met and mingled with great figures of the time. Many of these parties were given by socially prominent Negroes, but many of importance in Hughes's career were given by whites—editors, patrons, and other persons interested in getting "in on" the rebirth of blackness. A list of Hughes's friends and acquaintances of the period is most impressive; these acquaintances were, in themselves, the Harlem Renaissance: literary and political figures such as W. E. B. Du Bois, Mary McLeod Bethune, and Walter White ("who had the most beautiful wife in Harlem");[2] well-known names of the theater and music, such as Duke Ellington, Bojangles, Bessie Smith, Ethel Waters, Paul Robeson, W. C. Handy, and Richard B. ("DeLawd") Harrison. Perhaps the most predominant influences upon him at that time, via the whist-party circuit as much as via their writing, were such noted writers as Alain Locke, Countee Cullen, Arna Bontemps (". . . like a young edition of Dr. Du Bois"),[3] Claude McKay, Saunders Redding, Jessie Fauset, Charles S. Johnson, and James Weldon Johnson. One of the most renowned givers of parties was no less than Mrs. A'Lelia Walker, heir to the Madame Walker's Hair Straightening Process fortune, a "gorgeous dark Amazon, in a silver turban",[4] whose death in 1931 overlapped with the onslaught of the depression and the end of the Renaissance. Hughes's own description of her massive funeral, in one of his autobiographies (*The Big Sea*), underscores the impact of both events (the funeral was by invitation only!):

> That was really the end of the gay times of the New Negro era in Harlem, the period that had begun to reach its end when the crash came in 1929 and the white people had much less money to spend on themselves, and practically none to spend on Negroes, for the depression brought everybody down a peg or two. And the Negroes had but a few pegs to fall.[5]

Books

Hughes's first book, a book of poems entitled *The Weary Blues* (Knopf, 1926), published upon his entry that same year into Lincoln University in Pennsylvania (he had previously spent one year at Columbia, 1921–22), was made possible through his meeting Carl Van Vechten, an adviser with Alfred A. Knopf. The portrayals of Harlem life in this work were expressive of the flamboyance which to a great degree characterized black New York social life at the time. The book, however, met with mixed reviewing. One reviewer in the *Times Literary Supplement* found poems contained in the work "superficial" and "sentimental." Despite which, the book sold well enough (1200 copies for the first edition), and it served to launch Hughes's career. It contained the now-famous poem, "The Negro Speaks of Rivers," published also in the NAACP's *The Crisis,* a poem of black pride, of the new militancy which was as much a part of Hughes himself as of the Renaissance:

> I am a Negro:
> Black as the night is black,
> black like the depths of my Africa.[6]

His second book, published just one year later (Knopf, 1927), also a book of poems, entitled *Fine Clothes to the Jew,* a work on black culture, revealed, in the words of Charles S. Johnson, "a final, frank turning to the folk life of the Negro, striving to catch and give back to the world the strange music of the unlettered Negro—his 'Blues.' "[7] The title of the book derives from its first poem, "Hard Luck," about a man who was often so impoverished that he had to pawn his clothes in order to obtain money; to take them, as blacks would say, "to the Jews." While the book would no doubt be accepted today as a legitimate commentary on black life, it was met then by the black community with hostile condemnation. It was received reasonably well by the white press, but black newspapers criticized it with such phrases as "Langston Hughes' book of poems trash" (in the Pittsburgh *Courier*) and "Langston Hughes—the sewer dweller" (in New York's *Amsterdam News*), and even (to show that black reporters then were not above an occasional pun) a mention of Hughes as "the poet lowrate of Harlem" (in the Chicago *Whip*). It was generally accused by the black press as being a return to the dialect tradition—as "a parading of all . . . racial defects before the public."[8] Hughes himself suspected that black criticism of the book may have been brought on by an unfortunate choice of title. Yet, as Hughes notes in his autobiography, the same poems were being used some years later in black schools and colleges.

Not Without Laughter (Knopf, 1930) was his third book and first novel. It was published during an eventful year in Hughes's life. He received the Harmon award for literature, and a sum of four hundred dollars with it—which he used for a trip to Haiti during that same year (he stated then that he never before had "that much" money at any one time). The novel was well received, to say the least. It has been translated into eight foreign languages (Spanish, Dutch, French, Italian, Japanese, Russian, Swedish, and Swiss).

The story concerned a Negro family in Kansas, where Hughes spent his boyhood years. The characters are individuals through whom the reader may subjectively experience how rural blacks live and think. Despite its wide acceptance by the white world, it was, as was *Fine Clothes,* heavily criticized by blacks. While some praised it as containing understanding, tolerance, and beauty, others, like the editors of the NAACP's *The Crisis,* after first listing "books we must read," then listed *Not Without Laughter* under "books one may read." A brief note there called the work a study of "black peasantry in the Middle-West." Despite such luke-warm reception on the part of the black critics, the book was Hughes's first real commercial success, strictly in terms of sales. A letter from Bernard Smith of Knopf publishers, dated February 15, 1938, eight years after publication, states that "The sales of your books are as follows: *Not Without Laughter,* 6113; *Weary Blues,* 4356; *Fine Clothes to the Jew,* 2067." [9] Hence, in retrospect, we see that the sales of *Laughter* outsold his two earlier book-length publications.

Laughter was written when Hughes was a student at Lincoln during the three-year period 1926 to 1929:

> I wrote the book during the summer following my junior year at Lincoln. The authorities said that I might remain in [an] empty dormitory and write. For two weeks I didn't do anything. But the time passed like two days. Then I suddenly began with the storm, and my characters seemed to live in the room where I worked. Their chairs and tables were there, too, and the lamp. Then I wrote out short histories for all my characters as they came to life—how old they were, where born,

> things that had happened to them, and what might happen to them. Also why.
>
> These sketches and outlines I tacked on the wall above the table where I worked. Then I began the second chapter. At first, I did a chapter or two a day and revised them the next day. But they seemed bad. In fact, so bad that I finally decided to write the whole story straight through to the end before re-reading anything. This I did in about six weeks. Then I went to Provincetown for a vacation before classes opened in the fall.
>
> All that winter, my senior year, I re-read and re-worked my novel. The following summer, after graduation, I again stayed on the campus in a big, empty theological dormitory all alone. I began to cut my novel, which was far too bulky. As I cut and polished, revised and re-wrote, the people in the book seemed to walk around the room and talk to me, helping me write. Aunt Hager and Annjee and Jimboy were there. An oil light burned on my table—as in Kansas.[10, 11]

While at Lincoln, Hughes used to go to Harlem on weekends. His continuing interest in black pride and black protest was revealed in his extracurricular and cocurricular activities at Lincoln. Once, for a course in sociology taught by a Professor Labaree, he actually completed what would be called a sociological survey of student opinion. The study concerned what Hughes saw as an ironic inequity at Lincoln: The faculty of the university was dedicated to the training of "Negro leaders," and professed interest in doing all that was possible to attain this end and to do justice to the (all-black) students there. Yet the entire faculty was white; there seemed to be an unwritten law (they are always "unwritten," it seems) that no black person could be hired as a faculty member. This strange dichotomy—all-black student body and all-white faculty—disturbed Hughes deeply. He wanted to find out what other students felt. So he took the survey. Perhaps to his surprise (and perhaps not), he found that 63 per cent of the juniors and seniors favored an all-white faculty. Some of the students in his survey actually felt that blacks were *incapable* of being faculty members and teaching other blacks. Hughes wrote the survey in the form of a term paper for the course, and it evidently caused a stir, both on campus and off. Undoubtedly such experiences weighed heavily in his increasing militancy and rejection of "Uncle Toming" (his own words). And undoubtedly such experiences served only to increase the power and brilliance of his style.

At the end of the Renaissance period, two other books were published, in 1931: *Dear Lovely Death* (Troutbeck), a book of poems, and *The Negro Mother* (Golden Stair Press). This marked a departure from Knopf, the publisher of his first three books, and was evidently also a decline in association with Carl Van Vechten, his friend and editor from Knopf, who was instrumental in starting Hughes's career in published writing.

Prose and Drama

One is utterly staggered by the length of the list of Hughes's published work produced during the relatively (and regrettably) short Renaissance period, to say nothing of the vast number of publications that were produced *since* 1931 (a complete listing can be found in D. C. Dickinson's *A Bio-Bibliography of Langston Hughes,* 1902–1967, Hamden, Conn.: Archon Books, 1967). His writing spanned all classes and divisions of literature—books, poems, short stories, books edited, works in foreign languages for which there is no English edition, plays, and articles in both journals and in books edited by other scholars. (See Notes and Bibliographies for a listing of works [excluding poems] for the

1921 to 1931 period.) Clearly, one cannot comment on all his prose and drama, but a few significant pieces are worth mentioning: his contributions to *Messenger* magazine and its editor, the unusual genius Wallace Thurman; his short story, "Luani of the Jungle"; and his (then unproduced) play, *Mulatto.*

The *Messenger* brought to a limited public Hughes's first short stories. Founded in 1917 by A. Philip Randolph and Chandler Owen to further the cause of socialism, [12] the magazine, according to its editor, Wallace Thurman, was to "reflect the policy of whoever paid off best at the time." [13] Thurman was an amazing person. Hughes reports that he could read eleven lines of print at a time, and that he could read in one week a pile of volumes that it would take Hughes himself (who was no slouch in speed reading) one full year to read. And then he (Thurman) could discuss the contents at length. This man became a ghost writer for *True Story* and other publications about similar topics, and would write under such names as Ethel Belle Mandrake or Patrick Casey; he would write Irish, Jewish, and Catholic "true confessions" —and he was black! He would laugh bitterly at the white world, at his concocted "true" stories, and at the unsuspecting clientele. He created "adult" motion pictures; yet he had completely absorbed the works of Proust, Tolstoy, Dostoyevski, Melville. He liked to drink gin, but yet didn't like to drink gin; he liked to spend periods of time doing nothing, yet felt guilty about wasting time; he disliked crowds, but hated to be alone. Such paradoxes of his behavior perhaps serve only to underscore his great (yet frustrated) brilliance and potential. While Thurman had an impact upon the life of Hughes (he helped start the ill-fated journal *Fire,* to be discussed below), one does get the feeling from Hughes's own writing about him that he was beset by extreme bitterness during his most productive years. Yet he undoubtedly served as an inspiration for Hughes. If Hughes admired anyone, it was Thurman, even though the admiration was accompanied with mixed emotions.

The story "Luani of the Jungle," published in the November 1928 issue of *Harlem* magazine (a second major source of Hughes's stories during the period), begins as a black princess and her white husband arrive in Africa. A short time after the couple settles there, the husband sees his wife walking nude in the moonlight with a muscular African prince. The husband is most miserable, but can do nothing but return to the tent and brood. While one of Hughes's biographers, Dickinson, seems to criticize the story as "a rather naive contrast of black strength and white weakness," [14] its theme was most timely then, as it still is now. Both whites and blacks today, concerned over both the new sexual freedom and over black militancy, have themselves interwoven the threads of sex and racism tightly. It is interesting to note that Hughes saw the two as somehow relevant to each other—another indication of Hughes's prophetic abilities, and of his militancy and his perceptiveness.

A play, *Mulatto,* was evidently written during the Renaissance period but not produced on Broadway until much later. I note that a poem by the same title was published in 1926 in the *Saturday Review of Literature.* Hughes indicates that "I worked harder on that poem than on any other that I had ever written." [15] But his productivity in the writing of plays was indeed high, as was his productivity in virtually every other area of literature. A number of his plays were aired at *Karamu House* in Cleveland, Ohio, where he spent his high-school days (he graduated from Central High in 1920). The executive directors and founders of *Karamu,* Russell and Rowena Jelliffee, were close to him during the

Renaissance years, and remained so until his death in 1967.

Patron and Poems

In order to be able to have enough time to write, almost any budding artist must be free of the encumbrances of a job unrelated to his vocation. Thus, a number of talented writers of the Renaissance, Hughes among them, were financially supported by "patrons." Hughes's patron (whose name he refuses to mention in *The Big Sea*) evidently provided him well with funds, a chauffeured limousine, fine food, and fine bond paper, for he developed what he thought to be a strong friendship with her. It is doubtful that he was sexually active with her (he was generally busy with much younger women in Harlem), but his autobiography reflects the extreme sorrow which he experienced upon their separation.

This separation came as a direct result of two things: For one, Hughes was beginning to tire of the realization that he was, in effect, writing the kind of material that she wanted him to write. (She was able to interpret his many poems and stories as reflecting the primitive nature of blackness—an interpretation which she wanted to derive.) Secondly, after he had written a heavily satirical, sarcastic, powerful poem of black poverty, entitled "Advertisement for the Waldorf-Astoria," she did not like the poem ("It's not you" she told Hughes), and demanded that he not publish it. Naturally, Hughes felt this attitude on her part was unfortuante (perhaps he wrote the poem in order to "force her hand," so to speak). So he asked to be released—and the breakup was traumatic. A passage from the poem illustrates its power:

> Look! See what Vanity Fair says about the new Waldorf-
> Astoria:

"All the luxuries of private home . . . ."
Now, won't that be charming when the last flophouse has turned you down this winter?
Furthermore:
"It is far beyond anything hitherto attempted in the hotel world . . . ." It cost twenty-eight million dollars. The famous Oscar Tschirky is in charge of banqueting. Alexandre Gastaud is chef. It will be a distinguished background for society.
So when you've got no place else to go, homeless and hungry ones, choose the Waldorf as a background for your rags—
(Or do you still consider the subway after midnight good enough?) [16]

The patron did not like it. It wasn't the proud and primitive black prince that she wanted. And so Hughes wanted out. He asked that she give him no more money, but he did request that their friendship be retained; her friendship had been "so dear to me." [17] And he thought that she had liked him—not only his writing, but him, too. "But there must have been only the one thread binding us together. When that thread broke, it was the end." [18]

The split-up was so traumatic that Hughes suffered psychosomatic abdominal difficulties for weeks afterward.

Other Activities

There were other events that are significant in Hughes's life during the Renaissance: his first literary quarrel, with Zora Hurston, over the authorship of what was to be the first real black comedy play in history (entitled *Mule Bone,* never performed at Cleveland's *Karamu House,* for which it was originally intended); his close relationship with Carl Van Vechten; his poems published in the children's *Brownie's*

Book; his job as a cook's assistant on a steamer to Africa in 1923; his employment as a cook in a Paris nightclub in 1924, or his trip to Haiti in 1930. Yet, one more event deserves mention: his involvement with the magazine *Fire,* which cost its initiators (including Hughes) nearly a thousand dollars to produce (which took years to repay), and which only reached Vol. 1, No. 1, in production.

During the hot summer of 1926, Hughes and six other talented people decided to publish this "Negro quarterly of the arts." The six others were Wallace Thurman (the brilliant, eccentric, former editor of *Messenger*), Zora Hurston (with whom he later had the *Mule Bone* dispute), Aaron Douglas, John P. Davis, Bruce Nugent, and Gwendolyn Bennett. In Hughes's words, the title was intended to suggest the burning up of "old, dead conventional Negro-white ideas of the past," and provide youthful (and clearly nationalistic) black writers "with an outlet for publication not available in the limited pages of the small Negro magazines then existing, *The Crisis, Opportunity,* and *The Messenger*—the first two being house organs of interracial organizations, and the latter being God knows what." Predictably, the Negro establishment did not like the first (and only) issue. Rean Graves, then a critic for the Baltimore *Afro-American,* said:

> I have just tossed the first issue of *Fire* into the fire. . . . Aaron Douglas who, in spite of himself and the meaningless grotesqueness of his creations, has gained a reputation as an artist, is permitted to spoil three perfectly good pages and a cover with his pen and ink hudge pudge. Countee Cullen has written a beautiful poem in his 'From a Dark Tower,' but tries his best to obscure the thought in his superfluous sentences. Langston Hughes displays his usual ability to say nothing in many words.[19]

So, as Hughes states, *Fire* had "plenty of cold water thrown on it by the colored critics." To make matters worse, in what is certainly an irony to beat all ironies, several hundred undistributed copies of *Fire,* the last available, were destroyed by a basement fire.

But such unfortunate events did not deter Hughes. He went on to produce more and more poetry, and stories, and books, and plays. The end of the Harlem Renaissance marked the end of his patron, the end of A'Lelia Walker, the end of solvency for many other young artists and writers, and the end of white money to support new-found black causes. Hughes had won a few awards, but he would have to make his living on his own now. And so he determined to make it writing: "Shortly poetry became bread; prose, shelter and raiment. Words turned into songs, plays, scenarios, articles, and stories. Literature is a big sea full of many fish. I let down my nets and pulled. I'm still pulling." And up until his death in 1967, he still was.

CHAPTER 6

Major Themes in the Poetry of Countee Cullen

NICHOLAS CANADAY, JR.

Countee Cullen's first volume of poems, *Color* (1925), demonstrates convincingly that he is a poet of considerable scope who handles a variety of ideas and techniques with ease. The subsequent volumes—*Copper Sun* (1927), *The Ballad of the Brown Girl* (1927), *The Black Christ and Other Poems* (1929), and *The Medea and Some Poems* (1935)—although they do not present marked departures from the themes he introduces in the first volume, do indeed contain new variations and complexities within Cullen's major areas of concern. Here we shall demonstrate Cullen at his best, without regard to chronology, in each of the major thematic groups, noticing that the groups are by no means mutually exclusive because the themes are interrelated. Indeed, virtually every theme in Cullen's poetry—even including the exuberant spirit of his love lyrics—is found in his greatest poem, "Heritage." Our strategy will be to examine the several strands separately, and finally to observe how they are woven into the fabric of "Heritage."

It should not surprise us that the adopted son of the

Reverend Frederick Asbury Cullen of Harlem's Salem African Methodist Episcopal Church should have received from his father an abiding Christian view of the world, which is perhaps the most pervasive element in the younger Cullen's poetry. This faith is not without a countervailing tension of doubt. Many of Cullen's poems quite simply are about religious subjects: this fact in part explains why so many Negro preachers read Cullen's poems from their pulpits and why his poems remain popular as pieces for readings and recitations. Yet Cullen's religious background is also reflected by the frequency and variety of biblical allusion in his poetry, the use of religious imagery even in nonreligious contexts, and a marked tendency to cast poems in parable form.

Cullen's fondness for the parable form—usually brief, dramatic, poetic anecdotes with the meaning implied but not overtly expressed—shows the influence of a home in which the Bible was studied and discussed. A similar observation has long ago been made about another American writer, Stephen Crane, who was also reared in a Methodist parsonage. Crane rebelled in a bitter way that Cullen never did; but Cullen shows in what he thinks of as his pagan moments some of the proverbial behavior of the minister's son. His notable parables in verse include "Two Who Crossed a Line," companion poems about "passing," the poems "Incident" and "Uncle Jim," both about race, and "Ghosts," a poem about love. Many of his satiric epitaphs are also structured like parables in very brief form.

The poem which best seems to represent Cullen's religious posture is "A Thorn Forever in the Breast," from *The Black Christ and Other Poems,* and it is a poem primarily about idealism and not about religion at all. It begins by picturing the idealist as lonely and alien in the world of men. And then it tells of his end:

> This is the certain end his dream achieves:
> He sweats his blood and prayers while others sleep,
> And shoulders his own coffin up a steep
> Immortal mountain, there to meet his doom
> Between two wretched dying men, of whom
> One doubts, and one for pity's sake believes.

The poem is an Italian sonnet, and Cullen shows great skill in meeting the demands of this highly restrictive poetic form. When Cullen speaks of the alienation of the idealist in the real world, he sounds like John Keats, his favorite poetic model. To meet one's doom "between two wretched dying men" is the kind of biblical allusion that is so typical in Cullen's poetry and gives an added dimension of meaning to the fate of one who refuses to take the world as it seems. But Cullen's religious stance would also seem to be portrayed here: he is between two positions. One is doubt and the other is a belief prompted by fear. The latter would seem to be suggested by the one who "for pity's sake believes." The tension implicit in this stance is not resolved here or anywhere else in Cullen's poetry: he will rest neither in unbelief nor in an easy faith.

Overt religious motifs are found in such poems as "Simon the Cyrenian Speaks," "Pagan Prayer," "The Shroud of Color," the companion pieces "For a Skeptic" and "For a Fatalist," "Judas Iscariot," and "Gods"—all from his first volume, *Color*. "Simon the Cyrenian Speaks" is a dramatic monologue delivered by a black follower of Christ, drafted to carry his cross, who accepts his calling when he understands his Master's dream transcends race, that he is not simply being asked to bear another burden as a black man. "Pagan Prayer" is a short poem, the meaning of which relates to the central tension of Heritage.

> Our Father, God; our Brother, Christ,
> Or are we bastard kin,

the poet asks prayerfully. He speaks of his "pagan mad" heart and prays that all "black sheep" be retrieved, a nice irony given both the obvious biblical values associated with straying sheep, as well as what the phrase "black sheep" usually means. "The Shroud of Color" is the poem that first gained Cullen important attention; it was published in the November 1924 issue of H. L. Mencken's *American Mercury*. It begins:

> "Lord, being dark," I said, "I cannot bear
> The further touch of earth, the scented air;
> Lord, being dark, forewilled to that despair
> My color shrouds me in, I am as dirt
> Beneath my brother's heel . . ."

And the answer seems to be:

> *"Dark child of sorrow, mine no less, what art*
> *Of mine can make thee see and play thy part?*
> *The key to all strange things is in thy heart."*

This poem, too, is a kind of parable, with its dialogue between the poet and the divine voice. The poet's resolve is to go on living, even in the shroud of color, living anxiously, to be sure, close to nature, in a kind of trembling but joyful hope.

In the epitaphs "For a Skeptic"—which points out that the skeptic may have more faith than he knows but in the wrong thing—and "For a Fatalist"—which holds that such a person has his ship wrecked even before he can hoist his sail—two irreligious postures are rejected. "Judas Iscariot" is a sentimental poem depicting Judas as having willingly played the destined role of betrayer, taking the "sorry part" out of great love and being thus forever scorned by unknowing people. Finally, "Gods" is an interesting short poem because it shows paganism again in conflict with Christianity. The poet says:

I cannot hide from Him the gods
That revel in my heart,
Nor can I find an easy word
To tell them to depart . . .

Just as "gods" is not capitalized—they are the idols of a pagan impulse—neither is "word" capitalized. But the allusion to the Word that dispels such gods seems unmistakable. Yet the poet says he cannot find "an easy word," and thus the tension remains.

Since "The Black Christ" is a long narrative poem that gives its name to the 1929 volume of Cullen's poetry, it should be mentioned here under the rubric of religious verse. It is the story of a black boy who is lynched and then in resurrection appears to his mother and brother. The poem's message is overt and rather diffuse: have faith in the mercy of God. There is nothing of black messianism here in spite of the title—the idea that a suffering black Christ might ultimately redeem white America, though this idea had long before appeared in the writings of Du Bois and others.

Traditional lyric poets traditionally deal with love and death, and Countee Cullen is no exception. This second category of thematic concern contains the largest group of his poems, including many love lyrics of one mood or another. Let an early example stand for his frequent verses in the *carpe diem* tradition. In "To a Brown Girl" Cullen says it this way:

What if no puritanic strain
  Confines him to the nice?
He will not pass this way again,
  Nor hunger for you twice.

Since in the end consort together
  Magdalen and Mary,
Youth is the time for careless weather:
  Later, lass, be wary.

The inconstancy of love is also a traditional theme Cullen treated many times. The poems "There Must Be Words" and "Nothing Endures" from the 1929 volume may serve as examples. In the first he writes of love departing, leaving no external sign of its former presence:

After a decent show of mourning I,
As once I ever was, shall be as free
To look on love with calm unfaltering eye,
And marvel that such fools as lovers be.

And from the second:

Nothing endures,
Not even love,
Though the warm heart purrs
Of the length thereof.

Though beauty wax,
Yet shall it wane;
Time lays a tax
On the subtlest brain.

Let the blood riot,
Give it its will;
It shall grow quiet,
It shall grow still.

Claims made for paganism in love lyrics have been traditional through many centuries of English poetry, but since

Cullen writes out of the black experience, this strand has an added weight in his poems. We have already seen the opposing Christian/Pagan claims in his religious poetry. His advice in "To a Brown Boy" is:

> Lad, never dam your body's itch
>   When loveliness is seen.

And the word "dam" probably contains a deliberate ambiguity: neither condemn it nor attempt to obstruct its natural force. There is bliss, the poem continues, in "brown limbs,"

> And lips know better how to kiss
>   Than how to raise white hymns.

The imagery here, typical in Cullen's poems, opposes brown/sensuality/paganism to white/spirituality/Christianity. At the same time a cold sterility is also a connotation of the latter. Cullen does not honor an ascetic purity. On the contrary, the humorous epitaph "For a Virgin" illustrates his gentle scorn for the unfulfilled. The wry ironic tone is typical of Cullen's poetry as the virgin speaks from the grave:

> For forty years I shunned the lust
>   Inherent in my clay;
> Death only was so amorous
>   I let him have his way.

Another clearly identifiable group of Cullen's love poems deals with the subject of love for a brown maiden as opposed to a white. Sense and spirit are in general the opposing claims. In "A Song of Praise" Cullen says of his dark love:

> Her walk is like the replica
>   Of some barbaric dance
> Wherein the soul of Africa
>   Is winged with arrogance.

And from a later poem with almost the same title, "Song of Praise":

Who lies with his milk-white maiden,
  Bound in the length of her pale gold hair,
Cooled by her lips with the cold kiss laden,
  He lies, but he loves not there.

Who lies with his nut-brown maiden,
  Bruised to the bone with her sin-black hair,
Warmed with the wine that her full lips trade in,
  He lies, and his love lies there.

This thought accurately represents also the theme of Cullen's long narrative poem, *The Ballad of the Brown Girl,* published separately in 1927 as an illustrated and decorated book. The poem tells in ballad stanzas the story of Lord Thomas, who must choose between Fair London (the white maiden) and the Brown Girl. He chooses the latter, but on their wedding day Fair London appears and she is stabbed by the Brown Girl. Lord Thomas kills the Brown Girl and then himself, and all three are buried in a common grave. One could construct an allegory or explore motives and values in all this, but what Cullen primarily sought to achieve was a poem of haunting and sensuous beauty. A short poem called "Caprice" also illustrates the light/dark tension; it depicts the inconstancy of love and the forgiving nature of the lover. It has the structure of a parable—a brief episode dramatically presented—and its theme must be inferred by the reader. While awaiting her unfaithful lover, the black woman swears to dismiss him when he returns.

But when he came with his gay black head
  Thrown back, and his lips apart,
She flipped a light hair from his coat,
  And sobbed against his heart.

The poem "Ghosts" may summarize Cullen's achievement in writing love lyrics. It begins:

> Breast under breast when you shall lie
>   With him who in my place
> Bends over you with flashing eye
>   And ever nearing face;
>
> Hand fast in hand when you shall tread
>   With him the springing ways
> Of love from me inherited
>   After my little phase;

He warns that his own ghostly presence may be felt, and then continues:

> But never let it trouble you,
>   Or cost you one caress;
> Ghosts are soon sent with a word or two
>   Back to their loneliness.

The sexual imagery is specific and concrete: Cullen is here very conscious of reality. There is a joy in recalling "the springing ways of love" that gives also a lightness to the poem. Most characteristic is the tone of ironic detachment. The love was merely a "little phase" that is now over. Linked with the detachment is the physical awareness that the woman is now in the arms of another and his resulting loneliness. The achievement of the last stanza is that all three impulses are held in suspension simultaneously.

One poem may stand as the best example of Cullen on death. His poem "The Wise" echoes his master, John Keats, "half in love with easeful death." In a quiet, contemplative mood appropriate to the title, Cullen presents in rhymed triplets the several reasons why death is to be desired, what in fact are the elements of wisdom. In the first place, knowledge is gained through the dark glass, literally, of the earth, knowledge of ultimate natural mysteries:

> Dead men are wisest, for they know
> How far the roots of flowers go,
> How long a seed must rot to grow.

This knowledge is perhaps not commanding in an emotional sense, but in the second stanza the senses are stilled and there is no feeling of joy or pain. This aspect of death is emotionally more satisfying to the weary:

> Dead men alone bear frost and rain
> On throbless heart and heatless brain,
> And feel no stir of joy or pain.

Thirdly, the soul is at rest because the raging of love and hate is quieted:

> Dead men alone are satiate;
> They sleep and dream and have no weight,
> To curb their rest, of love or hate.

Thus the dead are the wise, and indeed a good definition of wisdom for the living would include the elements of knowledge, detachment, and peace. The poem concludes with a neat paradox:

> Strange, men should flee their company,
> Or think me strange who long to be
> Wrapped in their cool immunity.

In the concluding phrase "cool immunity" we have a particularly felicitous expression—appropriate to the tone, insightful, suggestive.

As we would expect of a lyric poet, Countee Cullen takes as his province the larger categories of religion, love, and death. Many of Cullen's poems, however, and here is added a new dimension of subject matter, are solely concerned with what he would call "color" or "race" and what we would call the black experience. Yet these divisions, as we have seen, are wholly arbitrary, for almost every poem already considered comes out of the black experience in one way or another. Many of them overtly refer to racial matters. Thus critics who assert that Cullen was not activist enough in orientation—and some are even harsher—would seem to have a rather narrow view of what a poet ought to be doing.

Before proceeding to this final category and its summary in "Heritage," it should be noted that Cullen was good at making short poems of social satire and that he also wrote poems about poetry and poets. These two minor categories contain some of his most often quoted lines, although they are not particularly related in any way except that the pervasiveness of the black experience is again apparent, as our examples will show.

Cullen delighted in humorous epitaphs, and we have already seen some examples. Here is one about prostitutes, replete with great irony:

Ours is the ancient story:
  Delicate flowers of sin,
Lilies, arrayed in glory,
  That would not toil or spin.

The daring but ironically appropriate allusion to the biblical passage accounts for the wit. These "lilies" neither toil nor spin any more than their natural counterparts, but the glory of their raiment is of a different order from that envisioned in the Gospel. Or take the well-known example of Cullen's wit in the epitaph "For a Lady I Know":

She even thinks that up in heaven
  Her class lies late and snores,
While poor black cherubs rise at seven
  To do celestial chores.

This will suffice to illustrate the type. There are several for men of letters—Keats, Conrad, and Dunbar. Perhaps the last of these is most poignant:

Born of the sorrowful of heart
  Mirth was a crown upon his head;
Pride kept his twisted lips apart
  In jest, to hide a heart that bled.

There are also other poems about poets and poetry—to Keats, Amy Lowell, and Emily Dickinson, for example. Cullen's poem "Yet Do I Marvel," about the struggle of being a poet, and more particularly about the struggle of being a black poet, may serve as a transition to our final section. It begins:

I doubt not God is good, well-meaning, kind,
And did He stoop to quibble could tell why
The little buried mole continues blind,
Why flesh that mirrors Him must some day die . . .

Through classical allusion the poem poses the great mysteries of life. Its conclusion is:

Inscrutable His ways are, and immune
To catechism by a mind too strewn
With petty cares to slightly understand
What awful brain compels His awful hand.
Yet do I marvel at this curious thing:
To make a poet black, and bid him sing!

On the surface of the poem the tone is a playful irony, treating great mysteries as "quibbles" or "curious things." Yet the Creator's work seems uneven, death is the end of all of it, and there are grave questions involving man's choice and freedom. But the most curious thing of all is—and Cullen understands the irony of this particular culmination to the great mysteries—"To make a poet black, and bid him sing!"

There is an implied ambiguity in the word "sing": one does not always sing for joy, though Cullen would not deny that even for a black poet there is a time for that too.

Of the poems that deal primarily with the black experience, it is appropriate to begin with two poems of initiation, both dramatic anecdotes presented in verse, one obviously based on an early experience in life and the other a later incident. The first is called "Incident." The subject matter of this poem is loss of innocence, and the impact of the poem depends partly on an incongruity between the subject matter and the form, as well as within the subject matter itself. Here is a smiling, friendly black boy eight years old—and to use the phrase "black boy" is to place it within context as part of a major motif in Afro-American literature—an innocent black boy who has an encounter with ugliness, evil.

Once riding in old Baltimore,
  Heart-filled, head-filled with glee,
I saw a Baltimorean
  Keep looking straight at me.

Now I was eight and very small,
  And he was no whit bigger,
And so I smiled, but he poked out
  His tongue, and called me, "Nigger."

There is, then, an incongruity between what a childhood experience ought to be and what it is. There is now a sad awareness in the last stanza; it was then shock.

I saw the whole of Baltimore
  From May until December;
Of all the things that happened there
  That's all that I remember.

What happened there wiped out all other memories; it is as

though a portion of innocence were destroyed. The tension between innocence and experience is also reflected in the ambiguity between subject matter and verse form. It is a child's verse, highly regular in rhyme and meter, simple in diction. It could be a poem in "A Black Child's Garden of Verse." By way of comparison, hear one of Robert Louis Stevenson's poems from *his* collection. No doubt Cullen would have known Stevenson's poems, perhaps even this one called "Singing":

Of speckled eggs the birdie sings
  And nests among the trees;
The sailor sings of ropes and things
  In ships upon the seas.

The children sing in far Japan,
  The children sing in Spain;
The organ with the organ man
  Is singing in the rain.

Children sing in Baltimore, too, and, sadly, one thing they sing is "Nigger." Speckled eggs and birds and ropes and things and ships upon the seas—these should be the stuff of childhood. Cullen's "Incident" is all about finding a spider in the Rice Krispies. The sadness of the last stanza is not unwarranted.

Another poetic anecdote recounts an experience with a bitter, pipe-smoking black uncle, who says only, "White folks is white," and waits for the poet to understand and to feel the meaning of the statement. The poem "Uncle Jim" begins:

"White folks is white," says Uncle Jim;
"A platitude," I sneer;
And then I tell him so is milk,
And the froth upon his beer.

His heart welled up with bitterness,
He smokes his pungent pipe,
And nods at me as if to say,
"Young fool, you'll soon be ripe!"

At the end of the poem the poet is in the company of a white friend, who shares deeply his joys and sorrows and his interest in poetry, but still the poet's thoughts return to Uncle Jim. He wonders why. The unspoken implication is that there is an impassable gulf between the white and the black experience, however intimate the friendship. So the poem as initiation experience deals with separation as a fact of life, Cullen would say a sad fact of the present. Whether inevitable or forever is a question I think not answered in Cullen's poetry.

Anger and ominous warning is the theme of Cullen's "From the Dark Tower," a poem that he places first in his second volume of poetry, *Copper Sun*. Another sonnet of considerable accomplishment, its octave reads:

We shall not always plant while others reap
The golden increment of bursting fruit,
Not always countenance, abject and mute,
That lesser men should hold their brothers cheap;
Not everlastingly while others sleep
Shall we beguile their limbs with mellow flute,
Not always bend to some more subtle brute;
We were not made eternally to weep.

The poetic diction—"bursting fruit" and "mellow flute"—makes the poem seem removed from reality, but the last line above—sad, angry, prophetic—is a sweeping line of ringing militancy: "We were not made eternally to weep." Ominous warning is also the theme of "Mood," a poem that captures an angry mood in the black experience. It begins:

I think an impulse stronger than my mind
May some day grasp a knife, unloose a vial,
Or with a little leaden ball unbind
The cords that tie me to the rank and file.
My hands grow quarrelsome with bitterness,
And darkly bent upon the final fray;
Night with its stars upon a grave seems less
Indecent than the too complacent day.

What are these cords that keep him from violence, that restrain him and his mass of brothers? Who controls them? Are they good restraints on an impulse toward destructive savagery or are they chains? And the ambiguous "final fray" may mean Armageddon. But who will win, or will all be destroyed? Such questions are implicit in this heavily suggestive poem. The impulse was later to be embodied in Bigger Thomas, and James Baldwin much later would say that no Negro living in America has not felt it, briefly or for long periods, in some varying degree of intensity. Yet it remains only an impulse for Cullen, as for Baldwin, his pupil in a Harlem junior high school, years later, who also had a minister father. The end of the poem reveals that Cullen's religious background is never far beneath the surface:

God knows I would be kind, let live, speak fair,
Requite an honest debt with more than just,
And love for Christ's dear sake those shapes that wear
A pride that had its genesis in dust,—
The meek are promised much in a book I know
But one grows weary turning cheek to blow.

Another familiar mood, the Negro as expatriate, is captured in one of the poems in the 1935 volume, a poem called "To France." Cullen praises that country as a place where blacks most feel free:

There might I only breathe my latest days,
With those rich accents falling on my ear
That most have made me feel that freedom's rays
Still have a shrine where they may leap and sear,—
Though I were palsied there, or halt, or blind,
So I were there, I think I should not mind.

The last poem in this last volume (not including, of course, the posthumously published *On These I Stand* of 1947) is perhaps the most militant protest poem that Cullen wrote. It is called "Scottsboro, Too, Is Worth Its Song," and it is dedicated to "American Poets." The clear but unspoken criticism in the poem is that the American poets who wrote eloquently about Sacco and Vanzetti (including Cullen himself) failed to notice the Scottsboro incident. It is appropriate that Cullen should choose to close his last volume of new poems with "Scottsboro." Cullen is the representative and symbolic figure of the Harlem Renaissance, and the Scottsboro tragedy of 1931 was the traumatic experience in the black community that ended this literary flowering. A few lines will reveal the tone of the poem:

I said:
Now will the poets sing,—
Their cries go thundering
Like blood and tears
Into the nation's ears,
Like lightning dart
Into the nation's heart.

And these were his reasons:

Here in epitome
Is all disgrace
And epic wrong,
Like wine to brace
The minstrel heart, and blare it into song.

We know the nation was not called to account by its poets. Here is Cullen's ironic conclusion:

Surely, I said,
Now will the poets sing.
  But they have raised no cry.
  I wonder why.

Cullen's relevancy, if it need be proved, is demonstrated forty years later with an incident at Jackson State College. The difference is that Scottsboro was not followed by its Kent State.

Thus many of the aspects of the black experience are reflected in Countee Cullen's poetry: awareness of a dehumanizing racism, uniqueness, and separatism, yearning for freedom, anger, and militant protest. And there is one thing more that adds to his scope. As the representative artist of the Harlem Renaissance, he may well have written the best poem about Harlem. It is called "Harlem Wine." It begins:

This is not water running here,
  These thick rebellious streams
That hurtle flesh and bone past fear
  Down alleyways of dreams.

The wine is a narcotic and at the same time a symbol of a dark race. All this is said in the poem: Whatever is running in Harlem is darker and more intoxicating, more vital than white water. It is rebellious because Harlem is a place apart, representing values other than those in white America. The wine gives courage when there may be fear; it represents a deep and dreamlike racial heritage. The primitivism of the poem concludes with the joy of music and dance presented in the imagery of lovemaking. All this is summarized in a place symbolizing human communication, personal relations, identity—the place is Harlem.

The heritage that is alluded to in "Harlem Wine" is fully developed in Cullen's finest poem, called "Heritage." A devastating irony pervades the poem, and part of the irony is the ambiguity of its title. What is the heritage of the Afro-American? It is Africa, of course, "three centuries removed," as Cullen rather wryly notes about his own case. But it is also the Western, that is, Christian, tradition. We have seen how this tension is a central motif in Cullen's poetry. The fact is that this tension is a central motif in black literature, never more explicitly and accurately stated than in Du Bois's famous passage about the quality of "twoness" in the black experience.

"Heritage" is not simply about Africa; nor is it simply an attack on Christianity. It says, however, something much better understood now than it was fifty years ago: that the part of Christianity which is merely the result of Western culture is an excrescence. Nor should "Heritage" be read on the simple level of tom-tom paganism. To Cullen Africa is a symbol; it is like the dark Harlem wine. One must not expect the real Africa to be depicted here; Cullen knew no more about the real Africa than did Keats about the real Provençal. Cullen has translated a myth into poetry in order to embody concretely, not to deny, the power of that myth. The poem begins:

> What is Africa to me:
> Copper sun or scarlet sea,
> Jungle star or jungle track,
> Strong bronzed men or regal black
> Women from whose loins I sprang
> When the birds of Eden sang?
> *One three centuries removed*

From the scenes his fathers loved
Spicy grove, cinnamon tree,
What is Africa to me?

As an example of a too literal response to this poem, one recent critic has objected to the presence of the cinnamon tree of Ceylon in these lines, a tree which the critic asserts is not found in Africa. No doubt Countee Cullen would have enjoyed this critical comment because he surely would have known the famous complaint about Keats choosing Cortez to discover the Pacific Ocean. With great irony, because with great self-knowledge, the poet asks what Africa can mean to him. His immediate response is clear: nothing. And yet this is not true either. "So I lie," begins the second stanza, and there follow three stanzas picturing the remorseless, inexorable pull of that African heritage. The rhythm of the poem pulsates from one wave of strong emotion such as this:

So I lie, whose fount of pride
Dear distress, and joy allied,
Is my somber flesh and skin,
With the dark blood damned within
Like great pulsing tides of wine
That I fear must burst the fine
Channels of the chafing net
Where they surge and foam and fret.

The "tides of wine" image symbolizing the African heritage, as in "Harlem Wine," is used again here. Then the poem subsides for a cool, ironic, "civilized" moment:

Africa? A book one thumbs
Listlessly, till slumber comes.

Such a book is, after all, the nearest the poet has come to a "real" experience with the "real" Africa. And then a swelling wave once again comes with an orgiastic culmination:

I can never rest at all
When the rain begins to fall
Like a soul gone mad with pain
I must match its weird refrain;
Ever must I twist and squirm,
Writhing like a baited worm,
While its primal measures drip
Through my body crying, "Strip!
Doff this new exuberance.
Come and dance the Lover's Dance!"

Then an introspective quiet couplet summarizes what is essentially the first part of the poem:

In an old remembered way
Rain works on me night and day.

Next the other part of the poet's heritage is put forth—the opposing claim, also powerful—the Western tradition: reason and distrust of emotion, civilization looking askance on primitive heathens, Christianity. Cullen proceeds quietly and with great irony, well aware of the self-righteousness of what he says:

Quaint, outlandish heathen gods
Black men fashion out of rods,
Clay, and brittle bits of stone,
In a likeness like their own,
My conversion came high-priced;
I belong to Jesus Christ,
Preacher of humility;
Heathen gods are naught to me.

Such is the counterclaim: patronizing, stuffy, superior, proud (as it is said) in all humility. In that voice the poet says he is superior because his belief is "high-priced"; it is not simply a matter of fashioning some idol out of whatever is at hand. One must pay; one must give up something. And what one denies always includes the Lover's Dance. Besides, African gods look like Africans. Cullen's irony is devastating because he is so well aware of what the Christian God looks like. He is above all proud, extremely proud, to belong to Jesus Christ, preacher of humility. This, too, is part of the black experience.

In the next stanza the ironic mask is put aside. The poet says he is playing a double part; the tension remains. The tone is reverent, confessional. If Christ were black, the poet says, he could be sure that Christ knew the pain of black men. Then Cullen returns to several lines of characteristic irony:

> Lord, I fashion dark gods, too,
> Daring even to give You
> Dark despairing features . . .

And then the quiet summary of this section:

> Lord, forgive me if my need
> Sometimes shapes a human creed.

The last stanza recapitulates but does not resolve the central tension of "Heritage." Returning to both strands of his heritage, he first addresses that part symbolized by Africa in these words:

> *One thing only must I do:*
> *Quench my pride and cool my blood,*
> *Lest I perish in the flood.*

And then for that part symbolized by the word "civilization":

> *Not yet has my heart or head*
> *In the least way realized*
> *They and I are civilized.*

Cullen says here: I know but I have not yet realized. This paradox would seem to be a great poetic statement of the "twoness" referred to by Du Bois—which is to say, a great poetic statement of the black experience.

And the black experience—I think Cullen would maintain—is part of the human experience. When the artist can discover and reveal the black experience in his art, he is thereby adding to our knowledge of the human experience. This is what Cullen's poetry succeeds in doing, still another marvel, now beyond the question of black and white.

CHAPTER 7

Claude McKay and the Cult of Primitivism

MICHAEL B. STOFF

When asked why he had never visited Gertrude Stein while they were both in Paris, Claude McKay replied, "I never went because of my aversion to cults and disciples."[1] McKay, a major poet and novelist of the Harlem Renaissance, was less than accurate in expressing a distaste for cults. In his art, he employed the images of the cult of primitivism in vogue among white contemporaries. Similarly, he pursued a primitive life-style as he struggled with the special problems of the black intellectual. McKay's success on the aesthetic level would not be matched in life.

" 'The most moving and pathetic fact in the social life of America today,' " wrote Malcolm Cowley about the 1920s, " 'is emotional and aesthetic starvation.' And what is the remedy?"[2] The search for that remedy elicited a multitude of responses, all of which seemed motivated by a frantic desire to escape. The physical act of expatriation and the spiritual immersion of the self in art were two mechanisms employed by young intellectuals to flee the materialism and artistic stagnation of modern America. The fear and repugnance engendered by the Machine Age also evoked a third response—the intellectual retreat into the primitive.

The cult of primitivism which gripped many American intellectuals during the 1920s manifested itself in a number of ways. The rising interest in jazz, the study of African art forms, and the examination of tribal cultures were all variations on the theme of the primitive. The Negro as the uncorrupted remnant of preindustrial man became the central metaphor in this cult.[3] Against the background of a tawdry culture stood the instinctive, sensual black man whose "dark laughter" represented a fundamental challenge to the effete civilization of white America. The Negro was transformed into a cultural hero serving as the protagonist in a series of white literary efforts. Eugene O'Neill's *The Emperor Jones* (1920) and *All God's Chillun Got Wings* (1924), Waldo Frank's *Holiday* (1923), Ronald Firbank's *Prancing Nigger* (1924), Sherwood Anderson's *Dark Laughter* (1925), and Carl Van Vechten's *Nigger Heaven* (1926) are merely a sampling of that new genre.

The primitivism in Claude McKay's art manifests itself even in his earliest efforts. As a Jamaican youth, McKay composed a series of dialect poems later published in two volumes: *Songs of Jamaica* (1912) and *Constab Ballads* (1912). Both thematically, through their emphasis on everyday peasant life, and stylistically, through their use of native dialect, these poems reveal McKay's fascination with Jamaican folk culture. They capture the exotic and earthy qualities of the black peasantry with a lyrical sensitivity reminiscent of Robert Burns. McKay might have been exposed to Burns through his acquaintance with Edward Jekyll, an English recluse living in Jamaica. Years later, McKay recalled the seminal role the Englishman played in awakening the young poet to the beauty of the Jamaican folk-art tradition:

> And when I sent them [his poems] on to Mr. Jekyll, he wrote back to say that each one was more beautiful than the last. Beauty! A short while before I never thought that any beauty could be found in the Jamaican dialect. Now this Englishman has discovered beauty and I too could see where my poems were beautiful. Also, my comrades and sometimes the peasants going to the market to whom I would read some of them. They used to exclaim, "Why they're just like that, they're so natural." And then I felt fully rewarded for my efforts.[4]

McKay derived a special satisfaction from the approval of his peers. That formative recognition reinforced his affection for the cultural roots of Jamaica and provided a base for a widening perception of other folk heritages.

McKay's depiction of the Jamaican peasant is integrally related to a stereotyped image of the world's peasantry. His peasants have a universality of condition and reaction which allows them to be exchanged with peasants of any nationality. This conception is consistent with McKay's later claim: "As a child, I was never interested in different kinds of races or tribes. People were just people to me." [5] In describing McKay's image of the Jamaican peasant, the French literary critic Jean Wagner has written:

> All things being equal, McKay's portrait of the Jamaican peasant is in substance that of the peasant the world over. Profoundly attached to the earth, he works the soil with a knowledge gained from age long habit; although a hard worker, the Jamaican, like his counterpart the world over, is condemned to exploitation.[6]

This perception of common qualities among the world's

masses later furnished McKay with a theoretical basis for his own peculiar vision of the ideal political state. At this early point in his life, the concept of a "universal peasantry" heightened his sensitivity to folk-art traditions of other cultures. That interest supplied him with a foundation for much of his work.

McKay emigrated from Jamaica in 1912 at the age of twenty-two. He carried with him not only a deep regard for the Jamaican peasantry but also a special vision of the island itself. He retained that vision until his death in 1948. The image of Jamaica as paradise permeates all his recollections of the island. In McKay's first American poems and in his later autobiographical material, Jamaica becomes the metaphorical equivalent of Eden. Its simplicity and freshness offered refuge from the complexities of a modern, industrialized world.[7] Two stanzas from the poem "North and South" are typical of the nostalgic, pastoral strains found in McKay's early work:

O sweet are the tropic lands for waking dreams!
There time and life move lazily along,
There by the banks of blue and silver streams
Grass-sheltered crickets chirp incessant song;
Gay-colored lizards loll all through the day,
Their tongues outstretched for careless little flies.

And swarthy children in the fields at play,
Look upward, laughing at smiling skies.
A breath of idleness is in the air
That casts a subtle spell upon all things,
And love and mating time are everywhere,
And wonder to life's commonplaces clings.[8]

The exotic setting and sensory images give a sensual flavor to the poem. These devices are re-employed in conjunction with themes of innocence and uncorruptibility in other Jamaican poems:

> What days our wine thrilled bodies pulsed with joy
> Feasting upon blackberries in the copse?
> Oh some I know! I have embalmed the days,
> Even the sacred moments when we played,
> All innocent of passion, uncorrupt,
> At noon and evening in the flame-heart's shade.
> We were so happy, happy I remember,
> Beneath the poinsettia's red in warm December.[9]

McKay did not lose the vision of Jamaica as an undefiled Eden where instinct and sensation reigned supreme. Although he never returned to his island home, he was forever swept back thematically to his preindustrial, peasant origins.[10] In 1947, a year before his death, McKay wrote, "I think of a paradise as something of a primitive kind of place where there are plenty of nuts and fruits and flowers and milk and wild honey. Jamaica has all of this." [11] Recapturing the lost innocence of that Eden provided one of the major themes in McKay's life.

McKay was also obsessed with describing the social role to be played by the intellectual. His membership in a visible and oppressed minority further complicated matters. In essence, the entire body of his art can be seen as a mechanism through which he sought to transform these personal problems into public issues.[12] Such a transformation entailed an insistent reference to a recurring pattern of images. That pattern was the juxtapositioning of the instinctive black man and the educated Negro. These images defined, with increasing precision, McKay's own concepts and made them salient within a broader cultural context.

McKay's earliest use of this construction came in the first of his three novels, *Home to Harlem*. The book was published in 1928, the sixth year of McKay's expatriation from America. Its appearance initiated a violent debate among the black literati over the propriety of its theme and subject matter. Many of McKay's peers agreed with Langston Hughes's evalution. Hughes argued that because it was so "vividly alive," *Home to Harlem* could legitimately be labeled, as "the first real flower of the Harlem Renaissance." [13]

The elder black literary figures and much of the established Negro press were revolted by what they believed to be overtly crude allusions in McKay's book. Claiming the book was not representative of Negro life, this Old Guard expressed its shock and indignation at the lasciviousness of the novel. Its very existence, they suggested, was a calculated affront to the black community. W. E. B. Du Bois's reaction was typical of the initial reviews:

> *Home to Harlem* for the most part nauseates me, and after the dirtier parts of its filth I feel distinctly like taking a bath. . . . It looks as though McKay has set out to cater to that prurient demand on the part of white folk for a portrayal in Negroes of that utter licentiousness which convention holds white folk back from enjoying—if enjoyment it can be labeled.[14]

The controversy enveloping *Home to Harlem* was merely the surfacing of an underlying tension engendered by conflicting visions of the Harlem Renaissance. The Old Guard saw the Renaissance as a vehicle for social amelioration. The Renaissance would not only demonstrate the intellectual achievements of the black man, but would also uplift the masses to some arbitrary level of social acceptability.[15]

It was precisely this view of the Harlem Renaissance, this venture in cultural pretension, that McKay's work fundamentally challenged. His notion of a renaissance was an aggregation of ". . . talented persons of an ethnic or national group working individually or collectively in a common purpose and creating things that would be typical of their group." [16] In 1929, McKay defined the problems one faced when speaking of a "racial renaissance." He delineated the tactics and sources to be employed in creating such a movement:

> We educated Negroes are talking a lot about a racial renaissance. And I wonder how we're going to get it. On one side we're up against the world's arrogance—a mighty cold hard white stone thing. On the other the great sweating army—our race. It's the common people, you know, who furnish the bone and sinew and salt of any race or nation. In the modern race of life we're merely beginners. If this renaissance is going to be more than a sporadic scabby thing, we'll have to get down to our racial roots to create it. . . . Getting down to our native roots and building up from our people is . . . culture.[17]

For McKay, this meant the conscious and studied illumination of a black folk-art tradition whose central themes would be the indestructible vitality of the primitive black man and the inextricable dilemma of the educated Negro.

Home to Harlem is a vivid glimpse of the lower depths of black life in urban America. Its peripatetic plot and dialect-oriented style are consistent with its thematic emphasis on the black man as the unrestrained child of civilization. Set in New York's black ghetto, the novel establishes Harlem as a carnal jungle. Our senses are subjected to a barrage of erotic images: "Brown girls rouged and painted like dark pansies. Brown flesh draped in colorful clothes. Brown lips full and pouted for sweet kissing. Brown breasts throbbing with love." [18] At the core of this physical world lies the cabaret Congo, "a real little Africa in New York." Forbidden to whites, the Congo is a distillation of Harlem life. Its atmosphere is filled with the "tenacious odors of service and the warm indigenous smells of Harlem." Its allusions to the unrepressed African culture provide an apt setting for the return of the novel's hero, Jake Brown.

Jake, an Army deserter, is introduced as the natural man whose actions are guided by intuition. He is the instinctive primitive, deeply rooted in the exotic mystique of Africa. As he walks down Lenox Avenue, he is overcome by the pulsations of Harlem life. "His flesh tingled," the narrator tells us, and "he felt as if his whole body was a flaming wave." Jake and Harlem are inexorably bound by a "contagious fever . . . burning everywhere," but burning most fervently in "Jake's sweet blood." That primitive passion sustains Jake and represents a profound threat to the cultural rigidity of modern society.

In contrast to Jake, McKay inserts himself as the Haitian immigrant Ray. Ray represents the cultivated intellect, the civilized black whose education has sensitized his mind but paralyzed his body. Intellectually, Ray can comprehend the cluster of sensations and emotions about him, yet he lacks the naturalness of action and spontaneity of response that are the hallmarks of a Jake Brown. Although envious of Jake, Ray harbors the obsessive fear that "someday the urge of the flesh . . . might chase his high dreams out of him and deflate him to the contented animal that was the Harlem nigger strutting his stuff." [19]

The result is a vision of the intellectual, and especially the black intellectual, as social misfit. Ray is capable of sensing and recording life, but he is unable to live it. "He drank in more of life," writes McKay, "than he could distill into active animal living." There is no outlet for his immense store of emotional energy. Robbed by his "white" education of the ability to act freely and impulsively, Ray remains little more than a "slave of the civilized tradition." Caught between two cultures, he is immobilized. "The fact is," he tells Jake as he flees to Europe,

> . . . I don't know what I'll do with my little education. I wonder sometimes if I could get rid of it and lose myself in some savage culture in the jungles of Africa. I am a misfit—as the doctors who dole out newspaper advice to the well-fit might say—a misfit with my little education and constant dreaming, when I should be getting the nightmare habit to hog in a lot of dough like everybody else in this country. . . . The more I learn the less I understand and love life.[20]

The implications of Ray's final statement are not only applicable to McKay's personal problems but related to a broader cultural phenomenon. Notions of escape, alienation, and crude commercialism were by no means uniquely black images. They were embraced by intellectuals of varying hues in the twenties.[21] McKay's use of these themes places the black experience into a larger cultural context. Blackness only added a further convolution to the already complex problem of the intellectual's social adaptability.

Ray's expatriation leaves the fundamental questions raised by the novel unresolved. The continuing focus on Jake, and his reunion with the "tantalizing brown" girl Felice, [22] imply that only the instinctive primitive can survive happily in white civilization, its dehumanizing tendencies are irrelevant to his innately free existence. The intellectual, defiled by the process of civilization, is doomed to wander in search of that potency of action he has irrevocably lost.

McKay's second novel, *Banjo,* published in 1929, pursues the issues raised in *Home to Harlem.* Although the scene has shifted to Marseille's harbor district, the structural dualism characterizing *Home to Harlem* is present once more. Lincoln Agrippa Daily, familiarly known as Banjo, replaces

Jake Brown while McKay again enters as Ray. The dichotomy is now expanded and more lucidly articulated.

In *Banjo* there is a sharpening of figurative focus and a widening of thematic scope. With the character Banjo, McKay adds a new dimension to the earthy black and provides a more concise definition of his own racial conceptions. At the same time, Ray's disposition has progressed from a confused uneasiness with American life to a coherent denunciation of western civilization. This increased clarity of imagery allows McKay to move toward a resolution to the quandary of the black intellectual.

The primitive black is given additional depth in *Banjo*. The loose plot, an account of the lives of a group of beach boys in the port city of Marseille, provides a background for the development of the protagonist, Banjo. He is the same intuitive vagabond originally described in *Home to Harlem* —with one significant difference. While Jake is nebulously characterized as a laborer, Banjo is depicted as an artist. He is a jazzman whose life is the embodiment of his art. Like the songs he plays, Banjo is unrestrained, free-spirited, and vibrantly alive. McKay immediately establishes the intimate relationships between Banjo and his music: "I never part with this instrument," Banjo says in the opening pages of the novel. "It is moh than a gal, moh than a pal; it's mahself." [23]

After equating the protagonist with his instrument, McKay explains the aesthetic function of the banjo:

> The banjo dominates the other instruments; the charming, pretty sound of the ukelele, the filigree notes of the mandolin, the sensuous color of the guitar. And Banjo's face shows that he feels that his instrument is first. . . . The banjo is preeminently the musical instrument of the American Negro. The sharp, noisy notes of the banjo belong to the American Negro's loud

> music of life—an affirmation of his hardy existence in the midst of the biggest, the most tumultuous civilization of modern life.[24]

The instrument is the cultural expression of American Negro folk-art, and Banjo represents the prototype black folk-artist lustily proclaiming the vitality of his race. His music, "the sharp, noisy notes of the banjo," is not derived from a pretentious adaptation of European culture. Drawing inspiration from the "common people," Banjo's art represents the truest expression of black culture.

Again juxtaposed to this earthy, intuitive black man is the intellectual Ray. Recently expatriated from America, Ray comes to Marseille in search of an artistic haven where he could "exist *en pension* prolitarian of a sort and try to create around him the necessary solitude to work with pencil and scraps of paper." [25] Ray has not given up his earlier passion for writing, and although he is occasionally forced to work as a laborer, he never renounces his "dream of self-expression." Once in the Vieux Port, he finds, instead of solitude, a band of beach boys whose free and undisciplined lifestyle is particularly appealing to Ray's vagabond sensibilities. As a result, he immediately establishes an intimate relationship with the members of the group and especially with their leader, Banjo. At this point, the linear progression of the plot becomes of secondary importance, and the novel is reduced to a vehicle for the delineation of Ray's (*i.e.*, McKay's) brief against civilization and the formulation of a solution to his intellectual quandary.

McKay's condemnation of Western civilization in *Banjo* is inexorably tied to the psychological problems arising from his blackness. In 1937 he wrote, "What, then, was my main psychological problem? It was the problem of color. Color-consciousness was the fundamental of my restlessness." [26]

And it is color-consciousness which is the fundamental of Ray's hatred for civilization. "Civilization is rotten," [27] Ray proclaims, and in the following passage, McKay defines the sociological basis of Ray's sentiments:

> He hated civilization because its general attitude toward the colored man was such as to rob him of his warm human instincts and make him inhuman. Under it the thinking colored man could not function normally like his white brother, responsive and reacting spontaneously to the emotions of pleasure or pain, joy or sorrow, kindness or hardness, charity, anger, and forgiveness. . . . So soon as he entered the great white world, where of necessity he must work and roam and breathe the larger air to live, that entire world, high, low, middle, unclassed, all conspired to make him painfully conscious of color and race. . . . It was not easy for a Negro with an intellect standing watch over his native instincts to take his own way in this white man's civilization. But of one thing he was resolved: civilization would not take the love of color, joy, beauty, vitality and nobility out of *his* life and make him like one of the poor masses of its pale creatures.[28]

Although the imagery utilized in the preceding passage is applied to the peculiar condition of the black man, this vision of a devitalizing, dehumanizing civilization is part of the larger, biracial indictment of American culture. While McKay's attack is rooted in color-consciousness, its targets remain remarkably similar to those of the general assault. McKay finds the fraudulence and duplicity of Western civilization in a multitude of situations beyond its psychological effect on individual black men. The arduous but profitable exercise of lifting the "white man's burden" was, for McKay, a particularly noxious undertaking of the civilized world. Under the guise of Judeo-Christian morality, Western civilization succeeded in its drive to commercialize and exploit the "uncivilized" masses of the earth. Furthermore, McKay saw the trend toward cultural standardization as effectively robbing the world of its "greatest charm"—ethnic diversity. The result was the creation of a sterile, monolithic culture in which "the grand mechanical march of civilization had leveled the world down to the point where it seemed treasonable for an advanced thinker to doubt that what was good for one nation or people was also good for another." [29] Yet Ray does commit the "treasonous" act of disputing this conceptualization. And it is in his dissent that he arrives at an uneasy resolution of the problem which has plagued him through two novels.

In the closing pages of the novel, Ray explains that he has always wanted "to hold on to his intellectual acquirements without losing his instincts. The black gifts of laughter and melody and simple sensuous feelings and responses." [30] It is in this rather untenable position that his problem lies. Given a world in which the terms intellect and instinct have been assigned opposing definitions, it seems improbable that one figure can plausibly synthesize both qualities. Ray's attempt at such a synthesis is achieved through his decision to join Banjo in the vagabond life. Thematically, this decision represents a rejection of the standardized white civilization and an affirmation of the cultural diversity of the beach boys' existence.

Nevertheless, we are uneasy with the solution Ray has developed, and in his closing monologue, he unwittingly defines the source of our dissatisfaction. Although he hopes to learn from Banjo how to "exist as a black boy in a white world and rid his conscience of the used-up hussy of white morality," [31] Ray realizes that "whether the educated man be white or brown or black, he cannot, if he has more than animal desires, be irresponsibly happy like the ignorant man who lives simply by his instincts and appetites."[32] However, "irresponsible happiness" is the essence of a Jake or a Banjo. Ray's inability to adopt this posture precludes the possibility of his successfully embracing their lifestyle or their method of survival in the white world. Despite his delusions, Ray remains the same "misfit" at the conclusion of *Banjo* that he was when he expatriated from America in *Home to Harlem.*

In *Banana Bottom,* the third and last of his novels, McKay achieves an aesthetic structure which permits the formulation of a viable resolution to the predicament of the educated black man. This resolution is viable in that it does not contradict any of the definitions set worth in the novel, and it is consistent with McKay's affirmation of the primitive elements of black life. This new form is attained by abandoning the structural dualism of his earlier works in favor of a single protagonist. In this way, McKay frees himself from the limitations imposed by the rigid polarizations of instinct and intellect in separate characters. No longer constricted by Ray's inability to reject even a part of his cerebral existence, or Jake's (and by extension, Banjo's) static, unattainable sensuality, McKay now produces a novel in which the main character can credibly embody both instinct and intellect.

The plot of *Banana Bottom* is relatively simple. Set in the West Indies, the story commences with the rape of a young Jamaican peasant girl, Bita Plant. Following the incident, Bita becomes the ward of the Craigs, a white missionary couple who, with an air of condescension, take pity on the girl. In the best Anglo-Saxon missionary tradition, they see in her the golden opportunity for demonstrating to their peasant flock "what one such girl might become by careful training [and] . . . by God's help."[33] As a result, they send her to a finishing school in England with the hope of "redeeming her from her past by a long period of education." [34] After a six-year absence, Bita returns to Jamaica only to find that, for all her education, she is irrepressibly attracted to the island's peasant life. Despite the Craigs' insistence on her marriage to a black divinity student and on the devotion of her life to missionary work, Bita rejects their civilized world in favor of the simplicity of peasant life.

The novel derives its power from the dynamic tension established between the conflicting value systems of Anglo-Saxon civilization and the Jamaican folk culture. This thematic dichotomy first manifests itself in the contrasting reactions to Bita's rape. Priscilla Craig expresses her shock and indignation with an unveiled sanctimony. The "oversexed" natives, she comments, are "apparently incapable of comprehending the opprobrium of breeding bastards in a Christian community." [35] On the other hand, the village gossip, a peasant woman named Sister Phibby, reacts with a knowing smile indicating her "primitive satisfaction as in a good thing done early." [36]

McKay expands and sustains the tension of contrary value systems through the ever-present antagonism between the civilized Christ-God of retribution and puritanical repression, and the African Obeah-God of freedom and primeval sensuality. Throughout the novel, the white missionaries and native ministers are constantly troubled with the problem of wandering flocks which "worship the Christian God-of-Good-and-Evil on Sunday and in the shadow of the night . . . invoke the power of the African God of Evil by the magic of the sorcerer. Obi [is] resorted to in sickness and feuds, love and elemental disasters." [37] And although the missionaries struggle desperately to win the native populace, it is the

Obeah-God who rules Jamaica, and it is the primitive African value system which is at the core of the peasant culture.

Of peasant origin and possessing a cultivated intellect, Bita Plant represents McKay's first successful synthesis of two cultures. When she finds it necessary to choose a life-style, it is a relatively easy decision. As opposed to Ray, she is not fraught with the vague uncertainties and questioning doubts over her ability to survive in either culture. Bita has readily internalized the concept of her blackness and willingly accepted her racial origins. Bearing no warping hatred for white civilization, she is characterized by an assertive self-confidence derived from a sense of her own innate worth:

> . . . a white person is just like another human being to me. I thank God that although I was brought up and educated among white people, I have never wanted to be anything but myself. I take pride in being colored and different, just as any intelligent white person does in being white. I can't imagine anything more tragic than people torturing themselves to be different from their natural, unchangeable selves.[38]

For Bita, intellect and education are the handmaidens of instinct. Her return to peasant life provides a source of sustenance and vitality for her total existence: "Her music, her reading, her thinking were the flowers of her intelligence, and he [Bita's peasant husband] the root upon which she was grafted, both nourishing in the same soil." [39]

In Bita Plant, McKay at last succeeds in framing an aesthetic solution to the black intellectual's problem of social incongruence. By rejecting not intellect nor education but rather the "civilized" value system in favor of the primitive values of a black folk culture, the intellectual can ultimately escape the stigma of "misfit." On the surface, this solution does not seem to differ from the one developed in *Banjo.*

Yet in *Banana Bottom,* McKay makes an important distinction not present in his earlier work. For the first time, McKay distinguishes between education, or the cultivation of the intellect, and the necessary acceptance of the value system implied by that education. Ray's failure to make this distinction is the source of his problem. Believing, on the one hand, that a rejection of civilization implies a rejection of intellect, and at the same time, desiring desperately to hold his intellectual acquirements, Ray is immobilized. He can neither remain in a white world which denies his humanity, nor move into a black world which denies his intellect. However, once the distinction is made, the element of conflict between instinct and intellect is removed. Bita, who rejects the civilized value system but not her intellect, can move easily from one world to another without impairing either instinct or intellect. Unfortunately, it is one of McKay's personal tragedies that although he is capable of making this distinction in his art, he is unable to make it in his life. "My damned white education," he wrote in his autobiography, "has robbed me of much of the primitive vitality, the pure stamina, the simple unswaggering strength of the Jakes of the Negro race." [40]

McKay's *art* can be seen as a coherent attempt to articulate and resolve the personal problems of the black intellectual through an aesthetic retreat into primitivism. His *life,* like the lives of most men, presents a less consistent pattern. If there is any overriding theme, it is found in the vision McKay holds of himself. "All my life," he wrote in 1937, "I have been a troubadour wanderer." [41] The role of artistic nomad is the thread connecting McKay's diverse preoccupations. By choosing this image, he transforms metaphor into reality and captures the elusive elements of instinct and intellect. The primitive, liberated black man, and the sensitive, eloquent artist merge in the vagabond poet who, like Bita Plant, is capable of sensually experiencing and rationally expressing life. However, the image is not the man. It is, rather, a convenient but unsuccessful vehicle through which McKay attempts to realize in life the primitive vision he sought so desperately in art.

In describing his Jamaican boyhood, McKay unwittingly identifies the two themes from which the image of the vagabond poet springs. These themes underlie McKay's life and ultimately destroy the efficacy of the role he adopts. The first of these is revealed in the following description of the changes which accrued as a result of McKay's early recognition as a poet: "People knew that I was a poet, and that made me different, although I wanted so much to be like them. . . . I tried to be as simple as simple, but they would never accept me with the old simplicity."[42] McKay sensed that becoming a poet made him different, and he associated that difference with a loss of the innate simplicity characteristic of his peasant culture. At the same time, McKay possessed a "romantic feeling about different races and nations of people until [he] came to America and saw race hatred at work in its most virulent form."[43] The second theme is the painful color-consciousness instilled by this virulent race hatred in a young, romantic Claude McKay. The vagabond poet was a mechanism designed to escape the denigrating effects of color-consciousness and to regain the lost simplicity and vitality of a primitive past.

McKay first struck the pose of the vagabond poet on his trip to Russia in 1922, the first year of his twelve-year expatriation from America. Describing himself as an "undomesticated truant,"[44] McKay explained, "I went to Russia as a writer and a free-spirit and left the same."[45] In reality, the "spiritual freedom" of McKay's truant pose is rigidly conditioned by the predispositions previously discussed. As in his Jamaican boyhood, two motivational streams are discernible. One is the overwhelming desire to "Escape from the pit of sex and poverty, from domestic death, from the cul-de-sac of self-pity, from the hot syncopated fascination of Harlem, from the suffocating ghetto of color-consciousness." [46] The other is the quest for lost simplicity and vitality. Both these needs would seek satisfaction in McKay's special vision of the Russian Revolution.

In March 1922, mere months before he left for Russia, McKay attended a performance of the Moscow Ballet in New York City and wrote a review comparing it to the American theater. His reaction was predictable but revealing: "A very vital thing is lacking [in the American theater], and one realizes what it is only after seeing naturally simple people like the Russians and Negroes on the stage." [47] Given his image of a universal peasantry, it is understandable that he would envision the hardy Russian stereotype as being derived from the same earthy stock as the Jamaican peasant. From here it is a relatively small step to the vision of the Communist revolution as a biracial, international movement of such kindred spirits as the Negro and the Russian. McKay wholeheartedly affirmed that vision [48] as it spoke directly to his desire for an escape from color-consciousness.

Concomitantly, the power of the Russian Revolution was particularly appealing to McKay, especially in the light of the unique goal he assigned to the movement. "For my part," he wrote in a *Liberator* article, "I love to think of communism as liberating millions of city folk to go back to the land." [49] Far from the destination Lenin, Trotsky, or Marx had in mind after the removal of the chains, this idyllic return to the simple life and values of the soil is typically McKay's. It fulfills the second of his driving motivations—

the quest for lost simplicity. The Russian pilgrimage thereby becomes a desperate effort both to lose color-consciousness and to recapture a primtive, pastoral life-style. Truancy has been transformed into frantic flight and pursuit, and freedom, rigidly controlled by these dual obsessions, into bondage. In the end, the vagabond poet becomes an untenable characterization because the metaphor of McKay's thought does not correspond to the reality of his actions.

The Russian experience was typical. The pattern of escape and quest under the guise of the vagabond poet was repeated; only the location differed. Interestingly enough, McKay's devotion to this image quite often caused sharp discrepancies between the recollection and the reality of a given event. In his autobiography, McKay described his stay in Marseille in terms conjuring up the image of the "troubador wanderer" who can immerse himself in the "great gang of black and brown humanity." [50] In a telling letter written during his stay, he related the following impressions of the city:

> And here I am . . . existing, trying to write, in swarms of flies and bugs and filth, when, maybe, my stories converted and sent to America might change my wretched situation a little. . . . Now I am terribly disappointed, utterly desperate, absolutely fed up. . . . Marseille is my last and cheapest stand. I don't want to be driven out of here by hunger and want. . . . After all, the few things I manage to turn out are the only joy I have.[51]

The self-portrait painted in this letter is quite different from the figure created in the memoirs. Instead of the vibrantly alive, vagabond poet, we now have the struggling artist "existing" amid filth and squalor. He derives joy not from the sensuous experience of life, as the autobiographical passage suggests, but rather from the "few things" he is able to write.

Unable to adopt fully the primitive life-style he pursues, McKay is destined forever to live, in his own words, "on the edge of native life," [52] always observing but never fully participating.

Claude McKay was an integral part of the American literary movement of the 1920s. Responsive to metaphors embodied in the cult of the primitive, McKay's art served to reinforce the image of the Negro as the simple, liberated, uncorrupt man. At the same time, his work provided the means by which McKay made his personal problem of social incongruence part of the larger cultural phenomenon expressing itself in the white expatriate movement. His life represented a less successful effort. Forever seeking fulfillment of his desires to escape color-consciousness and recapture lost innocence, McKay was doomed to an existence directly opposed to the life he apotheosized in his art. It is McKay's special and tragic irony that although he clung tenaciously to the conception of himself as a "free spirit," his obsessions condemned him to a life of slavery.

CHAPTER 8

Portrait of Wallace Thurman

MAE GWENDOLYN HENDERSON

Wallace Thurman arrived in New York on Labor Day in 1925 during the peak of the Harlem Renaissance. In less than a decade—nine years later—he died of consumption on Welfare Island in the charity ward of City Hospital. Before his death at the young age of thirty-two, Thurman became one of the central personalities of the Renaissance. Among his friends he was known as a *bon vivant* and bohemian.[1] It was perhaps his "erotic, bohemian" life-style, as Thurman himself described it, as much as his literary creations that made him one of the most fascinating and seductive of the Renaissance figures. During his last years, which he spent in New York, Thurman achieved his greatest successes and perhaps suffered his greatest disappointments. In many ways the course of his life parallels the brief, but colorful and intensely creative, period of the Renaissance itself. As Arna Bontemps described him, "he was like a flame which burned so intensely, it could not last for long, but quickly consumed itself." Indeed, his mind was ever alert and active, his life constantly hectic and searching. It was Thurman's way to plunge himself completely into whatever he became interested in. Writing to a friend, he once said, "I have always gone in for things until I exhausted myself then dropped them." [2] But for a brief period, no personality among the "New Negroes" shone so brilliantly as that of Wallace Thurman, who found himself on a floodtide of success with the publication of his first novel in 1929, and his well-known play, *Harlem,* later that same year. Although he published two novels afterward, Thurman's life, like the flow of the Renaissance, had already receded into an ebbtide.

There had always been an element of tragedy about this "strangely brilliant black boy," as Langston Hughes once described him.[3] Another friend, Harlem theater critic Theophilus Lewis, said it a different way, "Thurman's nature was rich in what I might call, for want of a better name, the Shelleyean essence," wrote Lewis.[4] Probably better than he realized, Lewis had succeeded in capturing the substance of that tragic shadow that seemed to hang so vaguely around Thurman. It was perhaps the consciousness of a failure that had as much to do with his personal life as with his artistic aspirations that gave him a constant expression of melancholy, tempered only by his own self-derision and cynicism. That Thurman recognized his failure as an artist—at least by his own standards—is apparent in his letter to a close friend. "I suddenly had . . . a vision of all artists as Matthew Arnold said of Shelley—futilely beating their wings in the luminous void. If *real* artists do that—how awful," wrote Thurman "must be the fate of folk like myself not exactly burned by the magic fire of genius, but nevertheless scorched." [5]

Thurman is described by one who knew him as a slender young man, dark skinned, "with hands and eyes that are never at rest." [6] His body was always rather fragile, probably due to his tubercular condition as well as a heavy addiction to alcohol. Many of those acquanited with him were struck with his "deep and resonant voice" and "rich, infectious laughter." Dorothy West, another friend, wrote that Thurman's voice was "the most remarkable thing about him, welling up out of his too frail body and wasting its richness in unprintable recountings." [7]

He was born in 1902 in Salt Lake City, Utah, and spent two years studying at the University of Utah. He probably left the Mormon state after having a nervous breakdown, hoping to restore his failing health in California. Although initially interested in medicine, at the University of Southern California Thurman rediscovered an earlier enthusiasm for writing and literature. Writing in the third person in his unpublished *Notes of a Stepchild,* Thurman said of his early interest in writing:

> At the age of ten he wrote his first novel. Three sheets of foolscap covered with childish scribbling. The plot centered around a stereoptican movie he had seen of Dante's *Inferno.* It concerned the agony of a certain blonde woman. At the age of twelve, being a rabid movie fan, he began to rewrite the contemporary serial thrillers, and was more prodigious with death defying escapades for his heroes and heroines, than the fertile Hollywood scenarists. On entering high school he immediately lost all interest in writing, and did not regain it until his last two years in college, when he spent many hours composing poems about gypsies, hell, heaven, love and suicide.[8]

In Los Angeles he wrote a column called "Inklings" for a local black newspaper. During this period he began to read about the "New Negro" movement in New York and made the acquaintance of Arna Bontemps, who was himself to become a participant in the new Renaissance movement. In an effort to establish a similar movement on the Coast, Thurman began to publish his own magazine, *The Outlet.* Unfortunately, the publication lasted only six months and Thurman gave up ideas of starting a New Negro movement in California. He came to New York where his friend, Arna Bontemps, had arrived some time earlier. At the Gurdjieff meetings in Harlem, Thurman soon met Jean Toomer, Dorothy Peterson, Eric Walrond, Langston Hughes, Dorothy West, Countee Cullen, Aaron Douglas, and other eager and talented young black artists like himself.

He found his first editorial job in New York through Theophilus Lewis on the staff of another short-lived publication, *The Looking Glass.* His job as "reporter, editorial writer, assistant make-up man, and errand boy" came to an abrupt end when the newspaper went bankrupt.[9] Thurman did not realize it then, but he had not yet seen his last unsuccessful venture in the magazine business. Several years later, he told his friend Lewis that his ambition was to become editor of a financially secure magazine.

Although he remained out of work for a while, Thurman soon obtained another editorial position, again through Lewis, who was at the time drama critic for the leftist-oriented *Messenger,* published by A. Phillip Randolph and Chandler Owen. When George Schuyler, then managing editor of *The Messenger,* went on a leave of absence from the magazine, Thurman was appointed acting editor. Although outwardly cynical about his work at *The Messenger,* which he described as a magazine "reflecting the policy of whoever paid off best at the time," a friend speaks of Thurman as "secretly elated to be doing the kind of work he had dreamed of doing." [10] As editor, he began publishing not only his own work, but that of other nascent Renaissance talent, particularly the poetry of Langston Hughes and Arna Bontemps as well as a series of sketches by Zora Neal Hurston and a short story by Dorothy West. His own contributions included a modest poem, a short story, several book reviews, and an occasional nonfiction article.

Upon Schuyler's return later that year, in the fall of 1926, Thurman left the magazine. He went to *The World Tomorrow,* a white publication, and became circulation manager. His job at *The World Tomorrow* brought Thurman into contact with many leading and influential people in the literary and publishing world. Probably he made connections there which would later prove useful.

Meanwhile, in the summer of 1926, a group of young black artists and writers—Zora Neale Hurston, Aaron Douglas, John P. Davis, Bruce Nugent, Gwendolyn Bennett, Langston Hughes, and Wallace Thurman—launched "a new experimental quarterly devoted to . . . younger Negro artists," as its editor, Thurman, described the first and only issue to appear of *Fire.*[11] Its enthusiastic young publishers named it *Fire* because, as Hughes said, "the idea [was] that it would burn up a lot of the old, dead conventional Negro-white ideas of the past, *épater le bourgeoisie* into a realization of the existence of the younger Negro writers and artists . . ." [12] Thurman and his friends were interested in a magazine that would give younger artists a chance to publish their works which was not offered elsewhere. Other black magazines of the period—*The Crisis, Opportunity,* and *The Messenger*—were all primarily political organs published by racial uplift organizations. *Fire,* on the other hand, was not concerned with "sociological problems or propaganda." Thurman regarded it as "purely artistic in intent and conception." He later wrote of the magazine:

> . . . hoping to introduce a truly Negroid note into American literature, its contributors had gone to the proletariat rather than to the bourgeoisie for characters and material, had gone to people who still retained some individual race qualities and

who were not totally white American in every respect save color of skin.[13]

These last remarks, of course, constituted an oblique attack on the older, more traditional, black writer of the period. Thurman felt that the black writer was doing a disservice to himself as an artist by constantly dwelling on the theme of racial struggle between whites and blacks. Such writers, he thought, tended to view their own people "as sociological problems rather than human beings." [14]

In an article published the following year in *The New Republic,* Thurman wrote that "the American Negro feels that he has been misinterpreted and caricatured so long by insincere artists that once a Negro gains the ear of the public he should expend his spiritual energy feeding the public honeyed manna on a silver spoon." The traditional black artist tried to suppress any aspects of the seamy or sordid side of life or the "low-down," common, everyday, black life-style, such as writers like Langston Hughes and Claude McKay wrote about in their works. Most blacks felt that they must always appear "butter side up" in public, and consequently, in literature. "Negroes in America," Thurman continued, ". . . feel they must always exhibit specimens from the college rather than from the kindergarten, specimens from the parlor rather than from the pantry." They are in the process of being assimilated and those elements within the race which are still too potent for easy assimilation must be hidden until they no longer exist." [15] Thurman felt that such writers limited themselves and "left a great deal of fresh vital material untouched." He reserved his praise for such black writers as Jean Toomer, Eric Walrond, Rudolph Fisher, and Langston Hughes, as well as such white writers as DuBose Heyward and Eugene O'Neill. He wanted the black author to "introduce a Negro note into American literature . . . by writing of certain race characteristics and institutions."

In *Fire,* Thurman hoped to establish sound artistic judgment and criticism for the literature of the Renaissance. While admitting that the Renaissance had given expression to "more articulate and more coherent cries for social justice," Thurman was more skeptical of its achievements in the arts. "[S]peaking purely of the arts," wrote Thurman, "the results of the renaissance have been sad rather than satisfactory, in that critical standards have been ignored, and the measure of achievement has been racial rather than literary." White critics had been so astonished at the phenomenon of blacks' writing that they had neglected traditional literary and critical standards in their often unqualified and unmerited praise of mediocre and ephemeral works. In an article published in *The Independent,* Thurman wrote:

> A man's complexion has little to do with his talent. He either has it or has it not, despite the dictates of spiritually starved white sophisticates, genius does not automatically descend upon one because one's grandmother happened to [be] sold down the river "befo' de wah" . . .[16]

In *The New Republic* he wrote:

> Genius is a rare quality in this world, and there is no reason why it should be more ubiquitous among Blacks than Whites.[17]

But Thurman's aspirations to promote a new Negroid note in American literature and to restore standards of artistic achievement were not to be achieved through *Fire.* Like its ill-fated predecessors, *Fire* proved to be a financial failure. The publication of a single issue had cost Thurman and his friends nearly a thousand dollars. Thurman spent his next three or four years paying the printer for the magazine.

It is worth noting that many of the older writers and critics of the period, including W. E. B. Du Bois, were harshly critical of the new magazine. The black press was just as uncomplimentary in their criticisms. Benjamin Brawley, black literary critic of the Renaissance, wrote of the magazine that "Its flame was so intense that it burned itself up immediately." [18]

Thurman had put everything into *Fire*. Long nights he stayed up getting the final drafts ready for the printer. He himself made all the arrangements for publication. The job of finding patrons and sponsors for the magazine also fell to him. He found himself constantly broke, despite his job at *The World Tomorrow*. At one point the editors at *The World* gave him a special check to purchase a new overcoat, so tattered and frayed had his old one become. During this period he wrote to Hughes, "*Fire* is certainly burning me."

But he was not yet disheartened, even after the failure of *Fire*. When he again found himself jobless, there were times when he was so broke, he could not even afford to pay for his room or purchase food. Not only was he out of work, but *Fire* had left him harassed with debt. Then he suddenly became ill. Boils, a swollen thyroid gland, and infected tonsils sent him to the hospital for an operation. "Truly I am akin to Lazarus," he wrote to Hughes.[19] Even so, all was not hopeless; at least he was writing. In 1927 he had several articles accepted by *The New Republic, The Independent,* and *The World Tomorrow*. It was largely as a result of these articles, as well as his editorship of *Fire,* that Thurman found himself a spokesman for the younger group of black Renaissance writers. In these articles, some of which have already been quoted, Thurman manifested that same skepticism which had shown itself in the pages of *The Messenger* and even earlier in his review of Alain Locke's *The New*

Negro in *The Looking Glass.* "In it [*The New Negro*]," Thurman wrote, "are exemplified all the virtues and all the faults of this new movement, even to a hint of its speciousness. Many have wondered what this Negro literary renaissance has accomplished other than providing white publishers with a new source of revenue, affording the white intellectuals with a 'different' fad and bringing a half dozen Negro artists out of obscurity." [20]

In the following year, 1928, Thurman wrote articles for *The Bookman* and *Dance Magazine.* Meanwhile he also began his first novel, *The Blacker the Berry.* But his real desire was still to become editor of his own magazine. Two years after the extinction of *Fire,* he published another magazine. *Harlem, A Forum of Negro Life* lasted little longer than had its predecessor. *Harlem,* however, appealed to a wider audience and at twenty-five cents a copy, it was much cheaper than the earlier magazine, which had sold for one dollar. But again expenses and lack of funds prevented Thurman from realizing his dream. *Harlem* folded after just two issues. Significantly, a critic later wrote of both *Fire* and *Harlem,* "It was a lack of money not a dearth of merit which caused [these] two magazines to disappear." [21]

Meanwhile Thurman found a job on the editorial staff of MacFadden Publications and published his first novel. Although *The Blacker the Berry* was acclamied by the critics, Thurman himself remained dissatisfied with the novel. The title, used by Thurman ironically, is borowed from an old black folk saying, "The blacker the berry, the sweeter the juice." The novel is a protest against forms of prejudice found within the black community. It deals with the problems of a dark-skinned girl, Emma Lou, among her own people of lighter skin. Like Thurman, Emma Lou came from a middle-class family in a small Midwestern town. Again recalling the author's own experiences, Emma Lou leaves the Midwest, going first to Los Angeles, then to New York's Harlem in a vain effort to escape the scorn and discrimination she has suffered among her own people because of her dark skin. Thurman himself hated small-town provinciality, which he thought bred petty prejudices. He once told a friend that he "hat[ed] every damned spot in these United States outside Manhattan Island." [22] He had Emma Lou's uncle express it this way: "People in large cities . . . are broad. They do not have time to think of petty things." [23] Both Emma Lou and to some extent Thurman were disappointed to discover even in the city what Thurman once described as "inter-racial schisms, caused by differences in skin color." [24] In his article "Harlem Facets," published in *The World Tomorrow,* Thurman had written of the prejudice against foreigners, particularly West Indians, that existed in the Harlem community. In another article, "Negro Life in New York's Harlem," Thurman wrote, "All people seem subject to prejudice, even those who suffer from it most . . ." [25]

On another level, Thurman attempted to deal with the phenomenon of race consciousness and self-hatred. Emma Lou, who used skin bleachers and hair straighteners, had unconsciously accepted the values of those who made her suffer so unjustly. Ultimately she is made to realize that part of the difficulty lay in herself and that she herself was to blame for much of her unhappiness:

> Although this had been suggested to her by others, she had been too obtuse to accept it. She had ever been eager to shift the blame on others when no doubt she herself was the major criminal . . . What she needed to do now was to accept her black skin as being real and unchangeable, to realize that certain things were, had been, and would be, and with this in mind begin life anew, always fighting, not so much for accep-

> tance by other people, but for acceptance of herself by herself.[26]

It is apparent, of course, that Thurman is trying to resolve some of his own problems concerning art and race and race consciousness in *The Blacker the Berry*. He had earlier expressed his disdain for so-called "progaganda literature" and wanted to free his own art "from all traces of interracial progaganda." In his novel he expressed a philosophy based on salvation for the individual. If an artist were talented and skillful enough, he could transcend racial barriers and limitations. But the desire to avoid propaganda did not mean that he must not write about blacks. He was not like those artists who thought they could produce better literature by writing about whites. These were artists who, like Emma Lou, were "trying to escape from a condition their own mental attitudes made more harrowing." Such artists "were inclined to forget that every facet of life could be found among their own people, and that Negroes, being human beings . . . had all the natural emotions and psychological reactions of other human beings." Continuing, he defines the role of the black artist:

> . . . if art is universal expression in terms of the particular he believed there was, if he had the talent, just as much chance for the Negro author to produce great literature by writing of his own people as if he were to write about Chinese or Laplanders. He would be labeled a *Negro* artist, with the emphasis on the Negro rather than on the artist, only as he failed to rise above the province of petty propaganda or failed to find an efficacious means of escape from the stupefying *coup d'états* of certain forces in his environment.[27]

But Thurman had not lived up to his own expectations; he had been disappointed to find that "after all his novel had been scorched with propaganda." It was true that he had avoided all interracial experiences between blacks and whites and attempted to deal only with "Negroes among their own kind." But in his effort to "interpret some of the internal phenomena of Negro life in America," he had blamed the existence of these conditions on race prejudice. To Thurman, such a manifestation "hung like a localised cloud over his whole work." [28] It is for this reason that he himself often deprecated the novel, while others, including the critics, acclaimed it. In one of his reviews, Lewis wrote that Thurman had written a novel, *The Blacker the Berry,* "of which he ought to be proud, but isn't." [29]

Meanwhile Thurman had become rather infamous among the more conservative circles of the Harlem literati, but quite a popular figure among the younger, more bohemian crowd. On his part, Thurman expressed only scorn and contempt for "society Negroes" and an outright rejection of established customs and traditional values. This rejection was expressed in his erotic, bohemian life-style and the group of eccentric companions with whom he chose to spend his time.

These were the days when downtown white artists, intellectuals, and thrill-seekers came to Harlem to drink bootleg liquor, eat fried fish, and pigs feet, and learn to do a dance called the "black bottom" at Saturday night rent parties and cabarets. Nightspots like the famed *Savoy* and *Cotton Club* catered especially to patrons from downtown who came seeking the primitive, the exotic, and the unusual in Harlem's night life. On Saturday nights, nearly everyone either gave parties or went to parties, including Thurman and the other members of the Harlem literati. Langston Hughes wrote in *The Big Sea* that "at Wallace Thurman's you met the bohemians of both Harlem and the Village." [30]

Downtown whites eagerly sought admission to these parties and cabarets. In fact, Thurman himself would frequently oblige those whites who were willing to make his efforts remunerative, and most of them did. He was known to escort these groups of pleasure-seekers and bohemians on frequent night excursions to Harlem's carbarets, parties, and bars. At these parties, he would often drink gin until he "pass[ed] out" and would have to "be carried bodily from a party." [31] Frequently he indulged in all-night drinking bouts with other young bohemians, would-be artists and artists who, like himself, had little regard for custom or convention. This was the period that he would later write about in his autobiographical novel, *Infants of the Spring.* In this second novel, a bitter and pessimistic satire, the Harlem literati, which he often found spurious in their pretensions and second rate in their productions, was renamed "Niggerati." His own house was christened "Niggerati Manor." Recalling those days, Lewis wrote several years later:

> Those were the days when Niggerati Manor was the talk of the town. The story got out that the bathtubs in the house were always packed with sour mash, while gin flowed from all the water taps and the flush boxes were filled with needle beer. It was said that the inmates of the house spent wild nights in tuft hunting and in the diversions of the cities of the plains and delirious days fleeing from pink elephants.

In a note of mild skepticism, Lewis continued:

> Needless to say, the rumors were not wholly groundless. Where there is smoke there must be fire. In the case of Niggerati Manor, a great deal more smoke came out of the windows than was warranted by the size of the fire in the house.[32]

Despite his growing popularity and his ever-widening circle of friends, however, Thurman could not escape a persistent feeling of barrenness in his life. Even the publication of his first novel and the approaching production of his play could not fill the void. There were times when Harlem living would get too hectic for him and he would seek the rest and quiet of the country where he could go for long walks in the woods, read prodigiously, and spend time writing. Occasionally he would go home to Salt Lake City, where his grandmother lived, and try to restore his failing health. At other times he would visit the homes of a couple of close friends just outside the city. Perhaps these were some of the feelings that led to Thurman's marriage to a young schoolteacher shortly after the publication of *The Blacker the Berry*. Unfortunately, the marriage was a failure, lasting only six months. Thurman went back to bohemia, and the schoolteacher later became active in the Communist party. The divorce and alimony payments left Thurman, who was already heavily in debt, in an even worse financial situation. And the tensions of a divorce, added to recurring health problems due to his tubercular condition, increased the strain.

When his marriage dissolved so quickly, it was rumored by some that Thurman "was not the marrying [kind]." "Scandalous things were said about the disunion," wrote Dorothy West, who herself denies any such allegations concerning Thurman. Even Miss West, however, allows that Thurman "surround[ed] himself with a queer assortment" of friends.[33] While there were a few women in Thurman's life, there can be little doubt that he had homosexual tendencies and that these inclinations contributed to his feelings of personal failure and inadequacy. The theme of homosexuality occurs repeatedly in his works and personal letters. In his autobiographical novel, *Infants of the Spring*, the hero, Raymond [Thurman], develops a relationship with a friend which has strong homosexual overtones. Perhaps most revealing is the letter Thurman wrote to a friend in which he tells how he found himself in a rather unusual situation involving overtures made toward him by a homosexual shortly after his arrival in New York. Another letter suggests that one of his friends living outside the city was, in fact, an intimate companion. Writing to a friend about his "disappearing act," Thurman explains:

> There are a number of good reasons for my keeping my whereabouts a secret—even from you, *pour le present.* More reasons than the obvious one that I like mysteries to crop up about myself. Some day when the censor (Freud's censor) is at ease I'll tell you . . .[34]

It would appear that Thurman saw his homosexuality as creating social as well as psychological difficulties.

In February 1929 the play, *Harlem,* opened at the Apollo on Broadway and skyrocketed its author to overnight fame. *Harlem* was an immediate hit, the most successful play of the period written by a black playwright. The critics acclaimed it as a realistic presentation on the lives and problems of blacks in Harlem. Although a white writer, William Jourdan Rapp, collaborated on the play, the plot and dialogue were written by Thurman. Rapp, who was a professional writer as well as a personal friend of Thurman's, helped to make revisions and adapt the play to a form suitable for stage production.

The play is based upon a short story entitled "Cordelia the Crude," which Thurman had published in *Fire.* It is a highly melodramatic story of a Harlem family who migrated from the South to Harlem, expecting to find an escape from the poverty, hardship, and bigotry of life in the South. They seek a "city of *refuge*" which becomes, instead, a "city of *refuse.*" In Harlem, the family must take in boarders in an already overcrowded apartment and give Saturday night rent parties in order to provide enough income to support itself. Most of the action centers on the older daughter, Cordelia, who leaves Basil, her West Indian lover, and gets involved with Roy Crow, an underworld character in the numbers racket. Roy is later murdered by his own partner, Kid Vamp, who accuses him of betrayal. The Kid then seduces Cordelia, who leaves with him, as Basil is left to take the blame for the murder. The play concludes as the Kid himself is approached by a rival band of white gangsters. Cordelia departs despite the pleas of her mother, who exclaims, "Lawd! Lawd! Tell me! Tell me! Dis ain't the City of Refuge." [35]

The play ran for over ninety performances and even went on the road to Los Angeles and Chicago, where it was also received warmly. As Langston Hughes commented, the play was "considerably distorted for box office purposes," although it remained "a compelling study—and the only one in the theater—of the impact of Harlem on a Negro family fresh from the South." [36] Again Thurman produced a work which focused on black life and society. Despite the rather overwhelming sensationalism of the production, he succeeded in dealing with a number of problems which were very realistic in the Harlem community—intraracial prejudice against West Indians, black migration from the South to the North, exploitation of the ghetto by black and white underworld racketeering, and lack of employment and decent housing conditions in the black community.

Describing the years between his "hectic hegira to Harlem" and the production of *Harlem,* Thurman had this to say:

> Three years have seen me become a New Negro (for no reason at all and without my consent), a poet (having had 2 poems published by generous editors), an editor (with a penchant for financially unsound publications), an erotic (see

> articles on Negro life and literature [in] *The Bookman, New Republic, Independent, World Tomorrow,* etc.), an actor (I was denizen of Cat Fish Row in *Porgy*), a husband (having been married all of six months), a novelist (viz: *The Blacker the Berry*. Macauley's, Feb. 1, 1929: $2.50), a playwright (being co-author of *Black Belt*). Now—what more could one do? (Author's note: *Black Belt* was later renamed *Harlem*.)[37]

Indeed, in the months and years that followed, Thurman discovered that there was much more to do, although he could not have known at the time that there remained for him but five short years.

After the production of *Harlem,* Thurman continued to write prolifically, sometimes ghostwriting books of the "true confessions" category. Later he wrote scripts for two lurid and second-rate movies. The pressure of his personal life and self-disillusionment as an artist had a debilitating effect on Thurman. His ailing health and his despair led him increasingly to gin, although the doctors advised against it. Finally, he determined that he would leave the city, go some place where he could exercise, read, write a little, and take a long rest. He went to Utah, then to Florida, Jamaica, and later to California, where he attempted to negotiate movie contracts for his works. Meanwhile he was also helping a young lady, who later became Rapp's wife, to write a novel based on his play, *Harlem*.

Most of his energies during the next two years were spent writing his second novel, *Infants of the Spring*. But he was not happy. The writing of this novel became a strain for him. It left him "depressed and enfeebled both mentally and physically." Written from his personal experiences and attitudes toward the Renaissance, the novel led its author into a journey of introspection that was often unpleasant or disturbing. Comparing his experiences with the new novel with those of the French novelist, Proust, in *Remembrance of Things Past,* Thurman wrote of his depression and illness:

> The diagnosis is of course: too much introspection. Continual mulling over the past, berating self for innate lack of will and self-control, consciously unreeling the past to do in my new novel what Proust succeeded in doing in his volumes.

Away from New York Thurman was lonely. He yearned for the busy social life he had led there. "I was never created to forego companionship," Thurman wrote in one of his letters. Finding few friends or diversions outside of the city, Thurman continued:

> I miss New York. I miss the chats I used to have with certain kindred spirits. I miss the occasional mad nights experienced in Harlem. And yet I know should I be in New York no work would be done.[38]

Trying to impose self-discipline, he determined to stay away from the city until he had completed more writing. Thurman finished the draft of his second novel in 1929, while in Salt Lake City. Upon the completion, he wrote to his friend Rapp:

> I finished the first draft of my novel about five A.M., yesterday morning. Writing it has been an adventure. I stood as one apart and watched it issuing forth from Wallace Thurman. It is the first thing I have ever let write itself, playing amanuensis to some inner urge . . .[39]

Most of Thurman's energies during the next couple of years were spent on *Infants of the Spring.* A white patron, Elizabeth Marbury, assisted him financially in the completion of his second novel. It appears that about this same time Thurman went through a series of personal changes in his attitude toward his life, although he himself doubted the permanence of this new "state of mind." Disclaiming "any great reformation," he does seem to manifest the beginnings of a new maturity and awareness. He is able to express a disinterest in the pursuits which used to occupy his time. "I have more or less outgrown them," wrote Thurman. He even tried to give up gin, restricting himself to what he called "civilized tippling." Looking back on his former life, he comments sardonically:

> Perhaps, after all, these past four hectic years in Harlem have not left me in a rut. I may still have my former capacity for experiencing sea changes. In which case, there is no telling what might happen next. Howbeit, Harlem holds no more charms for me.[40]

Thurman did not publish his novel until 1932. *Infants of the Spring* is an autobiographical statement of his disillusionment with the outcome of the Renaissance, as well as his own personal failure as an artist. His earlier skepticism toward the New Negro movement had now turned into bitter disappointment, and his own aspirations to become a great novelist had remained unfulfilled. Thurman had read all the great writers, including Proust, Melville, Tolstoy, Dostoyevski, Henry James, and others. Hughes wrote that "Thurman had read so many books because he could read eleven lines at a time." [41]

Comparing the literature of the Renaissance with the works of great writers made Thurman a severe critic, particularly of his own works. He puzzled over the reasons for what he considered to be the lack of productivity and creativity among the Renaissance artists. In his novel, he asked whether the failure was the result of "some deep-rooted complex [racial]" or an "indication of a lack of talent." [42] In most instances Thurman thought the black artist was hindered by a preoccupation with his racial identity. Thurman had grappled with this problem when writing his earlier novel, *The Blacker the Berry*. Earlier, in his *Notes of a Stepchild,* he had written of himself: "He tried hard not to let the fact that he had pigmented skin influence his literary or mental development."

There were two ways in which he felt the major black writers dealt with the fact of race identity in their works. In *Infants of the Spring,* Raymond [Thurman] rejects on the one hand those writers "who had nothing to say, and who only wrote because they were literate and felt they should appraise white humanity of the better classes among Negroes." Most of the early writers of the period fell under this condemnation. Those were the writers whom Thurman called the "propagandists" and whose contribution to the Renaissance he had earlier described as "sociological rather than literary." Another group of black writers was composed of those who wanted to escape their racial identity through a denial of everything black. Again speaking as Raymond, Thurman wrote: "He had no sympathy whatsoever with Negroes . . . who contended that should their art be Negroid, they, the artist, must be considered inferior." [43] Such artists "did not realize by adhering to such a belief" they were, in effect, "subscribing to the theory of Nordic superiority." [44]

The title of the novel comes from a verse in Shakespeare's *Hamlet* which Thurman quotes in the Preface:

> The canker galls the infants of the spring
> Too oft before their buttons be disclosed
> And in the morn an liquid dew of youth
> Contagious blastments are most imminent.

It was the canker and race consciousness which they could

not resolve which destroyed the young writers ["infants"] of the Renaissance ["spring"].

The weakness of the Renaissance was that all traits of individuality had been destroyed by the canker of a destructive race complex. That Thurman was only vaguely aware of his own preoccupation with race is indicated by his constant disavowals of such influences and his deliberate efforts to transcend the self-imposed limitations of race consciousness. He discovered the resolution through a philosophy of individuality. Raymond, the hero of his second novel, comments:

> Negroes are a slave race and a slave race they'll remain until assimilated. Individuals will arise and escape on the ascending ladder of their individuality.[45]

Such a statement, however, reveals the degree to which Thurman is a victim of his own self-hatred arising from his racial identity. In *The Blacker the Berry* he resolved this dilemma of race consciousnes and individuality through an acceptance of oneself and racial identity. In this, his second novel, the answer seems to be a rejection of one's racial identity through a doctrine of what he once described as Nietzschean individuality.

Niggerati Manor is the home of a group of young bohemian artists and would-be artists who live in a state of decadence and debauchery. Most of them spend their time attempting to justify their lack of creativity. Thurman sums up his attitude toward the Renaissance in a bitter passage which describes a rent party given by the inhabitants of Niggerati Manor:

> The lights in the basements had been dimmed, and the reveling dancers cast grotesque shadows on the tapestried

walls. Color lines had been completely eradicated. Whites and blacks clung passionately together as if trying to effect a permanent merger. Liquor, jazz music, and close physical contact had achieved what decades of propaganda had advocated with little success. . . . Tomorrow all of them will have an emotional hangover. They will fear for their sanity, for at last they have had a chance to do openly what they only dared do clandestinely before. This, he kept repeating to himself, is the Negro Renaissance, and this is about all the whole damn thing is going to amount to.[46]

The novel ends as Paul, one of the artists who had lived with Raymond at Niggerati Manor, commits suicide. He leaves behind his masterpiece, hoping that the publicity of his death would result in a successful posthumous publication of his novel. The fate of Paul, "a colorful, inanimate corpse," symbolized the ultimate doom of the Renaissance writers who would succeed in destroying themselves through voguish sensationalism. The endurance of their works, however, would be as ephemeral as Paul's, which had been rendered illegible by the overflow of water from the bathtub in which he drowned himself. Only the title sheet remained legible, where Paul had "drawn a distorted inky black skyscraper, modeled after Niggerati Manor."

The foundation of this building was composed of crumbling stone. At first glance it could be ascertained that the skyscraper would soon crumble and fall, leaving the dominating white lights in full possession of the sky.[47]

The Renaissance, represented by the destruction of Niggerati Manor, was inevitably doomed because it lacked the foundation to make it "something truly epochal." The pessimistic portrait of the Renaissance in this bitter satire was Thurman's final legacy to the New Negro movement.

His last novel, *The Interne,* written in collaboration with Abraham L. Furman, was also published that same year. *The Interne* is a muckraking novel which exposes, in a rather sensational way, the corrupt and abusive conditions at the City Hospital in New York. His last work symbolizes Thurman's final break and departure from the Renaissance. The story centers on the experiences of a young, white intern at the City Hospital. It was his only work which did not deal with black life and society.

Both of these novels were published by Macaulay, where Thurman became editor-in-chief in 1932. Two years later Thurman negotiated a contract with Foy Productions Ltd, to do the scenarios for two films, *High School Girl* and *Tomorrow's Children,* a film on sterilization which was censored in New York.

For a while he was content. He was making contacts, earning good money, and had a "very swank" office at the studio. But the strain and intensity of such a life was altogether too much for Thurman. Hollywood was hectic and mad. Thurman wrote to a friend, "Don't ever be lured into the studio except as a visitor. Am going thru the most insane experience of my life in this studio." [48] Finally he became nervous and started to lose weight. By the following summer his physical condition was getting dangerously worse. In May he returned to New York, where he proceeded to go on a drinking binge which lasted until he finally passed out. Ironically he was taken to the City Hospital, the institution which he had written of in *The Interne.* Thurman remained a patient in the hospital in the incurable ward for six long months. He made no effort to fight his condition. He died on Welfare Island on December 22, 1934. Lewis wrote, "To the very end (for he accepted it as the end when he was borne to the hospital), he was the *bon vivant,* the bohemian to the last." [49]

In terms of his literary contributions, Wallace Thurman has been regarded as one of the minor figures of the Renaissance. His significance, however, far exceeds the work he left behind. Not only was he tremendously influential upon the younger and perhaps more successful writers of the period, but his life itself became a symbol of the New Negro movement. Thurman had made his entrance into the Renaissance at the height of the movement. His life, brilliant and turbulent as it had been, ended after the Renaissance came to a close.

CHAPTER 9

Theophilus Lewis and the Theater of the Harlem Renaissance

THEODORE KORNWEIBEL, JR.

The most thought-out and consistent commentary on black theater to be produced during the Harlem Renaissance was the drama criticism of Theophilus Lewis. From September 1923 to July 1927 he wrote monthly columns in the *Messenger* magazine, which dissected in honest yet sympathetic ways the foibles and shortcomings of black theater as well as the white stage that produced works on black themes. Mere criticism was not his end; rather, he intended to help provide an ideology for the development of a national black theater which would be both a source of a racial ethos and a repository of the race's genius. In so doing Lewis was articulating a primary goal of the New Negro spirit: racial self-assertion in the arts would provide the race with a cultural foundation derived from its own historical and cultural roots.[1] Lewis's tools were alternately satire (of white stereotypes and of the lingering slave-psychology among blacks), compassion and sympathy (for the often amateurish efforts of little-theater groups), and exhortation (of playwrights to write serious drama, and of actors to demand serious and racially meaningful roles). Throughout, his columns were urbane and witty, at times biting, but never malicious.[2] His fundamental theme, that the primary need of blacks in establishing their cultural independence was for a national black theater grounded, above all, in the works of black playwrights, was a justifiable criticism. Even as harsh a critic of the Harlem Renaissance as Harold Cruse, who seems not to have known of either Lewis or his criticism, would probably admit that Lewis was articulating the cultural nationalism that Cruse deems the key to the success or failure of independent black cultural development.

Theophilus Lewis's knowledge of the theater was more intuitive than scholastic. A native of Baltimore, born March 4, 1891, Lewis had very little formal schooling—he has recently called himself a "dropout"—but from the beginning he had a great interest in the theater. He liked to go to shows, and as a teen-ager attended whatever and whenever he could: vaudeville, burlesque, anything that was available and that he could afford. Lewis came to New York before World War I and there met A. Philip Randolph and Chandler Owen, soon to begin publishing a radical magazine called the *Messenger*. When the United States became involved in the war, Lewis went into the service and was sent overseas with the AEF. After his discharge he lived in Detroit for three years but returned to New York in 1922 and secured a job in the post office.

Lewis started writing for the *Messenger* almost by chance. Given his long-standing interest in the theater, he naturally was drawn to the Lafayette Theater in Harlem and soon was a frequent visitor there. One day, after seeing a performance, he wrote a review of the play on a whim and showed it to his friend Randolph, although he had never before written any theater criticism. The editor of the *Messenger* liked the review and asked whether Lewis would write such pieces on a regular basis. There could be no remuneration, given the precarious finances of the magazine; all that could be offered was that the magazine would pay for the tickets. And naturally Lewis would have to do his play-viewing and writing after his regular work at the post office. But Lewis was nonetheless interested, and thus began a very fruitful association.[3]

The *Messenger* was lucky to have the services of Lewis. It, like the two other black magazines, *The Crisis* and *Opportunity,* was not founded as a literary periodical, but nonetheless became involved in cultural developments as the Harlem Renaissance writers began to emerge and demand publication of their works.[4] All three monthlies began to print a considerable volume of the new poetry and fiction, as well as book reviews and criticism. But the *Messenger* was the only one to have a regular drama critic. In addition to theater criticism, Lewis also reviewed important new books, such as Langston Hughes's first two volumes of poetry, and he brought to literary criticism the same New Negro perspective to be found in his theater reviews. Lewis also had modest aspirations as a creative writer and published four of his own short stories in the magazine in addition to collaborating with George S. Schuyler on the latter's satiric column, "Shafts and Darts."

However much Lewis may have lacked a formal education, he possessed considerable gifts which did not go unnoticed in the literary world. Arna Bontemps remembers him as an intellectual whose mind was widely respected among the black intelligentsia of Harlem. Wallace Thurman in particular, who later joined the *Messenger* staff through Lewis's influence, had a high esteem for Lewis and considered him to be a real scholar of the theater; so, too, did Langston Hughes and George Schuyler.[5] And despite the fact that the *Messenger* was not as well known as *The Crisis* or *Opportunity,* the word was circulated among young artists and writers that Lewis was the only drama critic that they could take seriously. Other than his writings, there was no reputable drama criticism at all in Harlem. The other "critics" rarely displayed any discrimination and did little more than promote any show that promised to be successful.[6] Given this paucity of good criticism, Lewis becomes all the more important.

Harlem was the black cultural capital of the country, just as was New York for the nation as a whole. What passed for a national black stage (which played a circuit of New York, Philadelphia, Washington, and sometimes Chicago) had its inspiration and headquarters in Harlem. The most common and most popular type of theatrical entertainment was the musical revue; most revues played either at the Lafayette or Lincoln theaters, both white owned and operated. They usually consisted of a series of dance and musical numbers with an inevitable chorus-line of beautiful girls. The degree of excellence of acting, dance, and music, as well as taste, ran an expected full gamut. High theater it was not, but Lewis and others recognized that its best examples provided something invaluable to black audiences, if only productions composed, written, and acted by blacks.

Lewis was of two minds about the revues and low-humor comedies. Some were often cheap and tawdry, yet others could be elevating in their joy, mirth, and infectious music and dancing. They might provide absolutely no challenge to acting skills, yet still be perfect vehicles for such genuine stars as Florence Mills and Irvin Miller. The major problem with the revues was that the supply of fresh ideas and new dance combinations was easily exhausted. The programs at the Lafayette and at the Lincoln changed frequently, due to the almost insatiable demand for new revues, and the productions were not presented in repertory fashion, so that even the best-known and most-talented writers and producers borrowed shamelessly from previous successes.

A brief cataloguing of the revues noticed by Lewis from September 1923 to May 1926 (after which date he ceased, with one exception, reviewing them) gives a pictorial view of the black comedy stage in Harlem in these years. *The Sheik of Harlem,* starring Hattie King Reavis and Irvin Miller, allowed mid-1923 audiences to see "the frothy side of Harlem life" with all its foibles and vices prominently displayed, as well as a chorus of "as sweet a collection of baby vamps" as it had been the reviewer's pleasure to see in many a month. (Lewis's commentary, while not always employing flapper terminology, was usually spicy and interlarded with his admiration for the charms and beauties of the female form.) That the standard of quality was uneven at the Lafayette is evident from a later paragraph in the same review which briefly noticed a succeeding production, *Raisin' Cain,* which was "ancient and seedy stuff." [7] Late in the same year Lewis caught *Follow Me* and thought it a poor piece, although the audiences liked it; this only proved to the reviewer how fastidious were the tastes of the Harlem showgoing public.[8] Succeeding shows reviewed were *Dinah,* with comic Irvin Miller, in late 1923, and *Come Along, Mandy,* early in 1924. Of a much higher standard of excellence was Lew Leslie's *Plantation Revue* (1924), starring Florence Mills. For this production Lewis did not reserve praise, although he attributed much of its success to Miss Mills, for whom he had unstinting admiration.[9]

Success bred imitation, and *Club Alabam* at the Lafayette,

following *Plantation Revue,* was merely a cheap replica of the former hit.[10] Mid-1924 saw a new show by the noted comedy and music team Noble Sissle and Eubie Blake, *Chocolate Dandies,* which enjoyed considerable success and impressed Lewis as being sophisticated and urbane.[11] The year ended with one of the most successful of all black shows of the twenties, *From Dixie to Broadway,* whose chief asset was Florence Mills. Lewis worshipped Miss Mills but was forced to admit that, on the whole, the show was an inferior production, most of which was "shoddy, garish and vulgar," with many of the ideas being "second-hand and cheap." Yet he predicted that it would make its producer, Lew Leslie, a wealthy man, and indeed the show was a great commercial success.[12] Once again the pendulum swung to the mediocre and Lewis panned in succession *The Demi-Virgin, Pudden Jones,* and *Blackbirds of 1926.* The second reflected no credit at all on the race, in Lewis's opinion, as it continued the old association of comedy with a coal-black Negro, a jail record, and the trappings of the minstrel show.[13] All that saved *Blackbirds* was Florence Mills; otherwise it was a rehash of older revues from which Lew Leslie had the gall to steal some songs and dance routines.[14]

The best examples of the revue, however, served good purposes and could be justified as art. Lewis was honest enough to admit that he more often than not enjoyed the dancing, bawdy jokes, and shedding of clothes, as well as the humorous comment. He recognized the special liberties allowed by the Roaring Twenties and that its freedoms and joys might well not last:

> I look upon these muscial shows and call them good. It is the business of the theater to satisfy spiritual craving. Whether the craving is refined or ethical is beside the point, so long as it's human. Since these shows satisfy a very definite and in-

> tense desire they are sound theater. So let us enjoy their verve, beauty and sin while we may, for the drear and inevitable day is coming when they will be against the law.[15]

One revue that in early 1927 reached this higher plane was *Gay Harlem.* Unlike many of its type, this was not only entertaining but intelligent as well in its humor and poking satire. It did not display racial buffooneries and stereotypes of blacks, but portrayed in honest fashion the foibles and libertinage of black life. As such Lewis unreservedly defended its seminudity against the charge of encouraging a decline in modesty. Rather, a general societal decline in modesty had resulted in nudity on the stage. And that was precisely why the scantily clad performers were a valuable contribution to contemporary life and theater, for this was nothing less than art holding up a mirror to life. This was the musical revue at its best.[16]

One of Theophilus Lewis's pet crusades was for an end to the belief that only light-skinned women were "beautiful." Nowhere was this color line more in evidence than in the choruses of the revues. The chorus line was often the highlight of an otherwise unspectacular production, and for many its scarcely clad, long-legged members were the main attraction of the evening's entertainment. But to see even a medium-brown girl was a rarity. The otherwise mediocre *Come Along, Mandy* had the "theatrical sensation of the decade—colored girls in the chorus!" [17] The chorus of *Club Alabam,* however, was the usual "high yaller." [18] And of the whole cast of *Blackbirds of 1926,* ironically, all the females but the two star actresses were "biological whites." [19] It was thus with great pleasure and relief that Lewis caught a dance performance of the National Ethiopian Art Theater in which two of the dancers were genuinely black women.[20] Lewis often attributed this discrimination to a psychology rooted in slavery, and it was certainly not confined to the musical stage; he was not successful in eradicating this judgment, however, and the white standard of beauty is still a burden on black performers to this day. Suffice it to say the "New Negro" perceived that along with a new definition of black culture would have to come new standards of aesthetics, of which color was a major problem.

The musical stage was not without importance, but Lewis, and probably any other serious student of the drama, would have insisted that it hardly served the functions of a race theater. It did provide employment for many actors and actresses and dancers, but only in the realm of comedy. The same held true for would-be playwrights: the musical stage was not the place for serious drama. And despite the protestations of James Weldon Johnson that the best musical revues broke completely with the minstrel tradition, there was certainly enough that was similar for younger critics to view it as a limited and stereotyped medium.[21] It was clear to Lewis that a truly racial theater based on black values and rooted in the black consciousness would come about primarily through the medium of serious drama, for serious drama was the repository of a society's (or race's) collective spiritual life, culture, and character.[22]

Some significant advances in the serious portrayal of blacks in drama were recorded by Lewis in the mid-1920s. First, there was promising activity coming from the (often short-lived) little-theater groups, of which more later. Equally as important was the occasional play, often written by a white, which presented blacks as believable and sympathetic characters and provided roles which were at the same time challenging to the competent actor, also sometimes white. Such a play was *Roseanne,* written by a white woman and starring in its original production in 1924 a white actress portraying a black character. Despite the lack of black personnel, Lewis praised it because it portrayed a believable Negro character "without sentimentality or exaggeration." Of the white actress he admitted he had "never believed a Caucasian could portray Negro feeling with such fidelity to the subject. It was simply astounding." Because of the truth of the whole production, Lewis felt that *Roseanne,* with the exception of Eugene O'Neill's plays on black themes, was the most significant dramatic work on black life up to that time.[23]

Around the same period (early 1924) Lewis viewed a production by one of the little-theater groups, the Ethiopian Art Theater, entitled *The Gold Front Stores, Inc.* He credited this play with being the first full-length dramatic piece by a black playwright (Caesar G. Washington) who showed a knowledge of how to construct a believable play. The work was, surprisingly, a farce. Lewis feared that the play would not be acceptable to most other reviewers, however, because it was too genuine, it had "too much niggerism" in it. But this was precisely what made it an important production.[24] The next important step he noted was taken by Eugene O'Neill in *All God's Chillun Got Wings* (mid-1924). Although Lewis thought it suffered by comparison with *The Emperor Jones,* he acknowledged that it was nonetheless a fairly authentic story in which Paul Robeson displayed some very sound acting. Lewis was of the opinion that this play was the most significant offering of the season because it showed that black people led lives, not in a vacuum, but in juxtaposition to others and to society. In addition the play gave black actors four major roles and in so doing greatly enriched black acting experience.[25]

It was nearly two years before Lewis recorded another significant advance in black drama. This play was *Lulu Belle,* and while not perfect in either execution or conception, it presented some extremely well-drawn characters who expressed universal human emotions in a believable manner. In fact, the main character was so genuine that the white critics were confounded—he did not carry a razor, shoot craps, believe in superstition, or do anything that they believed the typical black should do.[26] A year later, in 1927, another white-authored play was cited as an important contribution. *Earth* was "an elaborately camouflaged Greenwich Village conception of an Uncle Tom's Cabin version of the Book of Job." In fact the play was nowhere near portraying black life accurately, but its conception of the classic dimensions of the Job story was faithful and spiritually moving. Lewis called it "the best so-called Negro play since *The Emperor Jones*," and that was a compliment indeed. The acting was the finest he had seen from any black cast yet on Broadway, and he hoped that there would be more plays like it.[27]

The fact that Lewis could praise several white plays for contributing significantly to black drama does not mean that he disregarded the New Negro goal of developing black playwrights in order to ensure that the race's life would be accurately portrayed. He saw this problem indeed. What the foregoing paragraphs tell us is that he was also concerned about the development of competent dramatic actors and a theater tradition at the same time. Lewis spent no little energy decrying the paucity of serious black dramatists and showed clearly how critical this was. More than once he said that the playwright was more important than the actor in the long run, and thus acting should not be developed at the expense of drama. Actors contributed little to civilization except the moment of their performance, although that might become tradition. But great drama, great plays, were enduring in tangible form.[28] A playwright could create "the idealization of race character which in the last analysis is the real meaning of Negro drama." All this meant that the first item of importance in the theater was the drama; then came acting, audience, and production.[29] There were many sources to the problem of a lack of black dramatists—little public support, competing white drama, low public taste—all of which were valid complaints. But on occasion Lewis could not contain his disillusionment and disgust at the sorry state of black playwriting. In reviewing a play so bad he did not even name it, he noted that Charles S. Gilpin, probably the finest black actor then playing, had transformed his part into a thing of beauty. Yet why was he condemned to perform in such trash? Blacks simply would not write enough good theater to keep a fine artist like Gilpin well employed.[30]

Another obstacle to the development of black theater was that of audience. At whom should the theater be aimed? The answer to this question depended on several variables, such as the affluence of patrons, the types of themes available, and the type of drama to be presented. In general, Lewis was distrustful of the willingness of the upper classes of black society to support meaningful theater. That group strenuously objected to the miscegenation theme of *All God's Chillun Got Wings*:

> There is a lot of talk about "Art" in this community nowadays. The best people are all hot for it. But when a craftsman [O'Neill] unveils his work and the best people immediately begin chattering about its propriety instead of discussing the competence of the execution one is moved to wonder whether their esthetic fervor is not bogus.[31]

On the other hand, as Lewis admitted in a later analysis, much of the black audience was uncultured and coarse and thus many black entertainments naturally catered to this level. The result of this was that the more sensitive and intelligent actors were driven out of the theaters. Things would be better if the higher classes attended more often and in so doing demanded a higher degree of fare. This might have the effect of raising the mean of race culture. Yet that might merely result in the type of Victorian censorship suggested in the quotation above. The fundamental problem with the upper-class or "higher intellect" black theater patron was that he went to the theater and often ignored his own tastes as well as the desires of the lower classes in the audience and demanded instead that the performance be geared to a set of standards alien to both—to white standards. This patron often insisted on the black theater copying the suave manners and conventions of the white theater, which at base reflected the racial experience and heritage of a different tradition. The result, Lewis noted, was sterility and artificiality.

To make a decision to cater to either portion of the potential theater clientele was difficult indeed, but Lewis recognized that the issue should not be straddled. Weighing the alternatives, he decided that to direct the appeal of the theater to a small group with relatively high but artificial standards of taste might have short-term benefits, but that in the long run it would be best to appeal to the group with lower but nonetheless genuine standards. After all, the lower group was the greater in number of a potential audience—and numbers pay. Such drama would be much more healthy than a snobbish, artificial "high" theater, and it would also keep more theaters in existence and provide a corps of competent performers.[32] All this was not to say that the problems of a paucity of playwrights and of well-constructed plays and good roles would immediately cease to exist.

The weaknesses of the black theater were many, and most of them have already been touched upon. But two additional problems to which Lewis drew attention should be noted. One was the absence of actors with an understanding of the dignity of their calling. There were in fact plenty of black actors, but all too many were willing to play for low humor and obscenity. And it was plain that the black stage had more than enough low comedy already, even though Lewis could not resist taking some pride in this dubious achievement. The richness and variety of the black theater's lowest comedy, he claimed, far surpassed that found in the white theater, and in this respect the black stage enriched and helped to liberate the sexually repressed white world.[33]

A second weakness was not unrelated to the first. It concerned the ownership and control of the theaters in Harlem. Lewis cited figures showing that white owners controlled 50 per cent of the theaters and 75 per cent of the patronage of blacks in New York. These whites were not cultured persons linked to the white stage—they were cheap vaudeville entrepreneurs and sideshow vendors. Most of the black owners were alleged to be of the same generally low character. Neither was qualified to make cultural contributions to the community. If they managed to uplift the theater it would only be because that would pay immediate profits, which was very doubtful; experimental and high-level theater was bound to lose money and would have to be underwritten by money-making popular theater. The influence of the white theater promoters was doubly pernicious; not only did they produce jaded theater, but they produced it for the tastes of voyeuristic whites who wanted black-and-tan entertainment. The wishes of the black audience were generally not considered. The lesson was clear to Lewis: ". . . without economic autonomy the Negro stage can never become the flexible medium for the expression of the spirit of Negro people it ought to be." [34] Needless to say, the domination of Harlem's theater (as well as cinema) entertainment by an alien "cultural" force was a major impediment to the ideology as well as the realization of independent black dramatic expression.

If Harlem's established theaters could not be depended upon to sponsor serious and probably unprofitable drama, the task then lay with little-theater groups. Lewis paid attention to such groups and was often solicitous of their efforts even in the face of very pedestrian and amateurish performances. He always managed to say something good about a particular evening's offering, for he regarded the little-theater movement as perhaps the only foundation on which a truly national black theater could be built. So even the most pathetic attempts offered some encouragement and hope.

Of the six theater groups which found mention in Lewis's columns, perhaps the most durable was the National Ethiopian Art Theater (NEAT). The first performance recorded by Lewis has already been mentioned: *The Gold Front Stores, Inc.,* which was noteworthy for being a dramatic work of competence authored by a black writer. The one-act play, however, was the more usual fare in the little theaters, and three such were reviewed from a performance in October 1924. Two of the three Lewis thought were mediocre, but one, entitled *Gooped Up,* written by a student at the NEAT school, was good in mirroring the real drama of black life.[35] The NEAT also conducted dance classes, and it was at one of their recitals that Lewis had the pleasure of seeing a performance by genuinely black (as opposed to "high yaller") girls. The 1925 NEAT season closed with three one-acters, and the reviewer noted that the performances were encouraging and minus the gaucheries of previous productions. Two of the plays were of little value in themselves, but were good enough vehicles to be instructive to the actors.[36]

The other theater groups mentioned by Lewis were the

Tri-Arts Club, the Inter-Collegiate Association, the Sekondi Players, the Krigwa Players, and the Aldridge Players. The Krigwa Players Little Negro Theater was a project of W. E. B. Du Bois. In reviewing its first offering, Lewis was pleased to see that it had avoided spending all its energy on preparation and was instead getting out and actually performing. The acting could have been improved by being less reserved, but the evening was worth the time spent, since at least one of the plays (*Compromise*) proved to be a fairly serious discussion of real life, dealing with the theme of interracial, extramarital sexual relations.[37] By the time of the opening of this group's second season Lewis was overlooking their stumbles with a "tolerant eye." [38] Around the same period the Aldridge Players put on three short plays by the black writer F. H. Wilson. Although ranging in dramatic content from fair to mediocre, they were nonetheless important because they had highly actable roles which were of great significance in building up the repertory experience so necessary for the little-theater movement. A plentiful supply of meaningful roles was more important at that early stage than fine plays.[39]

Lewis's prescription for the health and vitality of the little-theater movement was a simple yet hard-to-achieve one: perform, perform, and perform some more. During its first year(s) of existence the most important thing was to keep putting on plays, mediocre though they may be. This would develop actors, and as they became more accomplished they would inspire dramatists to write good plays for them. And the frequent performances would create and begin to hold a public.[40] All of this could be done without resident geniuses in either the acting or playwriting departments. Several famous white little-theater groups, Lewis noted, had succeeded without such exceptional talent. The crucial task was to develop competent acting quickly. But to do this any company would have to become at least semiprofessional. Good acting could be acquired in only two ways: hire already trained and competent professional actors; or pay resident amateurs who showed promise, so that they could afford dramatic training. In either case money was necessary. Who would provide funds? Lewis was confident that there was a segment of the population that could be induced to support such endeavors, but in order to secure its cooperation the productions of the group should be geared in their direction. That group Lewis defined as those who desired theater entertainment but were so dissatisfied with what was currently available that they would contribute toward subsidizing new theater more in accord with their tastes.[41] But that returned the matter to the dilemma of the sophistication of the audience and its various ideas of artistic taste. There was no easy answer, and Lewis was perhaps more optimistic than was warranted; it was certainly not easy to keep a little theater alive during these years without some outside patronage or support which might or might not have strings attached.

Lewis saw the little-theater movement as a precursor and component of what he hoped would become a national black theater. To develop a race theater meant that a *national* theater must be constructed. It would have to be grounded on indigenous drama by its own playwrights or else it would become only the "sepia province of American Theater." Yet it must not isolate itself and address its appeal exclusively to black audiences. The problem lay in the nature of Harlem, where conditions were admittedly most propitious for the development of black theater. Even there only a fraction of the population, perhaps no more than five thousand, would initially support serious theater. Thus it must be on a low budget and repertory basis. It would have to educate and win its audience, and since much of that audience was conditioned by movies, the initial plays should be mostly melodrama, mysteries, and farce. But when the audience had been won over, more serious productions could be attempted. Finally, a nationwide network of several similiar repertory companies should be organized, so that productions could be exchanged. This was the stage at which a national race theater would come into being.[42]

What was to be done about the matter of popular taste? First, the race theater would have to develop outside the houses controlled by whites. This would be relatively uncomplicated, although perhaps not too simple in execution. But the more serious problem lay in the concept of legitimacy. Lewis went to the heart of the matter when he noted that one of the fundamental causes of weakness in the black theater derived from its unwritten philosophy that the only "legitimate" theater was the white stage, particularly Broadway. The black theater had wrongly tried to excel at the things Broadway did. Negro theater had taken its instruction from the white stage, which too often portrayed blacks only in caricature. The Lafayette Players, the only permanent company of adult performers in Harlem, took their cues from Broadway and performed ten-year-old, castoff plays from that stage. The Lafayette group had not only failed to encourage black playwrights but had not even kept pace with the white theaters it set out to emulate. Instead of crying for a "chance" on the white stage, Lewis asked, why not produce black drama on the black stage for black audiences. With a contribution of a hundred dollars monthly from the five richest black churches in New York City, a resident company could employ Charles Gilpin and Paul Robeson on a regular basis and offer the finest of drama to black audiences. But did the public really want this? Aside from his own fulminations on the subject and an occasional column in *Opportunity,* Lewis claimed to have heard no complaint from the black public or cultural critics. It was not surprising, then, that the only serious attempts to create a black theater up to that time had been fostered by whites. Lewis described the result in September 1924: "What we call the Negro Theater is an anemic sort of thing that does not reflect Negro life, Negro fancies or Negro ideas. It reflects the 100 per cent American Theater at its middling and cheapest." [43] This is precisely the criticism of the black theater which Harold Cruse has recently made, although he seems unaware that anyone in the twenties was this clear sighted.[44]

The cultural ethos of the New Negro balanced two views on the subject of the race's contributions. On the one hand, blacks should strive to develop their own cultural institutions and ideals so that for the first time an accurate representation of black life would be available. In so doing the spiritual part of the racial heritage would be preserved and fostered. On the other hand, the contributions blacks made to culture would be to the whole of culture. The New Negro saw himself as contributing not only to his race, but also to American (and world) culture. It was not to be a separatist movement. Theophilus Lewis voiced these concerns, sometimes in very articulate fashion. In describing the process of enriching the racial heritage he advised that

> the Negro stage should be a vital force in the spiritual life of the race; it should constantly delight . . . and . . . exalt . . . and it should crystallize that delight and exaltation in a form worthy of being preserved as a part of our racial contribution to the general culture of mankind.[45]

But he also saw the issue from a slightly more radical position, in which blacks would hold themselves somewhat aloof from American civilization, contributing to it, yet reserving judgment on whether or not to join it wholeheartedly. Lewis seemed to foresee the possibility of a Third World position from which dying civilizations could be viewed, but their contagion avoided. In other words, he was by no means sure that blacks should fuse themselves with white America and wholeheartedly embrace its destiny, cultural and otherwise:

> Now the Negro Problem is this: It is the question whether a youthful people living in the midst of an old and moribund civilization shall die with it or find themselves able to shake loose from its complexities and build their own culture on its ruins. . . . This condition of doubt will find its esthetic expression in dissonances of sound and color, and such explosive comedy and tragedy as results from the struggles of a passionate people to escape the restraints of the Calvinist version of the Ten Commandments.
>
> The task for the Negro artist, then, is to observe the confusion of rusting flivvers, vanishing forests, migratory populations and expiring faiths which confronts him and reveals its meaning in a felicitous manner. He will show us, perhaps, the convulsions of a world breaking down in chaos. Perhaps the nuclei of a new world forming in incandescence.[46]

Theophilus Lewis had a clear and consistent vision which made him, in Arna Bontemps's phrase, the "literary brain" of the *Messenger*. That magazine, as well as *Opportunity* and *The Crisis,* provided a valuable service to the black intellectual community. The daily and weekly press could not be depended upon for in-depth literary or theater criticism or book reviews, so it fell to the national magazines to fill this gap. Each of the three made unique contributions to the Harlem Renaissance, and the most significant offering of the *Messenger* was Lewis's commentary. Known and respected by those who could appreciate him best in the twenties, his subsequent obscurity is entirely undeserved.[47]

CHAPTER 10

Zora Neale Hurston and the Eatonville Anthropology

ROBERT HEMENWAY

Zora Neale Hurston is one of the most significant unread authors in America, the author of two minor classics and four other major books. What follows is openly intended to stimulate further interest in her art, and is part of a more extensive study of her life and work now in progress. My purpose here is not to provide a comprehensive account of her association with the Harlem Renaissance, but to articulate one intellectual problem facing her during that period. It should be acknowledged from the start that it is a white man's reconstruction of the intellectual process in a black woman's mind. That is not an irrelevant fact, either sexually or racially; people falsely impressed with the mythical "objectivity" of criticism and the presumed "universality" of literature will claim that it is. They are wrong. All men possess an anthropology which is less their own creation than a special burden of value and idea culturally imposed. Inevitably this anthropology—this view of man as he is—affects analytic efforts, but it is not a fact the critic can or should apologize for. A published author belongs in a special way to the world of culture—he is subject to the inquiry of any reader who would seek his example and learn his truth. When this process of inquiry is shared with others, it becomes criticism, and the success of criticism depends directly on the critic's ability to distinguish the parts of his cultural burden which can be responsibly shouldered from the parts to be shucked away forever because they limit his humanity. The existential irony making criticism frustrating is that one's acceptance or rejection of such burdens is a process of self-discovery, a condition of becoming. This leaves the critic in the same tentative position as the artist: he creates offerings. That is all the following essay presumes to be.

On January 16, 1959, Zora Neale Hurston, suffering from the effects of a stroke and writing painfully in longhand, composed a letter to the "editorial department" of Harper & Brothers inquiring if they would be interested in seeing "the book I am laboring upon at present—a life of Herod the Great." [1] One year and twelve days later, Zora Neale Hurston died without funds to provide for her burial, a resident of the St. Lucie County, Florida, Welfare Home. She lies today in an unmarked grave in a segregated cemetery in Ft. Pierce, Florida, a resting place generally symbolic of the black writer's fate in America. The letter to Harper's does not expose a publisher's rejection of an unknown masterpiece, but it does reveal how the bright promise of the Harlem Renaissance deteriorated for many of the writers who shared in its exuberance. It also indicates the personal tragedy of Zora Neale Hurston: Barnard graduate, author of four novels, two books of folklore, one volume of autobiography, the most important collector of Afro-American folklore in America, reduced by poverty and circumstance to seek a publisher by unsolicited mail. The letter makes the survival of three hundred pages of the "Herod the Great" manuscript all the more poignant; its posthumous destruction by county custodians was halted when a deputy sheriff extinguished its flame with a garden hose.

Herod the Great is a good beginning for understanding Hurston's role in the Harlem Renaissance, because it is unlike any of her Renaissance work. It is a straightforward, standard English, historical narrative of the ruler of Galilee from 40 to 4 B.C., the father of the Herod to whom Christ was sent for trial by Pontius Pilate. Hurston spent most of her energy over the last seven years of her life in the attempt to write this story, and yet even the most sympathetic reader concludes that the manuscript is not a major achievement, that it lacks the force, style, and significance of her other work. I think it fails because it illustrates how far Hurston had retreated from the unique sources of her esthetic: the music and speech, energy and wisdom, dignity and humor, of the black rural South. Her achievements during the Renaissance increase or diminish in direct proportion to her use of the folk environment which she had grown up in and would later return to analyze.

I

Zora Neale Hurston was born in 1903 in Eatonville, Florida,[2] an all-black town in central Orange County which claims to be the first incorporated totally black city in America. This fact of birth makes Hurston unique among black writers, and it was the major shaping force in her life. Growing up in Eatonville meant that Zora Hurston could reach the age of ten before she would realize that she had been labeled a "Negro" and restricted from certain social possibilities by chance of race. It meant that from early childhood she would hear the "lying sessions" on Mayor Joe Clark's storefront porch, the men "straining against each other in telling folks tales. God, Devil, Brer Rabbit, Brer Fox, Sis Cat, Brer Bear, Lion, Tiger, Buzzard and all the wood folk walked and talked like natural men."[3] It meant that the Saturday night music and the Sunday morning praying, the singing, working, loving, and fighting of black rural life would become the fecund source for her adult imagination.

The strong daughter of strong parents, Hurston was graced by the evangelical Christianity of her father's preaching and the permanent truths of her mother's rustic wisdom. Her parents and their neighbors had little formal education. They lived lives of rural poverty in a society of white racism, and they contributed to that elaborate mechanism of survival which makes Afro-American folklore one of the most remarkable products of ingenuity and intelligence in the human species. Hurston left the familial environment at fifteen, after her mother had died, working variously as a maid in a traveling Gilbert and Sullivan troupe, a manicurist in a barbershop catering to congressmen, and a servant for prominent black Washingtonians. She also finished high school and managed two years of credit at Howard University (where she studied under Alain Locke), before Charles S. Johnson, the editor of *Opportunity,* solicited her fiction and suggested she come to New York sometime. She arrived in January 1925 with "$1.50, no job, no friends, and a lot of hope."[4]

If one accepts the geography in the label, Zora Hurston's physical presence during the Harlem Renaissance could be overemphasized. She did not arrive on the scene until fairly late, and in February 1927 she left for four years of more or less continuous folklore collecting. Yet she was an important contributor to the Renaissance spirit, as any survivor of the age will confirm. She very quickly became one of the most dazzling émigrés of the influx of young black artists. A brilliant raconteur, a delightful if sometimes eccentric companion, she fit in well with the "Roaring Twenties"—both black and white divisions. Shortly after her arrival she was employed as Fannie Hurst's private secretary; she quickly became a favorite of the black intelligentsia and the recipient of a scholarship specially arranged for by a Barnard trustee. Her wit was lengendary; she called Negro uplifters "Negrotarians," and Carl Van Vechten claimed she combined Negro and literati into one of the famous ironic labels of the period: "Niggerati." Much of her personal success was built around her storytelling, which more often than not emphasized the Eatonville milieu. She could become a living representative of the Southern folk-idiom and she never failed to entertain with the material. Her stories, of course, were not unknown to Harlem, for black immigrants of the "great migration" could tell similar tales from neighborhood stoops. William Wells Brown, Arthur Huff Fauset, and other blacks had reported folklore sympathetically; Joel Chandler Harris's Uncle Remus stories had been popular among whites in the late nineteenth century.

But the folk materials seldom had been dramatized for the black artists and intellectuals of Hurston's acquaintance, and almost never for the white folks so often in attendance on the "New Negro." In fact, few of the literary participants in the Renaissance knew intimately the rural South; Hughes arrived from Cleveland and Washington, Bontemps from California, Thurman from Utah and Los Angeles; Cullen was from New York City, Toomer from Washington; the list can go on, but the point is obvious. Zora Neale Hurston represented a known, but unexperienced segment of black life in America. Although it is impossible to gauge such matters, there seems little question that she helped to remind the Renaissance—especially its more bourgeois members—of the richness in the racial heritage; she also added new dimensions to the interest in exotic primitivism that was one of the most ambiguous products of the age.

Yet the brilliance of her personality should not obscure her personal development. Hurston in New York was initially a country girl, wide-eyed, and if not altogether innocent, at least capable of being often impressed. She is still remembered at Howard by fellow students and retired faculty as merely a bright working girl, very rough about the edges. In the midst of her duties as Hurst's secretary, she could take time out to send a friend some matches shared one night by "Fannie Hurst, Stefansson (the explorer), Charles Norris and Zora Neale Hurston," adding that "Irvin S. Cobb was there also but he used another pack with Jessie Lasky and Margaret Anglin." [5] Later she would write the same friend about all there is to see in New York, admitting, "I won't try to pretend that I am not thrilled at the chance to see and do what I am. I love it!" [6] The sending of used matchbooks hardly constitutes jaded sophistication, and although Hurston could frequently hide behind masks, the youthful excitement here seems genuine. Her emotions are also the social analogs to her intellectual experience at Barnard.

Hurston came to New York in 1925 as a writer but left Barnard two years later as a serious social scientist, and although these are not incompatible vocations, they can imply different uses for personal experience. She had the relatively rare opportunity to confront her culture both emotionally and analytically, both as subject and object. She lived Afro-American folklore before she knew that such a thing existed as a scientific concept, or had special value as the product of the adaptive creativity of a unique subculture. This is extraordinary knowledge for one to learn about oneself, and Zora Hurston found it a fascinating and frustrating acquisition. Even before coming to New York there had begun to build within her a distance between the facts of her Eatonville existence and the esthetic uses she would make of it. Barnard conceptualized that distance between 1925 and 1927, the years of her most active participation in the cultural uprisings of Harlem.

The Barnard experience is seldom discussed when dealing with Hurston, but I believe it is central to understanding her role in the Renaissance and her subsequent career. She entered Barnard as a young, earnest scholar, feeling "highly privileged and determined to make the most of it." She was particularly impressed with her own admission—"not everyone who cries 'Lord! Lord!' can enter those sacred iron gates"—and with Barnard's "high scholastic standards, equipment, the quality of her student body and graduates." She quickly came under the influence of anthropologists Ruth Benedict, Gladys Reichard, and Franz Boas. By far the most important of these was Boas, one of the leading American scientists of the early twentieth century and a man of great personal magnetism. Boas recognized Hurston's genius almost immediately and urged her to begin training as a professional anthropologist. One can grasp how important Boas became to Hurston by reading her autobiography, *Dust Tracks on a Road* (1942).[7] Boas was "the greatest anthropologist alive," the "king of kings," and yet she was permitted to call him "Papa Franz." She admittedly "idolized" him. Perhaps the conclusive example of Hurston's serious commitment to Boas's training lies in her willingness to be equipped with a set of calipers and sent to Harlem to measure skulls—an act which many contemporaries feel only Zora Hurston could have gotten away with, and which only a dedicated student would be likely to attempt. Finally, in Febraury 1927, after she had completed the requirements for her B.A. degree, Boas arranged, through Carter Woodson's Association for the Study of Negro Life and History, to finance her on a folklore collecting trip to the South.

Going back was a difficult experience, one she describes with some anguish:

> My first six months were disappointing. I found out later that it was not because I had no talents for research, but because I did not have the right approach. The glamor of Barnard College was still upon me. I dwelt in marble halls. I knew where the material was all right. But, when I went about asking, in carefully accented Barnardese, 'Pardon me, but do you know any folk-tales or folk-songs?' The men and women who had whole treasuries of material just seeping through their pores looked at me and shook their heads. No, they had never heard of anything like that around there. Maybe it was over in the next county. Why didn't I try over there? I did, and got the selfsame answer. Oh, I got a few little items. But compared with what I did later, not enough to make a flea a waltzing jacket. Considering the mood of my going South, I went back to New York with my heart beneath my knees and my knees in some lonesome valley.
>
> I stood before Papa Franz and cried salty tears.[8]

The causes of her initial failure were varied, but at least one of them was philosophical. She was not returning to the South as a local girl home from college, but as a young, serious intellectual equipped with the analytic tools of anthropological theory and a desire to further the cause of science. In her experience with Boas she had tried to emulate what she called his "genius for pure objectivity," [9] but her academic training did not suffice once she was in the field. The problem went beyond techniques of collecting. Hurston had acquired a conceptualization for her experience. The Eatonville folk were no longer simply good storytellers, admirable in their lifestyles, remarkable in their superstitions, the creators of profound humor, the matrix for a vital, local-color fiction. Now they were a part of cultural anthropology; scientific objects who could and should be studied for their academic value. These are not irreconcilable positions, but for one who has previously conceived of such experience esthetically, it is a definite skewing of perception. Where before Eatonville had been considered a totally unique body of material known only to Zora Hurston (even her black fellow artists in the Renaissance knew little about it), now the town and her experience in it were abstracted to the level of science—a subculture created and maintained by adaptive techniques of survival, many of which had scientific labels and theoretical significance. The altered perception created in Hurston a dual consciousness.

A tension, perhaps latent since her removal from the Eatonville scene, became manifest between the subjective folk experience and the abstract knowledge of the meaning of that experience, and it was complicated by the stress on objectivity intrinsic to the Boas training. First in New York, and then in the South as a collector, Zora Hurston sought a scientific explanation for why her own experience in the black rural South, despite all her education, remained the most vital part of her life, and further, why the black folk-experience generally was such a source of vitality in literature. Moving between art and science, fiction and anthropology, she searched for an expressive instrument, an intellectual formula, that could accommodate the poetry of Eatonville, the theories of Morningside Heights, and the esthetic ferment she had known in Harlem.

This was a unique intellectual tension complicated by the personal factors of sex, race, and nationality, that whole complex of ambiguous identifications American culture imposes on its members. Hurston struggled with it during the Renaissance, and to some extent throughout her life. It is reflected in her unsuccessful attempt to return to Columbia for a Ph.D. in 1934—she told Boas, "You don't know how I have longed for a chance to stay at Columbia and study" [10]—her handling of her collected folklore in *Mules and Men* (1935) and *Tell My Horse* (1938); the attempts at esthetic resolution in her novels of the thirties (*Jonah's Gourd Vine,* 1934; *Their Eyes Were Watching God,* 1937; *Moses, Man of the Mountain,* 1939); and her final retreat from the issue entirely. Bitter over the rejection of her folklore's value, especially in the black community, frustrated by what she felt was her failure to convert the Afro-American world view into the forms of prose fiction, Hurston finally gave up. Her unsuccessful 1948 novel, *Seraph on the Suwanee,* is about white people; her later research interests were the Mayan Indian cultures of Central America; she spent the final seven years of her life writing a "nonracial" biography of Herod the Great.

II

Hurston's writing during the Renaissance years comes generally from the pre-Barnard or early Barnard period. After she became a serious Boas student, most of her energies were turned to the problems of folklore collecting. As a student at Howard she had been a striving English major, capable of such lyrics as "O Night":

O Night, calm Night,
Creep down and close my burning eyes,
Blot out this day of heavy sighs,
O Night.
Dam up my tears and hide my face,
Efface from mind this time and place,
O Night, black Night.[11]

"John Redding Goes to Sea," in Howard's *Stylus* for 1921 (later reprinted in *Opportunity*), is a sentimental story—the account of a rustic dreamer who achieves his wish of going to sea only after a heavy rain sends an errant log downstream with his corpse. Yet Hurston also realized early the rich possibilities of the Eatonville material, even if she did not quite understand her personal relationship to it. The first story sent in response to Charles S. Johnson's request was "Drenched in Light," published in *Opportunity* in December 1924, a month before her arrival in New York. It is a day in the life of Isie Watts, a "little Brown figure perched upon the gate post" in front of her Eatonville home. "Everybody in the country," knows "Isie Watts, the joyful," and how she likes to laugh and play, how she lives to the fullest every minute of her young life. Isie gets into various scrapes, including an attempt to shave her sleeping grandmother, and eventually is given a ride by a passing white motorist, despite her grandmother's disapproval. The point appears to be that Isie, poor and black, is far from tragic: rather, she is "drenched in light," a condition which endears her to everyone and presents her grandmother with a discipline problem. Isie is persistently happy, and the implication is that whites suffer from an absence of such joy; Isie's white benefactor ends the story, "I want a little of her sunshine to soak into my soul. I need it."

Hurston is probably manipulating white sterotypes of black

people here, but it is not a simple matter of satire. She remembered Eatonville as a place of great happiness, and "Drenched in Light" is clearly autobiographical. To realize how much so, one has only to read her autobiography, or her May 1928 article in *The World Tomorrow,* "How It Feels to be Colored Me." In this essay Hurston admits "My favorite place was atop the gate-post. Proscenium box for a born first-nighter. Not only did I enjoy the show, but I didn't mind the actors knowing that I liked it." She, too, used to take rides from white motorists if her family was not watching, and she admits to liking to perform for the white folks:

> They liked to hear me "speak pieces" and sing and wanted to see me dance the parse-me-la, and gave me generously of their small silver for doing these things, which seemed strange to me for I wanted to do them so much that I needed bribing to stop. Only they didn't know it.

There is an element of satire in both pieces, but it seems useful to place the emphasis on the Eatonville memory. The whole point to "How It Feels to be Colored Me" is that

> I am not tragically colored. There is no great sorrow dammed up in my soul, nor lurking behind my eyes. I do not mind at all. I do not belong to the sobbing school of Negrohood who hold that nature somehow has given them a lowdown dirty deal and whose feelings are all hurt about it . . . No, I do not weep at the world—I am too busy sharpening my oyster knife.

This is hardly a satiric tone, and Hurston is making a serious point: she is proud to be black, proud to be the product of a culture which endows her with a special response to the jazz of the "New World Cabaret." When the band starts playing she "follows them exultingly" and is amazed that "the great blobs of purple and red emotion" have not touched her white companion.

Hurston was as vulnerable as anyone to the cult of primitivism in the twenties, and some of the vulnerability is illustrated in the *World Tomorrow* article. Still, even before coming to New York, as the autobiographical "Drenched in Light" indicates, Hurston was trying to define her own special relationship to Eatonville, its folklore, the pastoral idyll that she associated with her first ten years there, and the implications of all of this for her art.

Hurston's use of Eatonville is also seen in her prize-winning story in the 1925 *Opportunity* contest, "Spunk." Spunk takes another man's wife, kills the cuckolded husband, and then rides to his death on the log at the saw mill—apparently the victim of the dead husband's return for vengeance. Eatonville is not exactly idyllic, although the violence just below the town's surface admittedly does not appear ominous. It is a place where superstition and "conjure" are everyday facts of life, and where existence has a continuity that transcends the moment. As the story ends: "The women ate heartily of the funeral baked meats and wondered who would be Lena's next. The men whispered coarse conjectures between guzzles of whiskey."

Not all of Hurston's writing during the Renaissance years deals with Eatonville, but certainly the best of it does. Her attempt to illustrate the Eatonville novice newly arrived on the Harlem cabaret scene, "Muttsy" (*Opportunity,* August 1926), is poorly plotted but provides a nice ironic touch to the *Pamela* motif; the girl preserves her innocence in capturing the worldly Muttsy, but the story ends with him going back to his gambling ways: "What man can't keep one li'l wife an' two li'l bones?" Her play "Color Struck," the second-prize winner in the 1926 *Opportunity* contest and later reprinted in *Fire,*[12] is sentimental, a somewhat unconvincing account of color consciousness within the black community, but its cakewalk setting has considerable vitality. Another play, "The First One," also submitted to the *Opportunity* contests and later printed in Charles S. Johnson's *Ebony and Topaz,* is a biblical account of the Ham legend, comic in its presentation of Ham's curse being a product of shrewishness in Shem's and Arrafat's wives; Ham is presented as a lover of dancing and music, a man of joy contrasted with his brothers' materialism.

More representative of Hurston's talent during this period is "Sweat," published in *Fire*'s single issue, and the "Eatonville Anthology," published serially in *The Messenger* between September and November 1926. The "Anthology" is a series of thirteen brief sketches told with great economy and humor. "Sweat" is probably Hurston's finest short story of the decade, remarkably complex at both narrative and symbolic levels. The account of a Christian woman learning how to hate in spite of herself, a story of marital cruelty, an allegory of good and evil, it illustrates the unlimited potential in the Eatonville material. The story centers on Delia and her husband Sykes. Sykes hates his wife, beats her, and lives with another woman; he finds excuses to be cruel. And yet Hurston sees through even such a distasteful character; one reason Sykes hates his wife is that she emasculates him by earning their living washing white men's clothes. His resultant behavior is perceptively analyzed by Joe Clark: "There's plenty men dat takes a wife lak dey do a joint uh sugar-cane. It's round, juicy an' sweet when dey gits it. But dey squeeze an' grind, squeeze an' grind an' wring tell dey wring every drop uh pleasure dat's in em out. When dey's satisfied dat dey is wrung dry, dey treats em jes lak de do a cane-chew. Dey throws em away. Dey knows whut dey is doin' while dey is at it, an' hates theirselves fuh it but they keeps on hangin' after huh tell she's empty. Den dey hates huh fuh bein' a cane-chew an' in de way." Sykes eventually tries to drive Delia from her own house by penning a rattlesnake near her back door, and then attempts murder by moving it to her clothes hamper. When the released rattler kills Sykes instead, even though Delia could have saved him, we understand how high Delia's "spiritual earthworks" of Old Testament vengeance have been built against Sykes; she truly hates him "like a suck-egg dog." But this makes the story Delia's tragedy, too, and when Sykes dies at Delia's feet with "his horribly swollen neck and his one open eye shining with hope," a burden is not lifted but newly imposed. Her situation testifies to the prevalence of evil in a world we shape with our own needs.

What these early Eatonville stories illustrate is that by 1925–26, Zora Hurston had taken the irrevocable step of the artist who must remove himself from his experience in order to give it form and meaning. The step was both physical—she had removed herself to Washington and New York, she had entered college—and mental: she was analyzing her experience for its esthetic possibility. When this removal was placed in an academic setting, the process of assigning meaning to her experience became transferred from the esthetic to the scientific, and the next four years of Hurston's life exhibit the ascendency of a scientific impulse toward the systematic collecting of folklore for serious academic purposes.

"Sweat" and the "Eatonville Anthology" were published during her last semester at Barnard, the time in which she became most closely associated with Boas and advanced anthropological study. Significantly, Hurston does not return again to Eatonville as a source for fiction until "The Gilded Six-bits," published in *Story* in 1933, an account of marital infidelity that led in 1934 to a contract for her first novel, *Jonah's Gourd Vine*. What happened to her in the intervening period is largely an untold or misunderstood story.

III

Hurston's 1927 collecting expedition lasted for six months, from February to October. Neither Woodson nor Boas was overly impressed. Woodson printed her article on Cudjo Lewis, a survivor of the last slave ship to America, in the *Journal of Negro History*,[13] but he apparently also used her as a common research hack. At one point she was copying legal documents from the Jacksonville, Florida, court records about a black-owned traction company of 1909. The folk material sent to Boas did not please, for it was similar to material collected by others, and her report to Boas on the conclusions of the expedition took only three double-spaced pages. Hurston had now, however, largely given up the writing of fiction to pursue a career as a scientist. Even though her field trip had not been a success, she is dedicated to anthropology, convinced of the need to collect her people's folklore before it is obliterated by the encroachments of modern civilization. In her report to Boas she stresses that material is slowly slipping away: "The bulk of the population now spends its leisure in the motion picture theatres or with the phonograph."[14] One cannot overemphasize the extent of her commitment. It was so great that her marriage in the spring of 1927 to Herbert Sheen was short-lived. Although divorce did not come officially until 1931, the two separated amicably after only a few months, Hurston to continue her collecting, Sheen to attend Medical School. Hurston never married again.

Hurston's return to her folklore collecting in December of

1927 was made possible by Mrs. R. Osgood Mason, an elderly white patron of the arts, who at various times also helped Langston Hughes, Alain Locke, Richmond Barthé, and Miguel Covarrubias. Hurston apparently came to her attention through the intercession of Locke, who frequently served as a kind of liaison between young black talent and Mrs. Mason. The entire relationship between this woman and the Harlem Renaissance deserves extended study, for it represents much of the ambiguity involved in white patronage of black artists. All her artists were instructed to call her "Godmother"; there was a decided emphasis on the "primitive" aspects of black culture, apparently a holdover from Mrs. Mason's interest in the Plains Indians. In Hurston's case there were special restrictions imposed by her patron: although she was to be paid a handsome salary for her folklore collecting, she was to limit her correspondence and publish nothing of her research without prior approval.

Hurston was financed by Mrs. Mason for an initial two-year period, from December 1927 to December 1929, and then was given an extension to March 31 of 1931. Although she spent time in the West Indies, most of her effort was in the South, and she collected a body of material which she would draw on for the rest of her life. Her correspondence during these years is remarkable for its enthusiasm. She feels that she is getting to the core of Afro-American culture, seeing it as an illustration of man's most basic impulses. She wants to present the material unadorned, letting it speak for itself as eloquent testimony for black creativity. She is impressed with the inherent beauty of the folklore itself, the way preaching is poetry, the way folk singing is more alive than classical music. She frequently rails against white distortions of this material, especially against Howard Odum and Guy Johnson, early white collectors in the field. In one letter she asks Boas point-blank if these men can be "serious scientists." [15] She also thought analytically about the material, formulating general principles to guide her study. She wrote Langston Hughes about theories of dialect: "Some laws in dialect. The same form is not always used. Some syllables and words are long before or after certain words and short in the same position. Example: you as subject gets full value but is shortened to yuh as an object. Him in certain positions and 'im in others depending on consonant preceding. Several laws of aspirate H." [16] In letter after letter Hurston emphasizes the uniqueness of black culture. She stresses the "basic drama" of black life, the ingenuity and wit in black dialect, the "asymmetry" of black art, the "dynamism" of black dancing, the originality of the entire Afro-American subculture.[17]

A measure of her sense of discovery and scientific commitment to it is the absence of her own creative effort between the fall of 1927 and the spring of 1930; even then she only began work with Langston Hughes on an ill-fated play, *Mule Bone,* itself a drama constructed out of a folktale. Hurston had previously used the Eatonville setting and its rural folklore as the stuff of fiction; now she is given to the collecting of songs, dances, games, conjure ceremonies, or anything else that can contribute to her body of information. As she told Hughes, "I am truly dedicated to the work at hand and so I am not even writing." [18] Her reports of her research are basically academic, apparently mainly by choice, although it was also a form approved by Locke and Mrs. Mason. She completed two pieces for the *Journal of American Folklore,* "Dance Songs and Tales of the Bahamas" [19] and the 110-page monograph, "Hoodoo in America." [20] She consulted with Boas and Benedict about her efforts and asked Boas's advice about the theories she was formulating—many of which were eventually published in a most unscientific volume, Nancy Cunard's *Negro* (1934). At one point she had planned seven books from her materials: "One volume of stories. One children's games. One dance and the Negro. One 'Mules and Men' a volume of work songs with guitar accompaniment. One on religion. One on words and meanings. One volume of love letters with an introduction on Negro love." [21] She was also interested in presenting on stage the true folk experience, eventually putting together a group of actors, singers, and dancers, and with Mrs. Mason's help producing an authentic folk concert at the John Golden Theatre on January 10, 1932. Extremely proud of her admission to the American Folklore Society, the American Ethnological Society, and the American Anthropological Society, she made sure that any news stories about her contained mention of these professional memberships. The Howard English major and the short-story writer of the Harlem Renaissance had apparently become a Barnard anthropologist, a folklore collector of considerable zeal and importance.

That transformation never fully took place, however, and although Hurston would continue to collect and use folklore for most of her career, establishing herself as the most important collector in the field, she grew away from the scientific view of her material. She came to doubt the efficacy of scholarly publication, pointing out to the Rosenwald Fund in 1934 that "it is almost useless to collect material to lie upon the shelves of scientific societies." [22] My own opinion is that she never became a professional, academic anthropologist, because such a vocation was alien to her exuberant sense of self, her admittedly artistic and sometimes erratic temperament. A good argument can be made for Hurston's never completely realizing this herself, but if there is a single theme which emerges from her creative effort during the thirties—her five books, her fiction, her essays—it is that eventually immediate experience takes precedence over analysis, emotion over reason, the self over society, the personal over the theoretical. She learned that scientific objectivity is not enough for a black writer in America, and she went on to expose the excessive rationality behind the materialism of American life, the inadequacy of a sterile reason to deal with the phenomena of living. She forcefully affirmed the humanistic values of black life, contrasting them to the rationalized inhumanity of white society, and she asserted early arguments for black cultural nationalism. Beginning with *Jonah's Gourd Vine* (1934), her writing exhibits a studied antiscientific approach, and in her nonfiction even the most technical data is personalized. Her rejection of the scholarly bias and the scientific form was a process instead of a revelation, forming a chapter in her personal history too complex to detail here. Its cultural context is relevant, however, for Hurston's intellectual experience is in some ways a paradigm for the much debated "Crisis" of the black creative intellectual of the Harlem Renaissance.

I think Hurston was predisposed in favor of an anthropological conception of Eatonville simply because she was a creative writer. Although that sounds paradoxical, it is actually a logical product of the environment of ideas surrounding her. The black writer is especially vulnerable to the prescriptions which an idolatry of western European "high culture" imposes on American artists. He is urged to aspire toward a "raceless ideal" of literature, which technically interpreted has meant that he should not write about race, that he should not create "Negroes" but "human beings"—as if they were mutually exclusive categories. Above all, he must never stoop to "propaganda." Such prescriptions were constantly offered during the Harlem Renaissance, and many of its participants aided and abetted such dubious aims. In fact, prior to the revolution in consciousness attending the current Black Arts Revoltuion, all black writers were badgered with such advice, the writer's success occurring in direct proportion to his ability to reject it. The attitude which invites the act of this prescribing, as well as the substance of the prescription, is a conception of the black condition as something which must be "overcome," since it is somehow manifestly less than human—a habit of mind institutionalized as American racism. All black American writers confront in some way this attitude and its resultant phenomena: the condition of black people. Thus, the dynamics of the culture make it as natural as breathing for the black artist to confront the issue of race.

In such a context, the attraction of a scientific conception for black experience becomes considerable for the writer-intellectual, especially if he has taken part in the formal educational system. The educational process in America is essentially one of assigning and reinforcing class structures through the creation of an educated middle class. This acculturative process informed Hurston that black sharecroppers were peasants (a pejorative term, especially within the self-enterprise mythology of American agriculture), that superstition was a crutch of the ignorant, that her folk experience was quaintly interesting but hopelessly unsophisticated. It is to Hurston's credit that she resisted much of this sort of knowledge, as is illustrated in an article she wrote for the *Messenger* in 1925, "The Hue and Cry About Howard University." Howard's white president liked to hear his students sing, and his motives are suspect at best. When the students objected, however, they did so for the wrong reasons; they argued that the spirituals were (a) "low and degrading, being the product of slaves and slavery"; (b) "not good grammar"; (c) "they are not sung in white universities."

Hurston supported the president for the right reasons, when she should have resisted his unconscious racism. Her prospiritual argument would later become a fight to make blacks aware of how "conservatory concepts" had corrupted native Afro-American music, and her awareness of the inadequacies in the antispiritual argument is part of her larger awareness of the black condition. For she *knew* that Joe Clarke and his Eatonville cronies were human beings of complexity and dignity, no matter what their grammar, no matter how unsophisticated their manner might be, no matter how much white society distorted them. This knowledge typifies a dilemma of the black intellectual, for knowing this fact, how does one assert its truth and assign it meaning in the midst of a country whose institutions are structured to deny it? For Zora Neale Hurston, and for others, one way has been to assert black humanity by emphasizing its anthropological confirmation, a particularly effective way of accounting for human truth in a technological society, and one which mostly sidesteps the purely esthetic issue of "universality" vs. "propaganda." Blacks can be measured, studied, and charted in the interests of proving the general equality of the races. One has only to cultivate a "genius for pure objectivity" and let the evidence prove the absurdity of racial prejudice. Moreover, because anthropology also proves the existence of particular cultural differences while simultaneously positing a basic sameness in the human condition, one can maintain the integrity of black culture without sacrificing it to the mythical American melting pot. The scientific collection of the data of black life, its folklore, comes to prove black humanity as it asserts the beauty of the culture; meanwhile the artist who affirms the same thing is accused of special pleading.

What I should like to conclude with is the hypothesis that one reason Zora Neale Hurston was attracted to the scientific conceptualization of her racial experience during the late twenties and early thirties was its *prima facie* offering of a structure for black folklore. That is, it offered a pattern of meaning for material that white racism consistently distorted into "Negro" stereotypes. A folk singer was a cultural object of considerable scientific importance to the collecting anthropologist precisely because his folk experience affirms his humanity, a fact that Hurston could know subjectively as she proved it scientifically. The scientific attraction became so strong that she was led into seriously planning a career as a professional anthropologst, and it continued to affect her writing even after she had rejected such a possibility. When she used Eatonville as fiction in *Jonah's Gourd Vine* (1934) and folklore as personal narrative in her collection, *Mules and Men* (1935), she was in the process of rejecting the scientific conceptualization, but had not yet reached the esthetic resolution in fiction that characterized her two masterpieces of the late thirties, *Their Eyes Were Watching God,* (1937), and *Moses, Man of the Mountain* (1939). Hurston never denied the usefulness of the Barnard training, but she made it clear that something more was needed for the creation of art. As she once told a reporter: "I needed my Barnard education to help me see my people as they really are. But I found that it did not do to be too detached as I stepped aside to study them. I had to go back, dress as they did, talk as they did, live their life, so that I could get into my stories the world I knew as a child." [23]

In sum, then, Zora Neale Hurston was shaped by the Harlem Renaissance, but by Boas as well as by Thurman and Hughes, by Barnard as well as by Harlem. This should not necessarily suggest that the Boas experience was of a superior quality; in many ways it seriously hindered her development as an artist. Nor should it suggest that the esthetic excitement among the Harlem literati failed to influence her thought. It does mean that the attraction of scientific objectivity was something Hurston had to work through to arrive at the subjective triumphs of her later books. But the ferment of the Harlem Renaissance should also not be underestimated. Hughes, in particular, showed Hurston the poetic possibilities of the folk idiom and she was continually impressed when a reading from Hughes's poems would break the ice with dock loaders, turpentine workers, and jook singers. The mutual effort involved in the creation of *Fire,* the nights at Charles S. and James Weldon Johnson's, the *Opportunity* dinners, even the teas at Jessie Fauset's helped make Zora Hurston aware of the rich block of material which was hers by chance of birth, and they stimulated her thinking about the techniques of collecting and presenting it.

Yet, even Wallace Thurman, the chief of the "Niggerrati," tacitly acknowledged that anthropology was Hurston's primary concern during the Renaissance years. In his 1934 novel, *Infants of the Spring,* a scarcely disguised account of the Harlem Renaissance, Thurman's Sweetie May Carr is transparent reportage of Zora Neale Hurston. Sweetie May is a storyteller from an all-black Mississippi town, "too indifferent to literary creation to transfer to paper that which she told so well." In one of his better jokes Thurman transfers Hurston's area of study and probably imposes some of his own cynicism on her character, but still suggests a preoccupation with scientific study: " 'It's like this,' she [Sweetie May] told Raymond. 'I have to eat. I also wish to finish my education.

Being a Negro writer these days is a racket and I'm going to make the most of it while it lasts . . . I don't know a tinker's damn about art. I care less about it. My ultimate ambition, as you know, is to become a gynecologist. And the only way I can live easily until I have the requisite training is to pose as a writer of potential ability.' "

One should be careful about accepting fictional characters as biographical evidence, but I hope the previous reconstruction suggests that Thurman was at least partially right. His insight provides a context for the study of Hurston's published books of the 1930s, a period in which she *did* give a tinker's damn, and created some of the best fiction ever written by a black American.

CHAPTER 11

Charles S. Johnson: Entrepreneur of the Harlem Renaissance

PATRICK J. GILPIN

Well, son, I'll tell you:
Life for me ain't been no crystal stair.
. . . .
So boy, don't you turn back.
Don't you set down on the steps
'Cause you finds it's kinder hard.
Don't you fall now—
For I'se still goin', honey,
I'se still climbin',
And life for me ain't been no crystal stair.

Langston Hughes, *Mother To Son*

Langston Hughes wrote in 1940 that Charles S. Johnson "did more to encourage and develop Negro writers during the 1920's than anyone else in America." [1] A generation later Arna Bontemps observed that Charles S. Johnson, along with Alain Locke, and others have "been called the nursemaids of . . . [the] Renaissance." [2] Yet, a decade after Bontemps's observation, Charles Spurgeon Johnson remains an enigma. Older, white intellectuals vaguely remember him as a sociologist in race relations. Black intellectuals, if they predate the era of Dr. Martin Luther King, Jr., remember him, of course. But they are most likely to recall that he was the first black president of Fisk University or that, for over a decade, he directed the Race Relations Institute at Fisk. Only recently have scholars begun seriously to evaluate the role of Charles S. Johnson in the generation that prepared the way for the Freedom Movement.[3]

In the area of popular culture, where the real value of the black cultural awakening will ultimately be measured, Johnson has no standing. In fact, the *Negro Almanac* does not even list his name. Lerone Bennett, Jr.'s valuable and popular history, *Before the Mayflower,* only vaguely alludes to Johnson. *Jet* magazine is an exception. For example, a July 1971 issue observed the month of his birth in the section "Yesterday in Afro-American History."

Yet, for four decades, Charles S. Johnson toiled quietly but incessantly in his efforts to combat white racism in preparation for the Freedom Movement. Later generations would use the base that he and others had established to launch the Freedom Movement and later the Movement for Black Liberation. A Renaissance man himself, Johnson moved from one area of quiet confrontation to another. He believed that progress anywhere was progress everywhere. At various times Johnson challenged oppression and racism in the social, economic, and cultural spheres of the nation of the white oppressor. This selection will concentrate on his contributions to black culture in the 1920s. But first, who was Charles S. Johnson?

Johnson was born in 1893 in Bristol, Virginia,[4] on the Tennessee border, the son of a Baptist minister. Almost half a century later, he recalled that his father's most "notable difference from the typical Negro minister" in southwest

Virginia, near the end of the last century, "was in the quality and security of his education." [5] At an early age Johnson was exposed to the classics of Western literature, theology, and history. By the time he went off to Wayland Academy in Richmond at the age of fourteen, he had sampled, "though not necessarily always absorbing," such works as the *Lives of the Saints,* the sermons of Spurgeon, Greek mythology, Gibbon's *Rise and Fall,* along with Alger's boys' stories and "countless dime novels." The son of a secure, middle-class, professional family, Johnson finished Virginia Union University in three years, graduating in 1916. From there he moved to graduate work at the University of Chicago and came under the influence of Robert E. Park. His work at Chicago was interrupted by the Great War. Although he saw action in the Meuse-Argonne offensive, as a regimental sergeant major in the 103rd Pioneer Infantry, and was under fire for twenty-two consecutive days, he later recalled that "much of the time in the war zone was whiled away resecuring and preserving the exposed books in shattered libraries of war torn French towns." [6]

In 1919 Johnson returned to Chicago to work under Park. But this was the same time that Eugene Williams' needless death sparked the Chicago riot. Johnson, who, Edwin R. Embree tells us, [7] was himself nearly killed during the riot, was uniquely qualified to react to the aftermath of the white-inspired violence of Chicago. Not only did Johnson have the training and middle-class *skills* necessary to analyze the riot systematically, but also, despite his middle-class origins, he had paid his dues as a black man in white America. For he had grown up in a "democracy" nurtured by the period that Rayford W. Logan calls the "nadir" in American history. As a child, Johnson traumatically experienced the "legal" implementation of jim crow.[8] Years later, when he was president of Fisk, he recalled that experience in some detail.[9] One of his childhood treats was riding the trolley to town, helping his mother shop, and then stopping at the soda fountain for refreshments. One day the security of his childhood world was shattered by the owner of the drugstore who told his mother that he "could not serve us any more at the counter." Johnson recalled that, in talking to his mother, the owner "had no defense against my mother's obvious dismay and sense of humiliating embarrassment. Nor could she explain to me with any more clarity what had happened and why it was happening. We simply went home in silence." [10] Of a similar experience with the once "familiar friendly face of the conductor on the little trolley car that passed our corner," Johnson says: "The Negroes could not believe their ears. . . ; but it was the beginning of a new self-consciousness that burned." [11] The well-educated, emotionally secure, and intellectually gifted Johnson would utilize his skills throughout his lifetime to ready America for liberation from segregation and all that it implied. Much of the inner drive that so many of Johnson's contemporaries speak of may have been that "new self-consciousness that burned."

As early as 1917, Johnson had headed the Department of Research and Investigations for the Chicago Urban League of which Park was president. As a young man who was well versed in the world of black Chicago, and who knew the available literature contained by the local Urban League, Charles S. Johnson was among twenty-four men suggested as a possible executive secretary to oversee the operations of Governor Frank O. Lowden's interracial commission to study the riot. As was typical of Johnson, when presented to the commission at the second meeting, he was prepared and "presented a tentative outline for investigating the riot." [12] Unfortunately, the white-dominated Chicago Commission, like the Kerner Commission a half century later, was not "ready" for a black man to be executive secretary of an interracial commission. The impressive Johnson, however, could not be overlooked, and he was named associate executive secretary at a salary fifteen hundred dollars less than the white executive director. Years later, the widow of the Executive Secretary, Graham Taylor, acknowledged that Johnson actually "-'set up the study' and was by far the stronger researcher of the two men." [13]

By March of 1920 the staff of the Commission was operating full scale. The next eleven months were spent in "compiling and presenting the data of the report." [14] Unlike many such commissions, Johnson and his colleagues were not willing to do merely a perfunctory job. As V.D. Johnston, reviewer of the Commission's report, noted:

> With the statement that the riot was only a "symptom of serious and profound disorders lying beneath the surface of race relations in Chicago" a thesis . . . [was] advanced to include an investigation of the migration of Negroes from the south, the Negro population of Chicago, the housing situation as related to Negroes in Chicago, racial contacts, crime, the Negro in Industry, and pubic opinion in racial relations. . . .[15]

In 1922 *The Negro in Chicago: A Study of Race Relations and a Race Riot* (Chicago: The University of Chicago Press) appeared. During its preparation, Johnson gained a national reputation in the field of race relations. He had received offers to do studies in other areas where the Great Migration was making an impact, such as Baltimore, Trenton, Buffalo, and Los Angeles.[16] He eventually accepted a position in 1921 with the National Urban League and went to New York as Director of Research and Investigations. For the next seven years he directed the economic and sociological research of the Urban League. At the same time he spent the last five and a half years editing *Opportunity: A Journal of Negro Life.* It was in this environment that he helped spawn the Harlem Renaissance of the 1920s.

On the eve of the Depression, Johnson left New York to return home to the Southland from whence he had come. At Fisk University he was to establish a nationally known Department of Social Sciences, the first Race Relations Institute in the South, and finally, in 1947, to be inaugurated as Fisk's first black president. His premature death in 1956 ended over four decades of combating white racism in preparation for the Freedom Movement.

In 1923, in addition to his duties as Director of the Department of Research and Investigations, Charles S. Johnson assumed the task of editing the new Urban League magazine, *Opportunity: A Journal of Negro Life.* It was John T. Clark, later executive secretary of the St. Louis Urban League, more than Charles S. Johnson, who first pushed the idea of a magazine. Even before 1920 Clark was asking the League to establish an official organ. Finally, in December of 1921, the *Urban League Bulletin* appeared with Johnson as editor; but Clark was not satisfied and continued to push for a more formal publication "with advertisements and second class mailing privileges." [17] Then, at the National Urban League meeting in Pittsburgh in October 1922, he got his wish. The first issue of *Opportunity* would be published in January 1923. In 1921 the League had begun receiving an annual grant of eight thousand dollars from the Carnegie Corporation for the establishment of a separate Department of Research and Investigations.[18] It was decided by the Urban League to allot part of these funds to finance *Opportunity.*[19]

During his five-and-a-half-year tenure as editor of *Opportunity,* Johnson applied the approach first learned under Park in Chicago and further developed during the writing of *The Negro in Chicago.* He was in tune with much of the National Urban League's philosophy of scientific investigation of the "facts" and the "education" of the public. In *The Negro in Chicago,* he had written:

> Because the "race problem" has been so vaguely stated, so variously explained, and so little understood, discussions of it and the conduct of whites and Negroes toward each other usually express feeling rather than intelligence.
>
> The public is guided by patterns of behavior and traditions generally accepted, whether sound or unsound. False notions, if believed, may control conduct as effectively as true ones. And pre-established notions lose their subtle influence when it appears that their basis is in error.[20]

Johnson believed that, in addition to economic causes, much of the Chicago riot could be explained by "isolation and misunderstanding" which led to "accumulated resentments" and "unchallenged mutual beliefs and resultant friction." [21] It was his judgment, then, that if:

> . . . these beliefs, prejudices and faulty deductions can be made accessible for examination and analysis, many of them will be corrected. If a self-critical attitude toward these prejudices can be stimulated by typical examples, a considerable step will have been taken toward understanding and harmony.[22]

Eugene Kinckle Jones, Executive Secretary of the National Urban League, set the tone of *Opportunity* when in the first issue he wrote that it would "depict Negro life as it is with no exaggerations. We shall try to set down interestingly but without sugar-coating or generalization the findings of careful scientific surveys and the facts gathered from research." [23]

Charles S. Johnson, while supporting Jones's position, noted an additional dimension that *Opportunity* would report, when in the next issue he wrote: "There are aspects of the cultural side of Negro life that have been long neglected." [24] Very quickly *Opportunity* was becoming more than a house organ of the Urban League. The journal was determined to be both readable and authoritative in the information it published. It was especially concerned with questions of two types: "those on which the results of dependable information were not available," and "those on which there was information which could not readily find its way into the general organs." [25]

Although *Opportunity* is most remembered for its role in the Harlem Renaissance, it was not restricted to spawning the new literary movement among black people. It devoted many pages to exposure, examination, and refutation of the pseudo-scientific racism rampant during the Era of Normalcy. It reported on scientific surveys of discrimination and conditions in the black community in the areas of housing, health, employment, and others. It was, of course, particularly interested in black migration, education, and other economic and sociological areas. But it was in its relationship to the Harlem Renaissance that Charles S. Johnson and *Opportunity* made their most enduring contribution.

At the end of his life Johnson said that "the importance of the *Crisis Magazine* and *Opportunity Magazine* was that of providing an outlet for young Negro writers and scholars whose work was not acceptable to other established media because it could not be believed to be of standard quality despite the superior quality of much of it." As if to vindicate the wisdom of the approach of education in race relations, Johnson went on to say: "What was necessary was a revolution and a revelation sufficient in intensity to disturb the age-old customary cynicisms. This function became associated with *Opportunity Magazine*." [26]

Although *The Crisis* was older and had a much larger

circulation than *Opportunity,*[27] it never seemed to capture the spirit of the Renaissance.[28] The orientation of W. E. B. Du Bois, editor of *The Crisis,* was more political than Johnson's and perhaps, as Bontemps suggests, "Du Bois had serious reservations about the tone and character of the new writing and art. He leaned toward the tidy, the well-mannered, the Victorian—literary works in which the Negro put his best foot forward, so to speak."[29] *Crisis* did publish many of the literary figures of the era, such as Langston Hughes, Countee Cullen, Alain Locke, Jessie Fauset, Arna Bontemps, and others. And, of course, the art of Aaron Douglas was presented. In fact, in most cases these figures first published in *Crisis.* But on the other hand, Du Bois saw the Harlem Renaissance as only one facet in the larger world. Apparently until she stepped down as literary editor in May of 1926, Jessie Fauset directed the literary end of *Crisis.* Du Bois was more concerned with Pan-Africanism, conventional politics, and the month-to-month battles of the NAACP against discrimination, racism, and colonialism.[30]

Opportunity did not neglect such things as Pan-Africanism, the international world, and the day-to-day struggle against discrimination, racism, and colonialism; it did, however, downplay conventional politics. But it was in reporting and promoting black *culture* in the United States and the world at large that Johnson and *Opportunity* found their forte. Sometimes entire issues were given over to black culture. For example, in the May 1924 issue, Alain Locke, Albert C. Barnes, and Paul Guillaume all contributed articles to a special issue on African art. Again, in the November 1926 issue, *Opportunity* presented a special "Caribbean issue." Among other features, it included poems by Claude McKay, an article by A. A. Schomburg on "West Indian Composers and Musicians," and W. A. Domingo's "The West Indies."

It was in the *Opportunity* contests and dinners, however, that Charles S. Johnson was most successful as an entrepreneur in promoting the new awakening of black culture. Johnson recognized the creative genius of the many black artists of the 1920s. But this genius was of limited value until the racial barriers of publishers were removed. Johnson, along with Urban League official William H. Baldwin, moved deliberately to bring the white publishers and the black writers together. They worked closely with Frederick Lewis Allen, then editor of *Harper's*. William H. Baldwin relates that "Allen invited a 'small but representative group from his field,' and Baldwin and Charles S. Johnson 'supplied an equally representative group of Negroes.' "[31]

The May issue of *Opportunity* reported the meeting of black writers, poets, and artists with great enthusiasm. On March 21 the Writers' Guild, "an informal group whose membership includes Countee Cullen, Eric Walrond, Langston Hughes, . . . and . . . others," had attended a dinner at the Civic Club. After a brief interpretation of the objective of the Guild by Charles S. Johnson, Alain Locke was introduced as master of ceremonies. He was asked to interpret the "new currents manifest in the literature of this younger school." The Civic Club gathering read like an honor roll of the Harlem Renaissance. W. E. B. Du Bois was just back from Africa and was introduced by the chairman with "soft seriousness as a representative of the 'older school.' " James Weldon Johnson was then introduced and acknowledged for the "invaluable encouragement [he had given] to the work of this younger group." Others included Carl Van Doren, editor of *Century;* Walter White, whose novel, *The Fire in the Flint,* had been accepted for publication; Montgomery Gregory, Director of the Department of Dramatics, Howard University; Albert C. Barnes, art connoisseur and "foremost authority in America on primitive Negro art"; along with Countee Cullen, Gwendolyn Bennett, J. A. Rogers, and many others. Jessie Fauset, literary editor of *Crisis,* whose novel, *There Is Confusion,* was due to appear soon, was given "a place of distinction on the program." [32]

Johnson and his colleagues, then, had succeeded in bringing together the black literati and the white publishers. No longer could publications such as *Survey, Survey Graphic, The World Tomorrow, Nation,* the New York *World,* and *Harper's* plead ignorance or talk about the lack of "qualified" blacks. Until the Depression black culture flourished as it moved from the narrow restrictions that white capitalists had placed upon it. It would still be at the mercy of white-controlled publications. And as a result, when the Crash came, black writers and artists would be the first "fired." But even during the bleak days of the Depression and after, aspiring black writers and artists would have a wealth of literary models worthy of emulation. As Charles S. Johnson would remark, the Civic Club dinner marked "the first significant transformation of vague hopes for the future into a material means for making that future possible. . . ." [33] No longer would it be necessary to look only to Paul Laurence Dunbar, who had "resorted to dialect verse to gain a hearing and then nothing but his dialect verse would be accepted." [34] No longer was Sutton E. Griggs the isolated exception to Charles W. Chesnutt. In fact, in all areas of black culture, one saw the influence of the Renaissance; and from Charles Gilpin to Paul Robeson, from Aaron Douglas to Richmond Barthé, from Bessie Smith to Josephine Baker, a new era had emerged. It would later decline, but only to be rediscovered and appreciated even more by later generations. In short, the March 21, 1924, meeting had secured broad patronage for the "New Negro Movement." While Harold Cruse and many others would later argue that a movement based upon white financiers was folly, it did seem at the time to Charles S. Johnson and his literary circle at *Opportunity* like one gigantic step. Certainly no one can gainsay the artistic and cultural contributions of the Harlem Renaissance. Its power structure is another matter.

Less than six months after the Civic Club dinner, Charles S. Johnson announced the first, of what was to be three, *Opportunity* contests. Now that white publishers were "alerted" to the potential of black artists, Johnson and *Opportunity* would act as agent to bring together and crystallize what had been developing at least since Claude McKay had penned *If We Must Die*. The September issue of *Opportunity* announced that "the Contest will include first, second, and third prizes for the following types of writing: Short Story— . . . Poetry—. . . Play—. . . Essay—. . . Personal Experience Sketch—. . . . For the next ten best stories, poems, plays, and essays there will be free criticism by competent authorities in each field of letters. The winning stories will be published."[35] Johnson further announced that the contest was "designed to stimulate creative effort among Negroes and quite without any notion of discrimination is confined to Negro contestants."[36]

Johnson's motivation in beginning the *Opportunity* contests appears to be that of a skilled, shrewd, and pragmatic entrepreneur who saw a flourishing of black culture as but another road for combating white racism while aiding black people. He pulled no punches in the September issue that announced the first contest. In the editorial he noted: "A new period in creative expression among Negroes is foreshadowed in the notable, even if fugitive and disconnected, successes of certain of the generation of Negro writers now emerging." From this premise he argued: "The body of experience and public opinion seem ripe for the development of some new and perhaps distinctive contribution to art, literature, and life. But these contributions demand incentives." Finally, in a lengthy conclusion, he wrote:

> The purpose, then, of *Opportunity*'s literary contest can thus be stated in brief: It hopes to stimulate and encourage creative literary effort among Negroes; to locate and orient Negro writers of ability; to stimulate and encourage interest in the serious development of a body of literature about Negro life, drawing deeply upon these tremendously rich sources; to encourage the reading of literature both by Negro authors and about Negro life, not merely because they are Negro authors but because what they write is literature and because the literature is interesting; to foster a market for Negro writers and for literature by and about Negroes; to bring these writers into contact with the general world of letters to which they have been for the most part timid and inarticulate strangers; to stimulate and foster a type of writing by Negroes which shakes itself free of deliberate propaganda and protest.[37]

It becomes apparent, then, that Johnson was not running a normal magazine contest for "amateurs." What he was doing was using his contacts with white capitalists of the publishing world to open an avenue for many black men and women. Johnson knew well that the work of Langston Hughes, Countee Cullen, Jessie Fauset, and many others was not the work of amateur artists. Heretofore, they were restricted, for the most part, to a few black journals such as *The Crisis.* This easily allowed white publishers to opt out of publishing the work of black authors with the age-old, but bogus, argument that such figures were writing mere "protest literature" of limited general interest. No longer would Johnson allow this. Furthermore, always the pragmatist, Johnson was applying his thesis of education first developed in *The Negro in Chicago.* He saw great advantages to blacks as an ethnic group, apart from individuals, "in the serious development of a body of literature about Negroes." It was not by accident, but by design, consistent with what was to become the pattern of his life's work, that Charles S. Johnson became the entrepreneur of the Harlem Renaissance.

But even before Johnson could announce the contest, there were tangible results from the Civic Club dinner. As he noted years later, "Out of this meeting came some of the first publications in the best publication tradition." In fact, Johnson went on: "Frederick Allen . . . [*Harper's* editor] made a bid for Countee Cullen's poems for publication as soon as he had finished reading them . . . ; and Paul Kellogg of the *Survey* sought to carry the entire evening's readings in an issue of the magazine. This fumbling idea lead to the standard volume of the period, *The New Negro.*" [38] Originally carried in the special March 1925 issue of *Survey Graphic,* under the editorship of Alain Locke, it was later combined with drawings by Winold Reiss (which had been done for *Survey*) into book form as *The New Negro.*[39]

Johnson continued to use the contests to promote black men and women of letters. Even while the first contest was in process, the "New Negro Movement" was making concrete gains. Part of Johnson's promotional scheme was to involve leading literary figures as contest judges. In all there were to be twenty-four judges involved in the first contest. In the October issue Johnson noted that the judges included such figures as "Fannie Hurst, one of America's foremost short story writers; Robert C. Benchley, dramatic critic and editor of *Life;* Witter Bynner, poet and anthologist; Alexander Woollcott, dramatic critic of the New York *Sun;* Henry Goddard Leach, editor of the *Forum;* . . . and James Weldon

Johnson, one of the best known of the Negro writers and anthologists." [40]

Almost every month Johnson used the contest to promote the mutual interest of the black literati and white patrons. In the January issue he revealed that Mrs. Henry G. Leach, wife of the editor of *Forum,* was the donor of the prizes to be awarded in *Opportunity*'s literary contest.[41] In April, on the eve of the *Opportunity* dinner, he reflected on the long-range benefits for black people. He noted that the "announcement of the prize winners will be by no means the end of the Contest." Once again, in his role as the pragmatic entrepreneur of black culture, he went on: "Its purpose from the beginning was to encourage creative effort among Negro writers and among those who have capacity for self-expression." The entrepreneur reminded the black artists that: "We have assurances that the interest of our judges will continue, and to those who see in the field of letters new channels for expression and for the adequate interpretation of Negro life. . . . The most vital function of the Contest has just begun." [42]

The May and June issues of *Opportunity* would practically be given over to what the New York *Herald-Tribune* editorially labeled a "Negro Renaissance." [43] Many of the winners, for the most part unknown to the white publishers, were well known within black literary circles. Many had published in black magazines such as *Crisis.* Now with *Opportunity* and Charles S. Johnson there was a medium for wider circulation and perhaps some royalties. John Matheus, Zora Neale Hurston, and Eric D. Walrond captured the first three prizes in the short-story division.[44] Langston Hughes and Countee Cullen won the first three prizes in poetry. E. Franklin Frazier, Sterling Brown, and Laura D. Wheatley did the same with their entries in the essays section. In the dramatic division [45] Zora Neale Hurston's *Color Struck* and Warren A. MacDonald's *Humble Instrument* shared second place, and Kelly Miller's daughter, under the name of Jean Ray, was third to a play listed as having been written by "FRANCES." Finally, the personal experience sketches prizes were captured by G. A. Steward, Fidelia Ripley, and J.C. Stubbs.[46]

Enthusiasm was running high by May of 1925. Charles S. Johnson was prepared to make the most of the March 21, 1924, meeting. He advised his readers once again that "the work of the contest is just beginning" and went on to "advise those of our contestants who are interested in this whole developing movement to *stand by*." [47] Under the section of *Opportunity* entitled "Pot-Pourri," Johnson reprinted a lengthy editorial from the New York *Herald-Tribune* with the lead, "A Negro Renaissance." With certain reservations, mindful of its white cultural racism, it seems fair to say that in many ways the *Herald-Tribune* had captured much of what was to become known as the Harlem Renaissance when it noted:

> These young people—and youth was another striking thing about this gathering—were not trying to imitate the white man nor repeating the professional white story-teller's dreary stencils of the "darkey." They were expressing their own feelings, frankly and unabashed, even if it took them back to the jungle. When rain threshes on the roofs of their Harlem flats they do not try to imagine what Wordsworth might have said about it. . . .
>
> A novel sight that dinner—white critics, whom "everybody" knows, Negro writers whom "nobody" knew—meeting on common ground. . . .[48]

The *Opportunity* dinner, itself, was a gala affair.[49] "Three hundred and sixteen persons—youthful prize winners, friends of Negro writers, critics and creators of American letters, editors, publishers, free lances, poets, novelists" took part in what Johnson called a "magnificent assemblage." The program began with a few brief remarks by Charles S. Johnson and closed with James Weldon Johnson who commented that "no race can ever become great that has not produced a literature." In between the two Johnsons the cerebral excitement was electrifying. John Erskine of Columbia University, and coeditor of the *Cambridge History of American Literature,* spoke as the chairman, talking about a new field in American literature. The audience was delighted as selections from the contestants were read in part or in their entirety. Langston Hughes's *The Weary Blues* and Countee Cullen's *To One Who Said Me Nay* were typical of the caliber of the evening's entertainment. The participants of the New Movement offered, in addition to samplings of their work, Alain Locke as their spokesman.

In evaluating the *Opportunity* dinner, Charles S. Johnson, always the practical man, noted the significance of the evening when he wrote: "It was not a spasm of emotion. It was intended as the beginning of something and so it was. The meeting . . . ended with . . . announcements, . . . which bound this initial effort to the future." Most important of the announcements was the reading of a letter from Casper Holstein. Holstein, a black West Indian, had guaranteed funds for a second contest.[50]

The dinner, while being "prearranged . . . was not stiffly formal." As a result, the pattern of the March 21 Civic Club mingling of artists and publishers was continued. For example, after James Weldon Johnson had read Langston Hughes's *The Weary Blues* aloud at the banquet, Carl Van Vechten approached Hughes that very night about the possibility of publication of a book of poems. From this came the book *The Weary Blues,* published by Alfred A. Knopf.[51]

From the first contest emerged many gains for black artists and for the further development of black letters. Not all gains were as spectacular or as immediate as those of Langston Hughes, but they were numerous. It was no small feat for the contest that "it located about 800 Negroes scattered through nearly every state in the union, . . . some of whom give promise of definite accomplishment in the field of letters. It marked, rather dramatically, the awakening of artistic effort among the newer Negroes." [52] In October Johnson was able to announce that John Matheus's prize-winning story "Fog" had been "recommended" by Dr. Blanche Colton Williams of Hunter College and Columbia University to the O. Henry Memorial Prize Committee "on its sheer merit as a short story." At the same time Zora Neale Hurston, "whose *Spunk* and *Color Struck* received prizes in the Contest will go to Barnard College on a scholarship. She will be its first colored student." [53]

Charles S. Johnson and *Opportunity* were less than modest when in the February 1926 issue Johnson pointed to the Boston *Transcript*'s reporting of Edward J. O'Brien's analysis of "best short stories of 1925." O'Brien had listed short stories by John Matheus, Zora Neale Hurston, Eloise Bibb Thompson, Marietta Bonner, Clement Wood, and Isabelle Eberhardt (translated by Edna Worthley Underwood) as "having distinction." For the most part, these were short stories by black artists, and all had been carried in the black journal, *Opportunity*. In this context Johnson's subtle reminder that "it should be remembered that this journal is not one of those devoted exclusively either to literature or to fiction" can be appreciated.[54] And so it was that the results continued to accumulate from the promotional activities of Charles S. Johnson, the entrepreneur of the Harlem Renaissance of the 1920s.

Some of the novelty may have worn off, but the contests continued for two more prolific years. The second *Opportunity* contest received 1,276 entries and was expanded to eight divisions.[55] In addition to the original five divisions of 1925 were added "Musical Compositions," "The Alexander Pushkin Poetry Prize," and "The F.C.W.C. [Federation of Colored Women's Clubs] Prizes for Constructive Journalism." Again the harvest was plentiful. Some of the old winners, such as John Matheus and Zora Neale Hurston, reappeared. Arthur Huff Fauset emerged as a double winner capturing the "short story" and the "essays" divisions. In perhaps the most competitive division, a new winner surfaced in Arna Bontemps, whose poem *Golgotha Is a Mountain* was rated over the work of such poets as Gwendolyn Bennett, Claude McKay, and Frank Horne.

Again, in May of 1926, the *Opportunity* Awards Dinner was held after elaborate preparations. This time the guest list reached over four hundred.[56] To many of the old figures, new participants were added. Supplementing the regulars, Carl Van Vechten, L. Hollingsworth Wood of the Urban League, and Alain Locke, were Paul Robeson, who "spoke for the plays," and Nathaniel Dett, who spoke "for the music," and many others.

As Johnson was wont to do, he once again involved a "blue ribbon" panel of judges. A random listing would include Jean Toomer, Carl Van Doren, William Stanley Braithwaite, James Weldon Johnson, Clement Wood, Alain Locke, Benjamin Brawley, Henry Goddard Leach, Nathaniel Dett, Robert Frost, Vachel Lindsay, and John Hope. The entrepreneur never overlooked the need for support from influential circles.

The June issue of *Opportunity* was designated as a "Contest Number." [57] The works of many of the winners, such as

Bontemps, Arthur Huff Fauset, Cullen, Bennett, and others, made up the bulk of the magazine.

As 1927 came, Johnson could look back on the previous year with much satisfaction. Again Edward J. O'Brien had honored *Opportunity* and its contestants in his anthology, *Best Short Stories of 1926*. Included were works by Arthur Huff Fauset, Dorothy West, Zora Neale Hurston, John Matheus, Louis L. Redding, Florida Ridley, and Benjamin Young. In addition, the *Opportunity* selection, *Black and White at the Negro Fair,* by the nonblack Guy B. Johnson was cited. Added to this honor, William Stanley Braithwaite's sesquicentennial edition of the *Anthology of Magazine Verse* had noted the works of Gwendolyn Bennett, Arna Bontemps, Countee Cullen, Waring Cuney, Joseph S. Cotter, Frank Horne, Georgia Douglas Johnson, Wallace Thurman, Helene Johnson, and Lucy Ariel Williams. Finally, Johnson reported that "the O. Henry Memorial Awards volume will also reprint Arthur Fauset's *Symphonesque.*" Johnson concluded: "Representation for Negro writers in these anthologies is the largest of any period in . . . history; . . . Their work now speaks for itself; and, to the glory of their skill, it speaks for Negroes." [58]

In the October 1926 issue Johnson announced the third *Opportunity* contest. It would not be known until much later that this was to be the last formal *Opportunity* contest. Again Casper Holstein put up the prize money. As was now the norm, Johnson used the contest for the purpose of reviewing and promoting black culture while involving white patrons. He noted, "The stories and poetry which have appeared in these pages, and which, indeed, with surprising frequency, have been republished elsewhere, with the stamp of authoritative approval, stand as their own testimony of the strength of this new literary fermentation." Again Johnson sought to "draw in for appraisal, the fugitive work of our scattered writers, . . . [and] with deliberate care . . . , to guide these prodigal energies to the most promising sources of power." With both lamentation and enthusiasm he remarked that "it is evident that a mine of material lies half buried. . . . But a world yet remains to be conquered." [59]

Johnson kept essentially the same format and promotional scheme. But some of the excitement and glamour was missing. For whatever the reason, the number of judges appears to have been reduced.[60] At the same time Johnson continued to involve a number of "big names," such as Theodore Dreiser, Eric D. Walrond, Robert T. Kerlin, Ridgley Torrence, Carl Sandburg, Paul Green, Benjamin Brawley, Paul Robeson, and others. *Opportunity* gave less space to the contest than in the past. The third *Opportunity* Awards Dinner was held in May. Johnson noted his satisfaction that many of the winners were "beyond the limits of the recognized culture centers." Perhaps the Harlem Renaissance was becoming a national movement. In the same editorial, however, in an unusual, cantankerous mood, he expressed irritation with the "too hasty work, in certain of the less successful entries." [61] The special contest issue of *Opportunity* was delayed this year until July.

Despite the contest's apparent lack of momentum, the winners in the third *Opportunity* contest were an impressive group.[62] Arna Bontemps again won the Alexander Pushkin Prize for his poem *The Return*. Georgia Douglas Johnson's play *Plumes* won first prize, and Frank Horne was another winner. But many of the giants were missing.

Finally, in the September issue of *Opportunity*, the contests were "suspended, . . . in all probability [to be] reopened in 1928." [63] But such was not to be the case, and the formal *Opportunity* contests were ended—never to be reopened. As an anticlimax, the Van Vechten Award, announced in the January 1927 issue for the best single contribution appearing in *Opportunity* in 1927, was awarded in the January 1928 issue. James Weldon Johnson, Robert Morss Lovett, an editor of the *New Republic,* and Charles S. Johnson were the judges. The two-hundred-dollar award was won by Dantes Bellegarde for his article, "Haiti Under the United States," in the December issue.[64] Among those in the impressive list of honorable mention were Eloise Bibb Thompson, William Pickens, Claude McKay, and Langston Hughes. In the November 1927 issue Johnson would note with pride that "the Barnes Foundation has admitted this year, into its restricted classes, two Negro students on fellowships; . . . Aaron Douglas and Gwendolyn Bennett, both familiar to readers of this journal and to a much larger public, . . . were selected for these first fellowships." [65] But *Opportunity*'s leadership in the Harlem Renaissance was waning on the eve of the Great Crash. Soon Langston Hughes's novel *Not Without Laughter* and the production of *The Green Pastures* would draw down the curtain upon an era.

During the five years or more that Charles S. Johnson, along with Alain Locke and Jessie Fauset, [66] reigned supreme as the entrepreneur of the Harlem Renaissance, he was not content with either the role of a participant or a promoter. He added the third dimension as that of interpreter. We have already seen to some degree how he cajoled, instructed, and encouraged whites in better understanding of the black literati. At the same time he did not shy away from advising black artists, nor from placing the New Movement into historical and sociological perspective.

In many ways Charles S. Johnson symbolized the paradox of the 1920s for many black people. It was a period in which there was a black awakening at many social, economic, and cultural levels. In the past, historians have tended to picture the Garvey movement, the rise of the black metropolis, and the cultural Renaissance as movements which were at loggerheads with one another. While this interpretation may still have much validity, it needs reexamining. Although it is beyond the scope of this selection, a new analysis of this period may reveal that the three movements had more in common than was once thought. Certainly a new and burning "race pride," along with a new desire to be free of the shackles of white racism, followed the period after the Great War. To the Garveyites, the Black Jesus, the Black Star Line, and the U.N.I.A. were a manifestation of "race pride" and a desire for liberation. In the Black metropolis, the mood was typified by the desire that Eugene Williams' death not go unavenged. And, of course, as the above indicates, the black literati had discovered a new beauty in "blackness." The new awareness, even in the Garvey Movement, is not to be confused with the white version of segregation. All three desired "first-class citizenship." Although the Garveyites found it in world citizenship, and other men in the street and the intellectuals found it in the areas of economics and culture, the motivations may have been similar. Perhaps Langston Hughes said it best in the *Nation:*

> We younger Negro artists who create now intend to express our individual dark-skinned selves without fear or shame. If white people are pleased we are glad. If they are not, it doesn't matter. We know we are beautiful. And ugly too. . . . We build our temples for tomorrow, strong as we know how, and we stand on top of the mountain free within ourselves.[67]

Johnson desired that black people seek "first class" citizenship within the "American system." For him, in the context of his generation, this did *not* mean becoming a black Anglo-

Saxon. To this degree, he was a kind of cultural pluralist of the 1920s. He saw great value to black people as an *ethnic group* in "the serious development of a body of literature about Negroes." As he himself later demonstrated, from his study of the folk Negro in *Shadow of the Plantation* (Chicago: University of Chicago Press, 1934) to his study of the black elite in *The Negro College Graduate* (Chapel Hill: University of North Carolina Press, 1938), black people were hyphenated Americans. At no time need, nor should, black people avoid their blackness. It was not by accident that most of the *Opportunity* contest divisions were limited "to subjects pertaining directly or indirectly to the Negro." [68] It was from this point of view that he praised Jean Toomer's *Cane,* Walter White's *The Fire in the Flint,* and Jessie Fauset's *There Is Confusion.*[69]

Johnson believed that "literature has always been a great liaison between races." [70] From this premise he argued that whites were "at as serious a disadvantage in writing about the subtle intricacies of Negro life and to its peculiar emotional experiences as the Negroes are of writing about them." In short, while he did not feel blacks should be restricted to writing about the black experience, he did urge blacks to exploit the black experience to build the body of literature about black people that was necessary for liberation from the isolated world of segregation. By avoiding writing about the black experience, blacks were allowing whites, "who have never yet been wholly admitted to the privacy of Negro thots [*sic*]," to continue to produce accounts that were "palpably unauthentic, frequently misleading, sometimes criminally libelous."

As the Renaissance years progressed, Johnson continued to warn against the dangers of blacks "whose only legitimate claim to distinction is their complexion" exploiting the

Movement.[71] He wrote that "if this awakening is to be a sound, wholesome expression of growth rather than a fad to be discarded in a few seasons, it must somehow be preserved from the short-sighted exploiters of sentiment; . . . [and from] a double standard of competence as a substitute for the normal rewards of study and practice." He warned in the 1920s, as he would all his life, that it was not sufficient to be "the best Negro." In short, "if a book or poem is bad or mediocre it is bad and should not beckon for the shroud of race to redeem it." Johnson believed, for example, that literary gains were curtailed by "pseudo-philanthropic teachers" who in integrated schools did not apply the same rigorous standards as are "applied to white students." Johnson's point was that "until the product of Negro writers can be measured by the same yardstick that is applied to all other writers, the Negro writer will suffer from the lack of full respect, and all that this implies." Needless to say, entries in the *Opportunity* contests were not faced with this problem.

In 1927 Johnson edited *Ebony and Topaz,* which was published by the National Urban League. In many ways it was a companion volume to Locke's *The New Negro.* In the introduction, Johnson went far toward defining the Harlem Renaissance.[72] He said of *Ebony and Topaz:* "It is a venture in expression, . . . [by artists] who are here much less interested in their audience than in what they are trying to say, and the life they are trying to portray." They did not seem to mind if "some of our white readers will arch their brows or perhaps knit them soberly at some point before the end." Nor were they overly concerned if some blacks objected, for "it is also true that in life some Negroes are distasteful to other Negroes." And Johnson, in agreement with what Langston Hughes had said in the *Nation,* wrote: "The

Negro writers, . . . are now much less self-conscious, less interested in proving that they are just like white people, and, in their excursions into the fields of letters and art, seem to care less about what white people think, or are likely to think about the race. Relief from the stifling consciousness of being a problem has brought a certain superiority to it." In short, Charles S. Johnson seemed to be saying that what he had envisaged in announcing the first *Opportunity* contest in the September 1924 issue of *Opportunity* had come true. The early creative promise of the Claude McKays, the Jean Toomers, and the writers in *Crisis* had matured. A significant number of black artists were now producing a "serious body of literature about Negro life." Finally, the writing was free of the "deliberate propaganda and protest" that so bothered Johnson. The protest now was subtle, artistic, and sophisticated.

Years later, near the end of his prolific life, Johnson had occasion in a speech at Howard University to look back at the Harlem Renaissance after a quarter of a century. Even though the movement *per se* was long dead, he seemed even more convinced of its success than he had been when he edited *Ebony and Topaz*. He recalled that the Harlem Renaissance was "that sudden and altogether phenomenal outburst of emotional expression, unmatched by any comparable period in American or Negro American history." Claude McKay's *If We Must Die* and Jean Toomer's *Cane* had been the harbingers. Unfortunately, Toomer had "flashed like a meteor across the sky, then sank from view." After McKay and Toomer had come Countee Cullen to give "a classic beauty to the emotions of the race," and Langston Hughes to give "a warm glow of meaning to their lives." Johnson remembered that in Hughes's writing there was "a wistful undertone, a quiet sadness." Johnson was to return the compliment paid him by Hughes in 1940 when he told the Howard audience in 1955 that "no Negro writer so completely symbolizes the new emancipation of the Negro mind" as does Langston Hughes. Johnson still saw the Harlem Renaissance in the context of cultural pluralism. He said of the 1920s:

> It was a period, not only of the quivering search for freedom but of a cultural, if not a social and racial emancipation. It was unabashedly self-conscious and race conscious. But it was race consciousness with an extraordinary facet in that it had virtues that could be incorporated into the cultural bloodstream of the nation.
>
> This was the period of the discovery by these culturally emancipated Negroes of the unique aesthetic values of African art, of beauty in things dark, a period of harkening for the whispers of greatness from a remote African past. . . . It was the period of the reaching out of arms for the other dark arms of the same ancestry from other parts of the world in a Pan-African Conference.[73]

In 1927, when *Opportunity* suspended the contests, Johnson may have known that the end of an era was approaching. For during the very month of the third Awards Dinner, Johnson was corresponding with President Thomas Elsa Jones of Fisk University.[74] He had been offered a position at Fisk. At first Jones tried to recruit Johnson on a part-time basis. Apparently Johnson was willing, for President Jones wrote the executive secretary of the Urban League that "Mr. Johnson has consented to come for at least one semester provided his work with you can be arranged." [75] Fisk was in the process of reestablishing a Social Science Department that would be closely related to the service of black people. On June 15, 1927, Eugene Kinckle Jones wrote the Fisk president that "the Steering Committee voted unanimously that it could not comply with your request for the services of Mr. Johnson." [76] Although not ready to resign from the Urban League, Johnson continued to keep in close touch with President Jones and with Fisk's plans for establishing a strong Social Science Department.[77] On September 3 he attended a conference at Chapel Hill with, among others, the well-known sociologist Howard Odum; the conference had been called by Thomas Elsa Jones in reference "to the department of our Social Science Research program at Fisk University." [78] Johnson followed this up with a memorandum on the subject.[79]

By 1928 Johnson was engaged in serious correspondence with President Jones about the possibility of coming to Fisk. The editor of *Opportunity* was beginning to consult others for advice. He sought the counsel of Robert E. Park, Edwin R. Embree, President of the Rosenwald Fund, and L. Hollingsworth Wood. In his letter of February 8 to President Jones, Johnson suggested some of the reasons for leaving *Opportunity* and returning South. He noted: "I have talked with Mr. Outwaite specially and frankly . . . , stating the reservations which I had entertained concerning my present organization, [and] the question of the magazine. . . . He is already aware that my research interest is definitely committed to the South. I have talked similarly with Mr. Hollingsworth Wood, and to both of these I think I made my first definite commitments about resigning the work here." [80] The correspondence continued during the early months of 1928. Finally, on March 13, 1928, Johnson wrote the president of Fisk: "Thus, to bring matters to a conclusion, I announced to Mr. Jones, the executive Secretary, that I had decided to resign the work here, to take up the duties at Fisk in the fall." [81]

Four years almost to the day after the tremendously successful Civic Club meeting, Charles S. Johnson had committed himself to leave New York to return to the South. Why? His motivation for leaving what looked like an ongoing successful venture to return to the region that was the bastion of racism was, like the man himself, complex. He was an extremely ambitious man. Yet, how much further could he go with the Urban League? He may have sensed that the economic bubble so important to the Harlem Renaissance would soon burst. Fisk was a great challenge and under the young President Thomas Elsa Jones seemed headed for a "Greater Fisk." Jones had practically urged him to write his own ticket. It is Johnson and not Jones who, in the correspondence, set the conditions under which he would come. As a middle-class black man, Johnson and his family could expect a materially comfortable, if segregated, life in a border state.

In the final analysis, it seems that his decision was influenced by the combination of the new and challenging position at Fisk and the less than optimistic outlook for the immediate future of the Urban League magazine *Opportunity*. Unlike *The Crisis, Opportunity* had never been a self-supporting venture. During Johnson's years it was always a part of the League's Department of Research and Investigations.[82] The Department itself was funded by an annual eight-thousand-dollar grant from the Carnegie Corporation.[83] From this basic eight-thousand-dollars came *Opportunity*'s limited budget. In 1927 the Carnegie Foundation support was discontinued.[84] When the League was unable to persuade Julius Rosenwald to pick up the tab, the budget of the Department of Research and Investigations became a responsibility of the entire League. At this time Eugene Kinckle Jones, who may have felt that the magazine and its editor were overshadowing the executive secretary and the National Urban

League, decided it was time to "consider 'the whole question of *Opportunity* Magazine and its future' to 'determine whether the magazine is an effective instrument for carrying out the League's purposes,' and, more immediately, whether it justified as much as $10,500 of the League's annual budget." [85] Johnson apparently saw little future for him in a department that was in search of funds, with the future of one of its major functions, namely *Opportunity,* in question.

After Johnson left the League, the director of the Department of Research and Investigations and the editorship of *Opportunity* were separated.[86] Ira DeA. Reid took over the task of director of Research and Investigations, while Elmer A. Carter was named editor of *Opportunity*. Although culture was not neglected, the magazine began to stress the "sociological and economic aspects of the Negro's relation to American life." [87] *Opportunity* came near going under during the Depression and New Deal years, only to be bailed out by "friends." [88] The wartime restrictions on paper, printing, and photoengraving supplies forced the magazine in 1943 to become a quarterly. In correspondence with Lester B. Granger, Johnson "offered . . . to resume the editorship in 'absentia' " from his post at Fisk in hopes of saving *Opportunity*. The idea was abandoned as the magazine's finances improved and Johnson became busy with *The Monthly Summary* at Fisk.[89] With the seven-page winter issue of 1949, *Opportunity* died.

Shortly after the exodus of its chief entrepreneur, the Harlem Renaissance was soon to end with a whimper. What had started with *If We Must Die* ended in *The Green Pastures* with "De Lawd." As Langston Hughes said:

> That spring for me (and, I guess, all of us) was the end of the Harlem Renaissance. We were no longer in vogue, anyway, we Negroes. Sophisticated New Yorkers turned to Noel Coward.

> Colored actors began to go hungry, publishers politely rejected new manuscripts, and patrons found other uses for their money. . . .
>
> The generous 1920's were over. . . .[90]

It is over half a century since Claude McKay and Jean Toomer built upon the work of James Weldon Johnson and W. E. B. Du Bois to usher in the "New Negro." Today the "New Negro" is no longer fashionable. Now the cry is heard for the "New Black Man." But few will deny the importance of the role of the "New Negro" in the development of the "New Black Man." As one looks back upon that extraordinary generation of the twenties, one theme keeps recurring. The entire movement was victimized by the economy. As Robert L. Allen, in using an economic approach, and Harold Cruse, in using a cultural approach, have demonstrated, the fuller development of black culture has too often been dependent upon foundations and white patrons.[91] Until this obstacle is removed, the kind of fully developed black culture that Charles S. Johnson believed in and worked for is still "over Jordan."

In reviewing the role of Johnson and of his generation in the Harlem Renaissance, one must always place him and his colleagues in the context of the 1920s and not in the context of the post-Watts era. In closing, it might be well to reflect upon what John O. Killens wrote in *Black World*'s special issue, "The Harlem Renaissance Revisited."

> Why is it important for us to know of Paul Robeson and Dr. DuBois and the men and women of the Harlem Renaissance? Because they are a vital and heroic part of our history. Because a people who are ignorant of their history are condemned to repeat their history. Because so many Black young people believe that the Black Liberation Movement began two or

> three hours after they joined the issues and that they themselves invented militancy. . . . We need desperately to know that this generation is not the first to produce artists and writers and historians who identified with Africa and proclaimed that Black was beautiful. . . .[92]

Even against the criticism of an Allen or a Cruse, Johnson stands up well when placed in the context of Killens's admonition. Perhaps Charles S. Johnson's favorite quotation, appropriately enough an African proverb, serves as the best epitaph for his years as entrepreneur of the Harlem Renaissance: "If you know well the beginning, the end will not trouble you much."

CHAPTER 12

Frank Horne and the Second Echelon Poets of the Harlem Renaissance

RONALD PRIMEAU

The Harlem Renaissance of the twenties and black-power movements of the sixties are often compared as times of rebirth and renewal in the life and arts of the black man. It is ironic, then, that we are forgetting the poetry of a man whose works span both periods. In 1925 Frank Horne's "Letters Found Near a Suicide" won the poetry prize in *The Crisis;* [1] James Weldon Johnson included many of Horne's poems in the various editions of *The Book of American Negro Poetry,* [2] as did Countee Cullen in his *Caroling Dusk* in 1927; [3] in 1937 Sterling Brown cited the "intellectual irony" and "race pride" in Horne's works; [4] and he was represented in Hughes and Bontemps' *The Poetry of the Negro, 1746–1949,* as well as in the new, revised edition.[5] But Bontemps and Hughes would remember, whereas today's editors have forgotten the poems of the twenties and passed over those of the sixties. The more recent comprehensive anthologies—from Emmanuel and Gross's *Dark Symphony* (1968) to Ruth Miller's *Blackamerican Literature* (1971), and Davis and

Redding's *Cavalcade* (1971)—omit Horne's works entirely.

The results are telling. We need the minor poets of the Harlem Renaissance to understand its full impact, and our study of the sixties should include the works of the older poets still making valuable contributions. The poetry of Frank Horne further links the two periods and deepens our understanding of the preoccupations of the poets of each time. Specifically, Horne's poems published in *The Crisis* and reprinted in anthologies can be divided into three groups: Christmas poems and poems with Christian imagery that demonstrate the intersection of the black man's religion and politics, his fervor and his militance; poems growing out of an historical consciousness of the black man's heritage; and poems centered on the quest motif, chiefly in the language of the athletic contest and the planning of a suicide. Works in all these groups appear predominantly in the twenties and the sixties and suggest a place of prominence so far not given to Horne's achievement.

The same is true of a number of the second echelon of poets of the Harlem Renaissance who increased the momentum for the creation and transmission of the black literary tradition. Among the figures often overlooked in the period, in addition to Frank Horne, are Georgia Douglas Johnson, Waring Cuney, Arna Bontemps, Helene Johnson, Gwendolyn Bennett, Donald Jeffrey Hayes, Angeline Grimke, and Anne Spencer. Together with the major writers of the time, these minor poets gave to the Harlem Renaissance what Sterling Brown has described as "temporal roots in the past and spatial roots elsewhere in America" and established its validity as a movement within "a continuing tradition." [6]

The Crisis published Frank Horne's "Letters Found Near a Suicide" in 1925 and "More Letters Found Near a Suicide" in 1929. In between, there appeared "Harlem" and "Nigger,

A Chant for Children." Taken together, these works over a five-year period are the chief examples of his combining a sense of history and the extended metaphor of an athletic contest in a quest motif.

"Letters Found Near a Suicide" is a collection of short poems exhibiting Horne's diversity of subject, theme, and style. The setting is that of a man preparing his death, facing his past, and addressing the many people in his life. The most widely read of the letters, "To James," is also the poem most central to Horne's philosophy.

> Do you remember
> How you won
> That last race . . . ?
> How you flung your body
> At the start . . .
> How your spikes
> Ripped the cinders
> In the stretch . . .
> How you catapulted
> Through the tape . . .
> Do you remember . . . ?
> Don't you think
> I lurched with you
> Out of those starting holes . . . ?
> Don't you think
> My sinews tightened
> At those first
> Few strides . . .
> And when you flew into the stretch
> Was not all my thrill
> Of a thousand races
> In your blood . . . ?
> At your final drive
> Through the finish line

Did not my shout
Tell of the
Triumphant ecstacy
Of victory . . . ?
Live
As I have taught you
To run, Boy—
It's a short dash
Dig your starting holes
Deep and firm
Lurch out of them
Into the straightaway
With all the power
That is in you
Look straight ahead
To the finish line
Think only of the goal
Run straight
Run high
Run hard
Save nothing
And finish
With an ecstatic burst
That carries you
Hurtling
Through the tape
To victory . . .

In an almost metaphysical development of the image of the footrace, the speaker links James's physical stamina with the endurance man needs in the midst of everyday struggles. Stylistically, the poem displays the vigor and consciseness characteristic of the twenties; thematically (although with the irony of the suicide underlying) it is an expression of the need for man to overcome difficulties by accepting them as part of the life process itself. A pivotal word is the "Live" in line 29 which divides the two movements away from and toward acceptance of difficulties in the poem. The first half, calm and reflective, is the speaker's flight to the past and to the remembrance of James's athletic achievements. But at the critical point of his "Live" the speaker extends his meaning beyond a footrace to a projection of life as a contest and struggle. The pace increases as the rhythm of the lines pushes to the finish, "hurtling" the reader through the tape "to victory." In structure and theme "To James" looks ahead to some of the more complex letters that develop in greater detail this quest motif.

The remaining "Letters" represent a panorama of the speaker's past experience. In "To All of You" he cries out of his alienation from the far shores that knew him not. The poem—like many in the Harlem Renaissance period—alludes to the black man's past and his cultural heritage:

> My little stone
> Sinks quickly
> Into the bosom of this deep, dark pool
> Of oblivion . . .
> I have troubled its breast but little
> Yet those far shores
> That knew me not
> Will feel the fleeting, furtive kiss
> Of my tiny concentric ripples . . .

Again we note the fusing of optimism and pessimism in the speaker's view that even by sinking into the deep, dark pool, he may have an effect on others in the form of his tiny concentric ripples which reach the shore. Thus on the brink of his own death, his concern is with future generations—a theme again central in the poetry of the times. But the optimism of "To James" seems to be at first entirely undercut by the mood of "To Chick." Although the speaker again develops his theme in terms of the athletic contest, now the "victory" has changed. We do not find here a forceful "Live" structuring the poem, but (in the imagery of the poem) a change of signals in which the speaker calls a play leading to oblivion. He has found his opening and has squirmed over the line to victory. But the finish line is now the "deep, dark pool of oblivion."

> You remember, Chick? . . .
> When you gaze at me here
> Let that same light
> Of faith and admiration
> Shine in your eyes
> For I have battered the stark stonewall
> Before me . . .
> I have kept faith with you
> And now
> I have called my signal,
> Found my opening
> And slipped through
> Fighting and squirming
> Over the line
> To victory . . .

Even here, while the speaker's attitude is negative in finding his answer in oblivion, he does not choose to run backward with the ball. Neither is his choice easy, since he too must fight and squirm. The game is the same: it's just that the goal is more complex and perhaps some of the rules have been changed. In "To Chick" also, then, there is a struggle, a quest, and a refusal to give up—an affirmation that comes only when the worst is faced.

Whether the speaker sees his victory as the positive act of ending his life or whether in facing death he has learned the value of life, the upswing in tempo and imagery at the conclusion of "To Chick" is clearly an affirmation that is supported by some of the other shorter letters.

In "To the Poets" the speaker sees the poets' task as singing "raptures to the grave." Reeling, from having drunk the "deceptive wine of life," he finds all knowledge in the face of death. In "To Henry" he feels that all attempts at knowledge made through the centuries could never succeed to the same extent as will the gun he is prepared to use. Only in the regions of oblivion will he know all. And in "To Alfred" the speaker is shocked at the sight of life coming forth from coldness—children, "little bits" of life born of an indifferent love. In his disgust, he chooses death over a life lacking passion. It is better to him to be genuinely insensate than to be capable of coldness and indifference while living.

The last letter in the collection, "To You," is a key poem in understanding the complexity of the speaker's overall attitude:

> All my life
> They have told me
> That you
> Would save my Soul
> That only
> By kneeling in Your House
> And eating of Your Body
> And drinking of Your Blood
> Could I be born again. . .
> And yet
> One night
> In the tall black shadow
> Of a windy pine
> I offered up
> The Sacrifice of Body

Upon the altar
Of her breast. . .
You
Who were conceived
Without ecstasy
Or pain
Can you understand
That I knelt last night
In Your House
And ate of Your Body
And drank of Your Blood.
. . . and thought only of her?

The note clearly is addressed to Christ and follows the conventional Christian imagery. Yet the speaker knows also about *her;* and in imagery of the Mass he offers his sacrifice on the altar of her breast. If the *her* of this note represents all of nature, of life in its ecstasy and in its pain, the meaning of the poem becomes clearer. In short, a wide gap has come between the speaker and his Saviour. Although Christ was also a part of nature, he was conceived without ecstasy or pain. The poet, on the other hand, has become so weighted down with the difficulties of the life experience, in the metaphor of the poem he has participated in the ritual and yet "thought only of her." Thus the poem focuses on the symbol of *her* which represents all that has obsessed the speaker, all that the Saviour he describes could not understand, all that has produced his alienation and made it necessary for him to offer the sacrifice of his body on the altar of her breast. But again, as in "To James," the speaker is not running away from but into the complexities he experiences.

Two other poems not included in the "Letters" represent a somewhat different facet of Horne's style. In "To a Persistent Phantom" his style is more conventional, the rhyme and meter are more regular, the language more sedate. The result is an atmosphere of calm, essential to the tone of the poem. But the subject is the same—the haunting, persistent phantom of the mystery of life itself. Finally, in "Symphony," Horne gathers into one thrust the pleasures and pains of the rhythm of human experience:

> Is this the dancing sunlight
> prancing through the windows
> of this limping room
> mocking us
> who strain
> and stagger
> with legs strapped in leather
> and braced
> with cold steel
> or tottering
> on crutch
> or cane. . . ?
> Is this carnival of light
> mocking
> the ponderous rhythms
> and stumbling pace
> and the tears
> and gasps of supplication
> to make quick
> the sickened limb. . . ?
> Does it taunt
> or does it beckon
> with warm affection
> and hope. . . ?
>
> Are prancing light
> and faltering crutch
> variations of the dance

of suns
and moons
and pain
and glory
point and counterpoint
to the baton
of the maestro
to whom
all rhythms
and periods
are the stuff
of the symphony
of life?

Thus, with detailed rhythmic progression, he again raises the central questions about the meaning of the stuff of life itself.

In "Letters" and "More Letters," then, Horne uses the quest motif and the imagery of an athletic event to express some of the most characteristic themes of the Harlem Renaissance. In "To All of You" "those far shores/ That knew me not" recalls Countee Cullen's "Heritage"; his "I have drunk deep/ At your crystal pool" in "To Lewellyn" echoes Langston Hughes's "I, Too, Have Known Rivers," and Arna Bontemps' "Nocturne at Bethesda"; if "Mother" stands for America in "To Mother," the speaker's "And yet as I go/ I shall know/ That you will grieve/ And want me back" suggests Garvey's Back to Africa Movement; and in "To Bennetti" the New Negro "freed" declares "I have climbed the heights/ Of white disaster." In fact, the entire movement of "To Chick," culminating in "Let's go . . . ," suggests the activity of Locke's New Negro on the way to "victory." Finally, "To Jean" echoes the poems of Jean Toomer and captures the rhythms of *Cane*:

When you poured your love
Like molten flame
Into the throbbing mold
Of her pulsing veins
Leaving her blood a river of fire
And her arteries channels of light,
I hated her. . .

These lines suggest "Blood-Burning Moon" in *Cane* and the poems "Song of the Son" and "Brown River, Smile." More than mere allusion to contemporary figures and works, these references demonstrate Horne's deep sense of history and his embodiment of the black man's traditions in his works.

Another group of Horne's poems arises more directly from his concern with history. In "Nigger, A Chant for Children," he creates sharp irony through the juxtaposition of the children's songs and the shouts of the bigot. In the language of children and from their viewpoint the speaker presents a catalog of heroic figures in literature and history. Through identification of the black boy of the last stanza with the figures cited in the poem—Hannibal, Othello, Crispus Attucks, Toussaint, and Jesus—and through repetition of the term "nigger" the poem creates a series of ironic contrasts. Horne's most successful experiment with dialect, "Harlem," appeared in *The Crisis* in June 1928. A picture of Harlem as seen through the eyes of a black minstrel, the poem serves as a perfect link between the major figures of the period and the works of its minor poets:

Harlem. . . Harlem
Black, black Harlem
Souls of Black Folk
Ask Du Bois
Little grey restless feet
Ask Claude McKay

City of Refuge
Ask Rudolph Fisher
Don't damn your body' itch
Ask Countee Cullen
Does this jazz band sob?
Ask Langston Hughes
Nigger Heaven
Ask Carl Van Vechten.

As an all-encompassing catalog of the sights and sounds of Harlem, the poem provides a short resumé of the entire period in its closing lines. The speaker singles out some of the major figures of the twenties—Du Bois, McKay, Fisher, Cullen, Hughes, and Van Vechten—and he frames his references in a form, style, and rhythm that were themselves part of the movement.

II

Many of Horne's religious poems of the sixties are Christmas poems uniting Christian imagery and political militancy.[7] In his 1965 "Balm in Gilead: A Christmas Jingle, Played with Trumpets and Muffled Drums,"[8] Horne presents a catalog of assassinations in the framework of a Brooklyn street fight. Mike calling Hyman "Christ-killer" leads to references to the five little girls bombed in a Birmingham church, Medgar Evers, and President Kennedy. The poem is actually a passion play at Christmas set in the ongoingness of time and the Christians' present participation in history whether for good or evil:

O, I learned
a long while ago
that Christ was killed
by Romans

and Jews
and Christians
and unbelievers . . . all—
and that He is crucified
again and again
when the soul of any man
is blasted
and we stand by
silent . . .

A year later, in 1966, on the occasion of the reissue of Robert C. Weaver's *The Negro Ghetto* (1947), Horne returns to the language of his 1928 "Harlem." Again in a catalog form and in the rhythm of "Go Down Moses," he tells the real-estate man, congressman, money-lending man, and slumlord to "let the ghetto/go." [9] Like Baldwin in *The Fire Next Time,* he uses the imagery of the flood and a purging, applying it specifically to the subject of housing: "Ain't gonna be no water/ next time . . . / burn, baby, burn—" "Let Go," then, structured around the religious imagery of "Go Down Moses" and biblical allusions, enacts a pattern of calm explanation forced to give way by frustration to violence:

I told you so
twenty years ago . . .
I tried to tell you
in orderly words
that you're supposed to
understand . . .
Listen to me now, baby
read it again, friend
So we can march together
. . . into the promised land
before the hell-flamed pit
fries together
all the Goodmans

and Chaneys
and Schwerners
—let go, man
let go—

The poem thus illustrates the doubled-edged calm and militancy of Horne's religious imagery.

Finally, in one of his most recent works, "He Won't Stay Put, A Carol for All Seasons," [10] he presents another crucifixion poem at Christmas, identifying the Christmas tree with the tree of the cross. At first lamenting his lack of the sparkling ornaments and the glitter of Christmas, the speaker links the black man's experience and the numerous political assassinations to the crucifixion: "there just ain't gonna be no Santy Claus/ this time" for Martin Luther King, Malcolm X, Bobby Kennedy, Medgar Evers, Goodman, Schwerner, and Chaney, the Biafran kids, and red-necked Mississippians. But he comes to a realization that he and all these people have "a sure nuff/ Christmas tree" on which they "hang him" every day, using thorns and spikes and twinkling blood for ornaments. This tree is with each man through use of his "inner eye." But in imagery of resurrection and renewal, the speaker shows how slain leaders "won't stay put" and people put down won't stay down.

III

The best concise review of the minor poets of the Harlem Renaissance is still Sterling Brown's discussion of "Contemporary Negro Poety (1914–1936)" in his *Negro Poetry and Drama.* And the best collection of their works is again Hughes and Bontemps' *The Poetry of the Negro, 1746–1970.* From the nature poems of Angeline Grimke and Anne Spencer, the poetry of ghetto life and racial heritage of Waring Cuney, Gwendolyn Bennett, and Helene Johnson, the religious motifs of Arna Bontemps, and the complex metaphors of the dream and the romantic imagination of Georgia Douglas Johnson, we discover lasting artistic expression that complements the works of Hughes and Toomer, McKay and Cullen.

Writing in 1937, Sterling Brown saw Anne Spencer as "the most original of all the Negro women poets" and pointed to her irony, sensitivity, and keen observation. For the most part, her poems rework rather conventional garden imagery in even patterns. But in "Letter to My Sister" and "At the Carnival" she creates a somber resonance, defying the gods and exposing "the dearth of beauty/ In its sordid life." [11] Similarly, Angeline Grimke's "A Winter Twilight" and "When the Green Lies Over the Earth" capture a freshness of nature that enhances the beauty of "your curls so shining and sweet." More complex is the imagery of the black hand in "Tenebris" and the questioning form reminiscent of Cullen's "Yet Do I Marvel" in "The Black Finger": "Why, beautiful, still finger are you black?/ And why are you pointing upwards?"

Alike too in their soft-toned, but forceful probing are the works of Donald Jeffrey Hayes, Gwendolyn Bennett, and Waring Cuney. Hayes's work displays considerable diversity ranging from the irony of "Haven"—again like Cullen's "Epitaphs"—to the horror of "Prescience": "Oh, that somehow I might contrive/ My first night dead to be alive. . . !" And in "Alien" the speaker expresses a longing for his roots, characteristic of the minor as well as the major poets of the times: "Let me escape safely from this gentle madness—/ Let me go back to the salt of sanity/ In the scent of the sea. . . !" Gwendolyn Bennett's "Heritage" shows the influence of Cullen, McKay, and Dunbar in its uniting tropical imagery and a solid identification with her people's experience in the ghettos of America. The poem is a longing in song for the black man's rightful place in his tradition:

> I want to see the slim palm trees,
> Pulling at the clouds
> With little pointed fingers. . . .
>
> I want to see little Negro girls,
> Etched dark against the sky
> While sunset lingers.
>
> I want to hear the silent sands,
> Singing to the moon
> Before the sphinx-still face. . . .
>
> I want to hear the chanting
> Around a heathen fire
> Of a strange black race.
> I want to breathe the Lotus flow'r,
> Sighing to the stars
> With tendrils drinking at the Nile. . . .
>
> I want to feel the surging
> Of my sad people's soul
> Hidden by a minstrel-smile.

"To a Dark Girl" expresses even more directly the poet's sense of the fusion of the African and American experiences in the black woman's heritage:

> Something of old forgotten queens
> Lurks in the lithe abandon of your walk,
> And something of the shackled slave
> Sobs in the rhythm of your talk.

Similarly in his 1926 prize-winning "No Images," Waring Cuney juxtaposes the beauty of the black woman's dancing under palm trees and her life "on the street" and "in the kitchen." Cuney's "Threnody" is indebted to Fenton Johnson's "Tired" in its despair in the face of unfulfilled dreams: "Only quiet death/ Brings relief/ From the wearisome/ Interchange/ Of hope and grief." Finally, Sterling Brown has again pointed to Cuney's absorbing something of the blues and the spirituals in his "I Think I See Him There," "Troubled Jesus," "Crucifixion," and "Wake Cry."

In the poetry of Helene Johnson, Arna Bontemps, and Georgia Douglas Johnson, we find a range and complexity approaching that of the more prominent figures of the time. Each makes a distinctive contribution to the Harlem Renaissance, and the three complement each other in style and theme.

Helene Johnson—like Frank Horne—combines an expression of unquenchable desires with realistic description of ghetto life and a discovery of the roots of her people. "Fulfillment" is in a sense an answer to Horne's "Letters Found Near a Suicide" in its catalog of intense experiences: "Ah, life, to let your stabbing beauty pierce me/ And wound me like we did the studded Christ,/ To grapple with you, loving you too fiercely,/ And to die bleeding—consummate with life." In her most famous work, "Poem," the speaker praises the whole way of being of a "little brown boy," calling him "a jazz prince" and celebrating her participation in his heritage:

> I'm glad I can
> Understand your dancin' and your
> Singin', and feel all the happiness
> And joy and don't-care in you.
> Gee, boy, when you sing, I can close my ears
> And hear tom-toms just as plain
> Listen to me, will you, what do I know

about tom-toms? But I like the word, sort of,
Don't you? It belongs to us.

As a follow-up, "Sonnet to a Negro in Harlem" can be thought of as addressed to the brown boy grown up, "disdainful and magnificent," with a tradition coming from a people "too splendid for this city street."

Sterling Brown finds the poems of Arna Bontemps primarily "meditative, couched in fluent but subdued rhythms." But the range and subject matter of the meditation is wide, from the *Cane*-like imagery of "A Black Man Talks of Reaping" to the horror of "Southern Mansion," which opposes the plantation myth with images of death, emptiness, and rattling chains. Bontemps' best-known poem is the 1928 contest-winning "Nocturne at Bethesda," a combination of biblical imagery and a longing for Africa that we have seen is central in the poetry of the period: "Is there something we have forgotten? some precious thing/ We have lost, wandering in strange lands?" The poem is really a transformation of its Christian framework through the speaker's identification with his homeland:

I may pass through centuries of death
With quiet eyes, but I'll remember still
A jungle free with burning scarlet birds
There is something I have forgotten, some precious thing.
I shall be seeking ornaments of ivory,
I shall be dying for a jungle fruit.

A similar fusing of Christian imagery and the experience the black man faces in America is achieved in the symbolism of "Golgotha is a Mountain." And in another prize winner, "The Return," the speaker combines images of the homeland and unfulfilled dreams in the new world: "Let us go back and search the tangled dream/ And as the muffled drum-beats throb and miss/ Remember again how early darkness comes/ To dreams and silence to the drums." Bontemps' poems—given more recognition during the Harlem Renaissance than they have been afforded later—demonstrate the diversity of the period, combining traditional religious imagery and a concern with the black man's history, his culture, and his present life of unfulfilled dreams in a land of promises.

Georgia Douglas Johnson's vision is that of the modern Romantic who stresses man's ability to transform his perception and create new realities through the dynamics of his own mind. Her emphasis on perception and the role of imagination is illustrated best in "The Poet Speaks":

> How much living have you done?
> From it the patterns that you weave
> Are imaged:
> Your own life is your totem pole,
> Your yard of cloth,
> Your living.

Similarly, "Conquest" is built on the pattern of the Romantic's internal quest: "I live my life running up a hill." In "Trifle," she stresses the creative role of dreams not in running away from difficulties but in helping man to experience them more fully and overcome them:

> Against the day of sorrow
> Lay by some trifling thing
> A smile, a kiss, a flower
> For sweet remembering.
> That when the day is darkest
> Without one rift of blue
> Take out your little trifle
> And dream your dream anew.

Finally "Your World" recalls Wordsworth's *Prelude* and the

poems of Wallace Stevens in its focus on man's quest to make his own world through his creative sensibility: "Your world is as big as you make it." And complementing the mind's creativity is the role of memory in sustaining man through times of unfulfilled dreams. In "Remember" the passing of love is relived through memory: "Love for a day, an hour and then—/ Remember through the night." Similarly, in "My Little Dreams" the speaker internalizes her realities to shield them from time's destructive powers: "I'm folding up my little dreams/ tonight, within my heart."

Georgia Douglas Johnson's Romanticism is the Romanticism of the best poetry of the Harlem Renaissance, a facing of life's difficulties through an intensification of experience and a transformation of reality, not an escape from it; it is a growing realization of life's potentialities and its unfulfilled dreams. "Old Black Men" combines the realism and Romanticism of the period in the contrast of the possibility of the first stanza: "They have dreamed as young men dream/ Of glory, love and power;/ They have hoped as youth will hope/ Of life's sun-minted hour," and the disillusion and acceptance of difficulty of the second stanza: "They have seen as others saw/ Their bubbles burst in air,/ And they have learned to live it down/ As though they did not care." But her poems show, of course, that the old black men do care; yet they dream, and their ability to sustain the dream makes possible their acceptance of reality and their ability to go on. Complementing "Old Black Men" is Georgia Douglas Johnson's mesage for young black men in "The Suppliant": "Soft o'er the threshold of the years there comes this counsel cool:/ The strong demand, contend, prevail; the beggar is a fool." This also is the message of the minor poets of the Harlem Renaissance, a theme learned from David Walker and Henry Garnet, and more immediately from such diverse figures as

Du Bois and Garvey, and then transmitted to Margaret Walker, to Malcolm X, and to Don L. Lee.

It was the responsibility and the accomplishment of the poets of the second echelon of the Harlem Renaissance to develop further the variety of themes and techniques in the tradition of black literature until that time and to transmit the tradition to the poets who followed.

CHAPTER 13

The Renaissance Re-examined

WARRINGTON HUDLIN

The Harlem artists did not constitute a "school" of literature in the traditional sense. These individuals (Langston Hughes, Arna Bontemps, Zora Hurston, Rudolph Fisher, Wallace Thurman, Eric Walrond, Jean Toomer, among others) were drawn primarily by the metropolitan charisma of New York City and word that "something" was happening. For writers the atmosphere of New York was quite attractive. The major publishing houses were located there, the theaters on Broadway, in Greenwich Village, and of course, Harlem. It is not simplistic to say Harlem became the black cultural center, because New York City was the white one. These individuals, young, talented, began to think of themselves as a group, as the result of their association with scholars such as Alain Locke and Charles S. Johnson. There was no single literary philosophy guiding them, nor even a uniform perception of what phenomenon was taking place around them. They were linked together, however, by a common black experience. It is necessary, therefore, to keep in mind, when one refers to the ideas and attitude of the

Harlem artist, that there will automatically be both exceptions and contradictions.

The foundation of the Renaissance was laid in the dialectical development of social and political thought during the turn of the century. The previous twenty years had been referred to as the "Age of Washington." This was a time when Booker T. Washington and the "men of Tuskegee" waged their campaign for self-help and race pride. Washington's program centered on economic nationalism. He argued that the "beggar demands" of social and political equality be abandoned in favor of an interdependence relationship with whites. Black and white Americans were to remain "separate as the fingers but united as the fist." In keeping with the self-help orientation, technical skills replaced higher education as a priority. White America found his presentation, if not his program, palpable. The philosophy, while it served as a basis for much positive self-improvement for blacks, did not constitute any confrontation or demand of white America. W. E. B. Du Bois was to constitute his opposition.

W. E. B. Du Bois was appalled by Washington's accommodation. He embraced the notion of "group economy," but felt far too much of Washington's position had implications of black inferiority. Du Bois instead proposed the utilization of the "talented tenth," educated blacks who could not only work in the group interest but serve as living examples of blacks fitness for equality. He avowed political and social equality as goals to be obtained through protest and agitation.

It was on the note of agitation, however, that Du Bois and a good number of the middle class parted. Many of the black middle class rejected the thought of confronting, even annoying, for the fear that they might jeopardize their chance for assimilation. Du Bois was considered a radical. Their mentality is comparable to that of many free blacks during the slavery era. They feared the antislavery agitation might return them to servitude.

This same middle class had a presence in Harlem during the Renaissance. Their demand of the Harlem artist was that he write "uplift literature." The Harlem artist, however, had transcended the propaganda criteria. (Du Bois also shared the demand for propaganda.) The Renaissance, however, owed its existence to this middle class. The Harlem artist was indebted to the middle class on the most basic level; without a middle class (leisure class) there can be no literature, which is precisely the reason why there is no literature written by field slaves during slavery times—when would they write? Clearly the financial status of the middle class afforded the time to produce what comprises the Afro-American literature of the 1800s. In the case of the Renaissance there was an additional development. The Harlem writers constituted an intelligentsia rather than a middle class, the distinction being that the intelligentsia are individuals who have broken with their middle-class backgrounds to form a community of free intellectuals. (There were, however, middle-class writers in Harlem.)

There also was a debt by the definition of the Renaissance as a point in the Afro-American literary tradition. The assimilationist goals and literature of the middle class provided the Harlem artists with a focus from which to "bounce off," or more specifically a factor in the dialectical process. Most of the literature was written in the Romanticist tradition, saturated with Victorian ideals, and consisted of appeals to white America to consider them equal or at least better than the common blacks. Their black experience was considered a plague from which they wished to escape. Having ignored the depth of their own experience, they wrote escapist literature that was usually shallow and artificial.

These were the roots of the Renaissance which synthesized all these forces .The assimilation was rejected, the separation was rejected, the accommodation, the agitation were all discarded, or rather transcended, for a new perspective of themselves and their relationship to the rest of society, hence a "New Negro." Having dealt with the assimilationist-separationist dichotomy, the political philosophy of the Harlem artist was what one might best call "conditional integration." Whites were neither all bad nor all good, they were the people with whom you had to deal. The relationship would be based on their behavior, for the moral advantage was the black man's. There was a commitment for a better understanding and adjustment. (This is a key factor in the eventual collaboration with the white artist and the larger white society.) Alain Locke spoke of "rehabilitating the race in world esteem," [1] and the reevaluation of the race due to cultural recognition, which he felt would "precede or accompany any considerable further betterment of race relationships." [2] Locke did not labor under any illusion that "if the Negro was better known he would be better liked or better treated"; he merely felt that mutual understanding is the basis for any subsequent cooperation and adjustment.[3]

A new appraisal of black Americans would neither be "fixed" nor at any price. "The Negro today wishes to be known for what he is, even in his faults and shortcomings, and scorns a craven and precarious survival at the price of seeming to be what he is not." [4] Thus an approach, qualitatively different from its propagandist forebears.

Race pride was the number one avowal. Folklore and the black African heritage were revered (Garvey's shadow on the

Renaissance) again in contrast to their black literary predecessors. The sense of cultural nationalism of the Harlem artist was tempered by the sense of "cultural dualism." He recognizes both Africa and America. Locke confirms: "The racialism of the Negro is no limitation or reservation with respect to American; it is only a constructive effort to build the obstructions in the stream of his progress into an efficient dam of social energy and power." [5] The goals of the new Negro are "happily already well and finally formulated, for they are none other than the ideals of American institutions and democracy." [6]

The forces that created the Renaissance were not created in an ethnic vacuum. Certain developments in white society and even world economics played an essential part in the emergence of the black cultural Renaissance. Synchronization of the literary and social revolt in the United States with the economic upswing that followed World War I brought about the mood necessary for a cultural Renaissance. The ingredients, a weakening of old ideas and values, a sense of adventure and rebellion among the intellectuals and tolerance among the status quo (all of which were facilitated by the economic upswing) created "the Roaring Twenties."

The literary avant-guarde became established, and there was a refocus on naturalism. Exoticism became the craze of Europe. The victims of its colonies throughout the world became subjects of concern and empathy. The intellectuals sought identification with the outcasts of society. A parallel development occurred in the United States. The plight of the American Indian became a topical concern for many intellectuals. Blacks constituted the logical extension.

The Renaissance can be divided into two parts; Arna Bontemps calls them Phase I and Phase II. Chronologically, it denotes the period of Primary Black Propaganda (1921–24) to the eventual additional impetus of white society (1924–31). The entrance of a new directional force marked the beginning of the second phase of the Renaissance. If this new force had a personified manifestation it would be the white literator, Carl Van Vechten. He did as much as, if not more than, anyone to bring the Renaissance into the public (*i.e.* white) eye.

During the first phase, however, the most outstanding supporters of the movement were *The Crisis* and *Opportunity* magazines. *The Crisis* was the official organ of the National Association for the Advancement of Colored People. W. E. B. Du Bois, its founder, served as editor. *Opportunity: A Journal of Negro Life* served a similar function for the Urban League. Charles S. Johnson was its editor. These two publications not only devoted space to exhibition and review of the work of the Harlem artist, but also held literary contests with cash prizes. The Charles Chesnutt Honorarium, offered through *The Crisis,* was a considerable distinction during this period. Their efforts did much to create literary interest in the Harlem community. They clearly destroyed the barrier that forced black writers in the past to feel as lepers, barred from print or relegated to some obscure publishing house, many times at their own expense. It was not unusual for a writer to resort to presenting his work anonymously.

The Harlem artists, themselves, also responded to the need to develop interest in the Harlem community. Countee Cullen and Langston Hughes offered a special edition of their poetry at a drastically reduced price to come within reach of the common man's budget. This move was of considerable importance, since paperback books were not printed in the United States during this era and hard-bound books were quite expensive.

In 1924, Charles S. Johnson gave a "coming out" party for

the Harlem artists. Prominent white artists, publishers, and wealthy patrons attended. The meeting was a fateful one. Several of the writers obtained patrons, who supported them while they devoted time to their work. The stipends received were modest but allowed them to live comfortably. On occasion a patron would attempt to dictate to his protege, which would result in a break between the two. Langston Hughes was involved in such a situation. The patron/advisor relationship with several prominent whites in no way meant the Harlem artists would submit to paternalism.

The Harlem writers had a twofold reason for establishing this type of relationship with the white intelligentsia. First, the white intelligentsia had access to publishing mechanisms that were essential to the young artist. Their greater experience and literary training must have also attracted the Harlem artists. There was, too, the sense of contributing to a better social understanding, as well as being understood. Alain Locke qualifies the reasoning, . . . the desire to be understood would never in itself have been sufficient to have opened so completely the protectively closed portals of the thinking Negro's mind. There was still too much possibility of being snubbed or patronized for that. It was rather the necessity for fuller, truer self-expression, the realization of the unwisdom of allowing social discrimination to segregate him mentally, and a counterattitude to cramp and fetter his own living–and so the "spite wall" that the intellectuals built over the color line has happily been taken down.[7]

The white intelligentsia seem to have had a different motivation. Their involvement with the black artist appears to have been merely a part of their fascination with the exotic. Blacks represented the uninhibited man that they idealized. He was the noble savage, the carefree child of nature. These were the days of the "Roaring Twenties" with their sexual revolution, bathtub gin, and jazz. The Harlem writers and their art would be the new fad for white society. This was not true of all the whites professing interest, but it was true of far too many. The Harlem writers were not oblivious to this development and felt betrayed and bitter. Langston Hughes remarked in *Fighting Words,* "Here are our problems; in the first place, Negro books are considered by editors and publishers as exotic. Negro materials are placed, like Chinese materials or Bali materials into certain classifications. Magazine editors tell you, 'we can use but so many Negro stories a year.' (That 'so many' meaning very few). Publishers will say, 'We already have one Negro novel on our list this fall.' When we cease to be exotic, we do not sell well."

The stage was set. Carl Van Vechten's *Nigger Heaven* depicted Harlem and its residents as exotic, so many blacks capitulated. Not all blacks to whites intentions seriously. Zora Neale Hurston suspected the interest was a fad and decided to play it for whatever it was worth. It is difficult to say to what extent the Harlem writer internalized the sense of exoticism. Claude McKay in his novel *Home to Harlem,* outdid Van Vechten.

The Harlem Renaissance with its black cultural revival and goal of a greater social understanding was abdicated for a vogue. The new Negro became merely a new stereotype. The Harlem artist could only try to raise his voice higher than the vogue rumblings and salvage what he could.

Meanwhile, whites flocked to Harlem; some were sincere, with real appreciation of black folk-culture; others were merely curiosity seekers; still others were simply slumming. The Harlem community observed this odd procession and the hustlers in the group made some extra money.

In 1929 the stock market crashed. The effects were not immediately felt in Harlem. By 1931, however, the depression had taken its toll. One by one the artists began to leave Harlem. America had resolved to tighten its belt, leaving no room for the Harlem writers. The "good times" were over; a new environment was created that would produce a new writer in a new tradition. Many of the Harlem writers would continue to produce works, often excelling their Harlem contributions.

The legacy of the Harlem Renaissance is its art, its artists, and its idea. The reactions they encountered are for our education. The Harlem writers did not leave any "stone and mortar" institutions, but rather lived on as "living institutions." What better institution than Arna Bontemps? While the essence of the Renaissance was captured in the literature, what all this meant was concretized in the manifestos. Alain Locke's *New Negro,* Langston Hughes's "The Negro Artist and the Racial Mountain," contemporary issues of *The Crisis* and *Opportunity* magazines, all speak to the phenomenon that was occurring in Harlem.

The activity in Harlem should be considered political, even though this opposes the usual appraisals. The political quality of the Renaissance is the result of its having synthesized the dialectical forces that had polarized the black intellectual community in the previous decade. The Renaissance's political philosophy, that of "conditional intergration," is no less a political philosophy than separation, assimilation, Pan-Africanism, or any other. The philosophy in essence rested on a single axiom: It will be necessary for blacks to change their perspective of their selves before whites will change their image of them. The Harlem artists were neither didatic nor dogmatic about their belief. In fact, there seemed to be an air of transcendence about its acceptance. "We Negro artists who create now intend to express our individual dark skinned selves without fear or shame.

If white people are pleased, we are glad. If they are not, it doesn't matter. We know we are beautiful and ugly too. If colored are pleased, we are glad. If they are not, their displeasure doesn't matter either. We build our temples for tomorrow, strong as we know how, and we stand on top of the mountain, free within ourselves." [8]

It is difficult to write about the Renaissance without reaction to criticism leveled against it. There have been analyses of this era in which the Harlem artists were viciously indicted, as if they were superhuman architects, consciously constituting the period, rather than ordinary human beings in the grip of a series of events that would have remarkable historical significance. The hindrance of close historical proximity is never considered. Still, what occurred in Harlem needs neither apology nor qualification. The situation, the alternatives were all created by the forces of the period, just as the environment of the next decade would, with its repressive forces, create black protest writing. There is a certain naïveté in much of the criticism. How does one expect mass participation in the art of the Harlem writers when literature by definition is bourgeois? The Harlem writers did not have any illusions about this. Langston Hughes wrote: ". . . there were mostly intellectuals doing the thinking. The ordinary Negroes hadn't heard of the Negro Renaissance, and if they had, it hadn't raised their wages any." Who but intellectuals have time to think? [9]

The Harlem Renaissance is a point in the evolution of Afro-American literature. It is ludicrous to criticize beginnings; rather they should be placed in perspective to compute its significance. It "opened the door" for the black writing of today. The Renaissance will aways be remembered for this reason. It will be valued for its merits. It will come again to importance because of its idea.

Notes and Bibliographies

CHAPTER 3
Bibliography

Bone, Robert A., *The Negro Novel in America* (New Haven, Conn.: Yale University Press, 1958).

Bontemps, Arna, "The Negro Renaissance: Jean Toomer and the Harlem Writers of the 1920's," Herbert Hill, ed., *Anger and Beyond* (New York: Harper & Row, 1966).

Hughes, Langston, *The Big Sea* (New York: Hill & Wang, 1940).

Margolies, Edward, *Native Sons* (Philadelphia: J.P. Lippincott, 1968).

Mason, Clifford, "The Harlem Renaissance Revisited," *Black World,* Vol. XX (Chicago: Johnson Publishing Co., 1970).

Redding, Saunders, *To Make a Poet Black* (Chapel Hill: University of North Carolina Press, 1939).

Rosenfeld, Paul, *Jean Toomer, Men Seen* (New York: Dial, 1925).

Toomer, Jean, *Cane* (New York: Harper & Row, 1923).

Toomer, Jean, "Earth-Being," unpublished.

Toomer, Jean, *Essentials.* Private Edition (Chicago, 1931).

Toomer, Jean, *Natalie Mann.* Unpublished.

Toomer, Jean, *The Sacred Factory.* Unpublished.

Turner, Darwin, "The Failure of a Playwright," *The College Language Association Journal,* 1966.

CHAPTER 4
Jessie Fauset
Notes

1. Frances E. W. Harper, *Iola Leroy, or Shadows Uplifted* (Boston: James H. Earle, 1895), p. 281.
2. *Fire 11,* Vol. I, No. 1 (November 1926).

3. Langston Hughes, *The Big Sea* (New York: Hill and Wang, 1963), p. 223.
4. William S. Braithwaite, "The Negro in American Literature," *The Crisis,* Vol. XXVIII, No. 4 (September 1924), p. 210.
5. Alain Locke, "Enter the New Negro," *Survey Graphic,* Vol. VI, No. 6 (March 1925), p. 632.
6. James Weldon Johnson, "What the Negro Is Doing for Himself," *The Liberator,* Vol. I, No. 4 (June 1918), p. 30.
7. Claude McKay, "To Ethiopa," *The Liberator,* Vol. III, No. 2 (February 1920), p. 3.
8. W. E. B. Du Bois, "Criteria of Negro Art," *The Crisis,* Vol. XXXII, No. 6 (October 1926), p. 292.
9. Alain Locke, "Negro Youth Speaks," *The New Negro* (New York, Atheneum 1969), p. 52.
10. *Ibid.,* p. 48.
11. *Ibid.,* p. 52.
12. *The Big Sea, op cit.,* p. 218.
13. Robert Bone, *The Negro Novel in America* (New Haven, Connecticut: Yale University Press, 1968), p. 58.
14. W. E. B. Du Bois, "The Younger Literary Movement," *The Crisis,* Vol. XXVII, No. 4 (February 1924), p. 162.
15. William Stanley Braithwaite, "The Negro in American Literature," *The Crisis,* Vol. XXVIII, No. 4 (September 1924), p. 210.
16. Jessie Fauset, *The Chinaberry Tree* (New York: Negro Universities Press, 1969), p. ix.
17. Jessie Fauset, *loc. cit.*
18. Claude McKay, *A Long Way from Home* (New York: Lee Furman, 1937), p. 112.
19. *The Big Sea,* p. 247.
20. Claude McKay, "A Negro Extravaganza," *The Liberator,* Vol. IV, No. 12 (December 1921), p. 24.
21. *Fire 11, op. cit.,* p. 47.
22. William Stanley Braithwaite, "The Negro in American Literature," *The New Negro, op. cit.,* p. 35.
23. Marion L. Starkey, "Jessie Fauset," *The Southern Workman,* Vol. LXI, No. 5 (May 1932), p. 219.
24. Marion L. Starkey, *loc. cit.*
25. Jessie Fauset, *There Is Confusion* (New York: Boni and Liveright, 1924), p. 14.
26. *Ibid.,* p. 297.
27. Robert Bone, *op. cit.,* p. 101.
28. William Stanley Braithwaite, "The Novels of Jessie Fauset," *Opportunity,* Vol. XII, No. 1 (January 1934), p. 26.
29. Hugh Glouster, *Negro Voice in American Fiction* (Chapel Hill: The University of North Carolina Press, 1948), p. 133.

30. William Stanley Braithwaite, "The Novels of Jessie Fauset," *op. cit.*, p. 27.
31. Jessie Fauset, *Plum Bun: A Novel Without a Moral* (New York: Frederick A. Stokes, 1929), p. 11.
32. *Ibid.*, p. 12.
33. Jessie Fauset, *loc. cit.*
34. Jessie Fauset, *loc. cit.*
35. *Ibid.*, p. 116.
36. *Ibid.*, p. 243.
37. *Ibid.*, p. 275.
38. *Ibid.*, p. 88.
39. *Ibid.*, p. 209.
40. *Ibid.*, p. 218.
41. William Stanley Braithwaite, "The Novels of Jessie Fauset," *op. cit.*, p. 28.
42. Robert Bone, *op. cit.*, p. 102.
43. Jessie Fauset, *The Chinaberry Tree, op. cit.*, p. 2.
44. *Ibid.*, p. 8.
45. *Ibid.*, p. 44.
46. Jessie Fauset, *Comedy: American Style* (New York: McGrath, 1969), p. 143.
47. William Stanley Braithwaite, "The Novels of Jessie Fauset," *op. cit.*, p. 28.
48. Alain Locke, "Enter New Negro," *Survey Graphic, op. cit.*, p. 631.
49. Jessie Fauset, "The Gift of Laughter," *The New Negro, op. cit.*, p. 166.
50. Claude McKay, "The Negro Dancer," *The Liberator*, Vol. II, No. 7 (July 1919), p. 20
51. Robert Bone, *op. cit.*, p. 101.
52. Pauline Elizabeth Hopkins, *Contending Forces: A Romance Illustrative of Negro Life North and South* (Boston: Colored Co-Operative Publishing Co., 1900), p. 13.
53. LeRoi Jones, "The Myth of a 'Negro Literature,'" *On Being Black*, C. Davis and D. Walden, eds. (Greenwich, Connecticut: Fawcett, 1970), p. 295.
54. *The Big Sea, op. cit.*, p. 334.
55. Zora Neale Hurston, "What White Publishers Won't Print," *Negro Digest*, Vol. VIII, No. 6 (April 1950), p. 85.
56. *Ibid.*, p. 88.
57. Jessie Fauset, *The Chinaberry Tree, op. cit.*, p. x.

Bibliography

I. WORKS OF JESSIE FAUSET

A. Novels:

The Chinaberry Tree, (New York: Negro Universities Press, 1969).

Comedy: American Style, (New York: McGrath, 1969).
Plum Bun, (New York: Frederick A. Stokes, 1929).
There Is Confusion, (New York: Boni & Liveright, 1924).

B. Stories:

"Double Trouble," *The Crisis,* Vol. XXVI, No. 4 (August 1923), pp. 155–9 and Vol. XXVI, No. 5 (September 1923), pp. 205–9.
"The Sleeper Wakes," *The Crisis,* Vol. XX, No. 4 (August 1920), pp. 168–73; Vol. XX, No. 5 (September 1920), pp. 226–9; and Vol. XX, No. 6 (October 1920), pp. 267–74.

C. Poems:

"Courage: He Said," *Double Blossoms; Helen Keller Anthology,* ed. Edna Porter (New York; Lewis Copeland, 1931), p. 39.
"Dilworth Road Revisited," *The Crisis,* Vol. XXIV, No. 4 (August 1922), p. 167.
"Douce Douvenance," *The Crisis,* Vol. XX, No. 1 (May 1920), p. 42.
"Here's April," *The Crisis,* Vol. XXVII, No. 6 (April 1924), p. 277.
"La Vie C'est la Vie," *The Crisis,* Vol. XXIV, No. 3 (July 1922), p. 124.
"Rain Fugue," *The Crisis,* Vol. XXVIII, No. 4 (August 1924), p. 155.
"Rencontre," *The Crisis,* Vol. XXVII, No. 3 (January 1924), p. 122.
"Song for a Lost Comrade (To O. B. J.)," *The Crisis,* Vol. XXV, No. 1, (November 1922), p. 22.

D. Articles and Book Reviews:

"As to Books," *The Crisis,* Vol. XXIV, No. 2 (June 1922), pp. 66–8.
" 'Batouala' is Translated," *The Crisis,* Vol. XXIV, No. 5 (September 1922), pp. 218–9.
"Dark Algiers the White," *The Crisis,* Vol. XXIX, No. 6 (April 1925), pp. 255–8, Vol. XXX, No. 1 (May 1925), pp. 16–20.
"The Enigma of the Sorbonne," *The Crisis,* Vol. XXIX, No. 5 (March 1925), pp. 216–19.
"The Eucalyptus Tree," *The Crisis,* Vol. XXXI, No. 3 (January 1926), pp. 116–17.
"Henry Ossawa Tanner," *The Crisis,* Vol. XXVII, No. 6 (April 1924), pp. 255–58.
"Impressions of the Second Pan-African Congress," *The Crisis,* Vol. XXIII, No. 1 (November 1921), pp. 12–18.
"Looking Backward," *The Crisis,* Vol. XXIII, No. 3 (January 1922), pp. 125–6.
"New Literature on the Negro," *The Crisis,* Vol. XX, No. 2 (June 1920), pp. 78–83.
"No End of Books," *The Crisis,* Vol. XXIII, No. 5 (March 1922), pp. 208–10.
"Nostalgia," *The Crisis,* Vol. XXII, No. 4 (August 1921), pp. 154–8.

"On the Book Shelf," *The Crisis,* Vol. XXII, No. 2 (June 1921), pp. 60–4.
"Out of the West," *The Crisis,* Vol. XXVII, No. 1 (November 1923), pp. 11–18.
"Pastures New," *The Crisis,* Vol. XX, No. 5 (September 1920), pp. 224–6.
"Rank Imposes Obligation: A Biographical Essay on Martin Robinson Delaney," *The Crisis,* Vol. XXXIII, No. 1 (November 1926), pp. 9–13.
"Saint-George, Chevalier of France," *The Crisis,* Vol. XXII, No. 1 (May 1921), pp. 9–12.
"Sunday Afternoon," *The Crisis,* Vol. XXIII, No. 4 (February 1922), pp. 162–4.
"The Symbolism of Bert Williams," *The Crisis,* Vol. XXIV, No. 1 (May 1922), pp. 12–15.
"This Way to the Flea Market," *The Crisis,* Vol. XXIX, No. 4 (February 1925), pp. 161–3.
"In Talladega," *The Crisis,* Vol. XXXV, No. 2 (February 1928), pp. 47–8.
"What Europe Thought of the Pan-African Congress," *The Crisis,* Vol. XXIII, No. 2, (December 1921), pp. 60–7.
"When Christmas Comes," *The Crisis,* Vol. XXV, No. 2 (December 1922), pp. 61–3.
"The 'Y' Conference at Talladega," *The Crisis,* Vol. XXVI, No. 5 (September 1923), pp. 213–6.
"Yarrow Revisited," *The Crisis,* Vol. XXIX, No. 3 (January, 1925), pp. 107–9.

E. Translations:

"Kirongozi," by G. D. Perier, *The Crisis,* Vol. XXVII, No. 5 (March 1924), pp. 208–9.
"The Pool," by Amedee Brun, *The Crisis,* Vol. XXII, No. 5 (September 1921), p. 205.
"La Question des Noirs aux États-Unis," by Frank L. Schoell, *The Crisis,* Vol. XXVIII, No. 2 (June 1924), pp. 83–6.
"The Sun of Brittany," *The Crisis,* Vol. XXXIV, No. 9 (November 1927), pp. 303.
"To a Foreign Maid," by Oswald Durand, *The Crisis,* Vol. XXV, No. 4 (February 1923), p. 158.

F. Letters:

Postcard to Mrs. James Weldon Johnson, from Algiers, Africa (January 19, 1925).
A letter to Claude McKay (September 7, 1934).
Eight letters to Harold Jackman, (December 21, 1924), (December 3, 1933), (May 13, 1935), (November 18, 1936), (September 15, 1939), October 5, 1939), (September 21, 1939), (January 19, 1942).

A Letter to Miss Roberts Bosley (November 1942).
These letters are kept in the James Weldon Johnson Collection at Yale University Library.

II. GENERAL:

Arden, Eugene, "The Early Harlem Novel," *Images of the Negro in American Literature,* S. L. Gross and J. E. Hardy, eds. (Chicago; The University of Chicago Press, 1966), pp. 106–14.
Bennett, Gwendolyn, "Review of *Plum Bun,*" *Opportunity,* Vol. VII, No. 9 (September 1929), p. 287.
Bone, Robert A., *The Negro Novel in America* (New Haven: Yale University Press, 1965).
Braithwaite, William Stanley, "The Negro in Literature," *The Crisis,* Vol. XXVIII, No. 4 (August 1924), pp. 204–10.
———, "The Novels of Jessie Fauset," *Opportunity,* Vol. XII, No. 1 (January 1934), pp. 24–8.
Burgum, Edwin Berry, "Review of *The Chinaberry Tree,*" *Opportunity,* Vol. X, (1932), pp. 88–9.
Du Bois, W. E. B., "Review of *The Chinaberry Tree,*" *The Crisis,* Vol. XXXXI, No. 4, (April 1932), p. 138.
———, "The Younger Literary Movement," *The Crisis,* Vol. XXVII, No. 4 (February 1924), pp. 161–3.
Glouster, Hugh, *Negro Voice in American Fiction* (Chapel Hill: The University of North Carolina Press, 1948).
Davis, Charles and Daniel Walden, eds., *On Being Black* (Greenwich, Conn.: Fawcett, 1970).
Hughes, Langston, *The Big Sea* (New York: Hill and Wang, 1963).
Hurston, Zora Neale, "What White Publishers Won't Print," *Negro Digest,* Vol. VIII, No. 6 (April 1950), pp. 85–9.
Locke, Alain, "Enter the New Negro," *Survey Graphic,* Vol. VI, No. 6 (March 1925), pp. 631–4.
———, "Harlem," *Survey Graphic,* Vol. VI, No. 6 (March 1925), pp. 629–30.
———, *The New Negro* (New York: Atheneum, 1969).
McKay, Claude, *A Long Way from Home* (New York: Lee Furman, 1937).
Starkey, Marion L., "Jessie Fauset," *The Southern Workman,* Vol. LXI, No. 5 (May 1932), pp. 217–20.

CHAPTER 4
Nella Larsen
Notes

1. Robert Bone, *op. cit.,* p. 97.
2. W. E. B. Du Bois, "Review of *Quicksand,*" *The Crisis,* Vol. XXXV, No. 5 (June 1928), p. 97.

3. Nella Larsen, *Quicksand* (New York: Negro Universities Press, 1969), p. 136.
4. *Ibid.*, p. 137.
5. *Ibid.*, p. 196.
6. *Ibid.*, p. 207.
7. Nella Larsen, *loc. cit.*
8. *Ibid.*, p. 140.
9. *Ibid.*, p. 209.
10. *Ibid.*, p. 208.
11. *Ibid.*, p. 215.
12. *Ibid.*, p. 273.
13. *Ibid.*, p. 302.
14. *Ibid.*, p. 194.
15. *Ibid.*, p. 216.
16. Robert Bone, *op. cit.*, pp. 105–6.
17. *Quicksand, op. cit.*, p. 301.
18. Nella Larsen, *Passing* (New York: Negro Universities Press, 1969), p. 187.
19. *Ibid.*, p. 214.

Bibliography

I. Works by Nella Larsen.

Passing (New York: Negro Universities Press, 1969).
Quicksand (New York: Negro Universities Press, 1969).
Twenty-one letters to Carl Van Vechten are kept in the James Weldon Johnson Collection at the Yale University Library.

II. General.

Bone, Robert, *The Negro Novel in America* (New Haven: Yale University Press, 1965).
Du Bois, W. E. B., "Review of *Quicksand*," *The Crisis*, Vol. XXXV, No. 6 (June 1928).
Glouster, Hugh, *Negro Voice in American Fiction* (Chapel Hill: The University of North Carolina Press, 1948).

CHAPTER 5

Notes

1. From one of Hughes's autobiographies, *The Big Sea*, p. 228.
2. *Ibid.*, p. 248.
3. *Ibid.*
4. *Ibid.*, p. 245.
5. *Ibid.*, p. 247.
6. From Hughes's *Selected Poems*, p. 8.

7. C. S. Johnson in *The New Negro Thinking Years Afterward,* R. Logan *et al.*, eds., 1955.
8. *Big Sea,* p. 266.
9. D. C. Dickinson, *A Bio-Bibliography of Langston Hughes,* 1967, p. 56 and n. 80.
10. *Big Sea,* pp. 304–05.
11. Hughes's reference to "as in Kansas" in the last line refers to his own residence in Lawrence, Kansas, 1902–14. He was born in 1902 in Joplin, Missouri, and was moved to Kansas that same year. The book (*Not Without Laughter*) may be interpreted as autobiographical, but only in part.
12. Dickinson, p. 52.
13. *Big Sea,* pp. 233–34.
14. Dickinson, p. 53.
15. *Big Sea,* p. 262.
16. *Ibid.*, p. 321.
17. *Ibid.*, p. 325.
18. *Ibid.*
19. *Ibid.*, p. 237.

Publications

(Note: Following is a list of all publications of Hughes during the period 1921–31, abstracted from D. C. Dickinson, *A Bio-Bibliography of Langston Hughes, 1902–67,* preface by Arna Bontemps (Hamden, Conn.: Archon Books, 1967).

I. Books Written:

The Weary Blues, Knopf, 1926.
Fine Clothes to the Jew, Knopf, 1927.
Not Without Laughter, Knopf, 1930.
Dear Lovely Death, Troutbeck, 1931.
The Negro Mother, Golden Stair, 1931.

II. Books Edited:

Four Lincoln University Poets. Lincoln U. P., 1930.

III. Anthologies which contain contributions by Hughes:

Africa Sings, 1929.
An Anthology of American Negro Literature, 1929.
Book of American Negro Poetry, 1931.
Caroling Dusk, 1927.
Four Negro Poets, 1927.

Golden Slippers, n.d.
Four Lincoln University Poets, 1930.
Lyric America, 1930.
Book of Poetry, 1926.
Modern American Poetry, 1930.
Negro Poets and Their Poems, 1923.
Poems of Justice, 1929.
Portraits in Color, 1927.
Readings from Negro Authors, 1931.
Twentieth Century Poetry, 1929.

IV. Prose and Drama:

1. Published in 1921:
Gold piece, *Brownie's Book,* July 1921.
In a Mexican city, *Brownie's Book,* April 1921.
Mexican games, *Brownie's Book,* January 1921.
Those who have no turkey, *Brownie's Book,* November 1921.
Up to the crater in an old volcano, *Brownie's Book,* December 1921.
The virgin of Guadelupe, *The Crisis,* December 1921.
2. Published in 1923:
The Negro artist and the racial mountain, *Nation,* June 1923.
Ships, sea, and Africa, *The Crisis,* December 1923.
3. Published in 1925:
Burton moon, *The Crisis,* June 1925.
4. Published in 1926:
Fascination of cities, *The Crisis,* January 1926.
5. Published in 1927:
Bodies in the moonlight, *Messenger,* April 1927.
The little virgin, *Messenger,* November 1927.
Washington, our wonderful society, *Opportunity,* August 1927.
The young glory to him, *Messenger,* June 1927.
6. Published in 1928:
Luani of the jungle, *Harlem,* November 1928.
7. Published in 1930:
A certain sculptor, *Opportunity,* November 1930.
Greetings to Soviet workers, *New Masses,* December 1930.
Listen boy, *Revista de la Habana,* July/August 1930.
Party for white folks, *New Masses,* July 1930.
8. Published in 1931:
A letter from Haiti, *New Masses,* July 1931.
People without shoes, *New Masses,* October 1931.
Scottsboro limited, *New Masses,* November 1931.
Southern gentlemen, white prostitutes, mill owners and Negroes, *Contempo,* December 1931.

CHAPTER 7

Notes

1. Claude McKay, *A Long Way From Home,* Arno Press, 1969, p. 248.
2. Malcolm Cowley, *Exiles Return* (New York, 1951), p. 77.
3. *Ibid.* See also Frederick J. Hoffman's discussion of the image of the black man in the cult of primitivism in his *The Twenties* (New York, 1949), pp. 306–08.
4. Claude McKay, "My Green Hills of Jamaica" (1947), unpublished manuscript in Claude McKay Folder, James Weldon Johnson Collection, Yale University Library, hereafter referred to as McKay Folder. By kind permission of Hope McKay Virtue, p. 62.
5. *Ibid.,* p. 51.
6. Jean Wagner, *Les Poètes Nègres des États-Unis* (Paris, 1963), p. 220, quoted in Wayne Cooper, "Claude McKay and the Negro of the 1920's," *Phylon* (Fall, 1964), pp. 297–306.
7. Claude McKay's *Harlem Shadows* (New York, 1922) contains many of the Jamaican poems alluded to in this paragraph (*e.g.,* "Flame-Heart," "North and South," "Home Thoughts," "The Tropics in New York"). The poems cited here have been more recently reprinted in Claude McKay, *The Selected Poems of Claude McKay* (New York, 1953). The biographical material can be found in McKay's "My Green Hills" and "My Boyhood in Jamaica," *Phylon* (June 1953), pp. 134–45.
8. McKay, *Harlem Shadows,* p. 17.
9. *Ibid.,* "Flame-Heart," p. 9.
10. It is unclear from either McKay's autobiography *(A Long Way)* or his personal letters (McKay Folder), why he never returned to Jamaica. His later emphasis on the degenerating effects of civilization and Anglo-Saxon education suggest that the answer might lie in the admonishment of his favorite author, D. H. Lawrence. "Man," wrote Lawrence, ". . . can't successfully go back to Paradise— There is a gulf in time and being. I could not go back so far. Back to their uncreat condition."
11. McKay, "My Green Hills" (Fragmentary MS), p. 8.
12. This vision of the intellectual as one who seeks to make public issues of personal problems was first introduced to me in a series of lectures given by Warren I. Sussman at Rutgers University. For a more concise definition of the concept, see Warren I. Sussman's "The Expatriate Image" in *Intellectual History in America, Vol. II,* pp. 145–57.
13. Letter from Langston Hughes to Claude McKay, 5 March 1928 (McKay Folder).
14. W. E. B. Du Bois, "The Browsing Reader," *The Crisis* (June 1928), p. 202. For additional examples of similar responses see Aubrey Bower, *Amsterdam News,* 21 March 1928; "Ferris Scores Obscenity,"

Pittsburgh Courier, 31 March 1928; Burton Roscoe, "The Seamy Side," *The Bookman* (April 1928), p. 183.

15. See McKay's *A Long Way* (pp. 306–23) for a more detailed account of this conflict as well as his description of the New Negro movement and the Harlem Renaissance.
16. *Ibid.,* p. 321.
17. Claude McKay, *Banjo* (New York, 1929), p. 200.
18. Claude McKay, *Home to Harlem* (New York, 1928), p. 8.
19. *Ibid.,* p. 264.
20. *Ibid.,* p. 274.
21. For a discussion of these themes among white expatriates see Malcolm Cowley's *Exiles Return.*
22. Felice is a black girl Jakes meets in the opening chapters of the novel. He subsequently loses her. Translated from the Spanish, her name signifies joy or happiness.
23. McKay, *Banjo,* p. 6.
24. *Ibid.,* p. 49.
25. *Ibid.,* p. 66.
26. McKay, *A Long Way,* p. 245.
27. McKay, *Banjo,* p. 163.
28. *Ibid.,* pp. 163–64.
29. *Ibid.,* pp. 324–25.
30. *Ibid.,* pp. 322–23.
31. *Ibid.,* p. 322.
32. *Ibid.,* p. 323.
33. Claude McKay, *Banana Bottom* (New York, 1933), p. 17.
34. *Ibid.,* p. 31.
35. *Ibid.,* p. 16.
36. *Ibid.,* p. 15.
37. *Ibid.,* p. 135.
38. *Ibid.,* p. 169.
39. *Ibid.,* p. 313.
40. McKay, *A Long Way,* p. 229.
41. *Ibid.,* p. 354.
42. McKay, "My Green Hills," p. 69.
43. *Ibid.,* p. 51.
44. McKay, *A Long Way,* p. 150. McKay often used truant to express the same primitive energy, simplicity, and innate freedom implied in his use of the term vagabond. For a more complete discussion of McKay's concept of the black man as truant, see his short story "Truant" in his *Gingertown* (New York 1932), pp. 143–62.
45. Letter from Claude McKay to James Weldon Johnson, 8 May 1935 (McKay Folder). By kind permission of Hope McKay Virtue.
46. McKay, *A Long Way,* p. 153.
47. Claude McKay, "What Is Lacking in the Theater," *The Liberator* (March 1922), pp. 20–21.

48. Claude McKay, "How Black Sees Green and Red," *The Liberator* (June 1921), pp. 17–20.
49. *Ibid.*
50. McKay, *A Long Way,* p. 277.
51. Letter from Claude McKay to Louise Bryant Bullitt, 24 June 1926 (McKay Folder). By kind permission of Hope McKay Virtue.
52. McKay, *A Long Way,* p. 332.

CHAPTER 8
Notes

1. Theophilus Lewis, "Harlem Sketchbook," New York *Amsterdam News* (January 5, 1935). Yale University, James Weldon Johnson Collection, Wallace Thurman Folder. (Hereafter referred to as Thurman Folder.)
2. Letter to Harold Jackman from Wallace Thurman, August 1930. Thurman Folder.
3. Langston Hughes, *The Big Sea* (New York: 1940), p. 234.
4. Lewis, "Harlem Sketchbook."
5. Letter to Jackman from Thurman, May 1928. Thurman Folder.
6. Richard De Roachement, "Harlem a Fraction of a Mirror," New York *Sun* (March 4, 1929).
7. Dorothy West, "Elephant's Dance," *Black World,* Vol. XX, No. 1 (November 1970), p. 77.
8. Thurman, *Notes of a Stepchild,* unpublished manuscript. Thurman Folder.
9. Lewis, "Harlem Sketchbook."
10. Hughes, pp. 233–34; Letter from Arna Bontemps to Jackman on Thurman, (March 25, 1942). Thurman Folder.
11. Thurman (ed.), *Fire.* Thurman Folder.
12. Hughes, p. 235.
13. Thurman, "Negro Artists and the Negro," *The New Republic,* Vol. LII (August 31, 1927), p. 297.
14. Thurman, "Nephews of Uncle Remus," *The Independent,* Vol. CXIX (Sept. 24, 1967), p. 39.
15. Thurman, "Negro Artists and the Negro," p. 38.
16. Thurman, "Nephews of Uncle Remus," p. 298.
17. Thurman, "Negro Artists and the Negro," p. 39.
18. Benjamin G. Brawley, *The Negro Genius.*
19. Letter to Langston Hughes from Wallace Thurman, December 8, 1927. Thurman Folder.
20. West, pp. 78–9.
21. Theophilus Lewis, "Wallace Thurman is a Model Harlemite," New York *Amsterdam News,* no date. Thurman Folder.
22. Lewis, "Wallace Thurman is a Model Harlemite."

23. Wallace Thurman, *The Blacker the Berry* (New York: Collier Books Edition, 1970).
24. Wallace Thurman, *Notes of a Stepchild.* Thurman Folder.
25. Wallace Thurman, "Negro Life in New York's Harlem," *Little Blue Book,* No. 494, edited by E. Haldeman-Julius. Thurman Folder.
26. Thurman, *The Blacker the Berry,* pp. 226–7.
27. Thurman, *Notes of a Stepchild.* Thurman Folder.
28. *Ibid.*
29. Lewis, "Wallace Thurman is a Model Harlemite."
30. Hughes, *The Big Sea,* p. 234.
31. West, p. 80.
32. Lewis, "Harlem Sketchbook."
33. West, p. 80.
34. Letter to Jackman from Thurman, May 1928. Thurman Folder.
35. Doris E. Abramson, *Negro Playwrights in the American Theatre 1928–1929* (New York, 1969), p. 37.
36. Hughes, *The Big Sea,* p. 235.
37. Abramson, p. 33.
38. Letter to William Jourdan Rapp from Wallace Thurman, no date. Thurman Folder.
39. Letter to Rapp from Thurman, 1929. Thurman Folder.
40. Letter from Thurman to Jackman, August 1930. Thurman Folder.
41. Hughes, p. 234.
42. Thurman, *Infants of the Spring* (New York, 1932), p. 62.
43. *Ibid.,* p. 91.
44. *Ibid.,* pp. 108–09.
45. *Ibid.,* pp. 141–2.
46. *Ibid.,* p. 187.
47. *Ibid.,* p. 284.
48. Letter to Jackman from Thurman, March 13, 1934. Thurman Folder.
49. Lewis, "Death Claims Noted Writer," New York, *Amsterdam News,* (December 29, 1934). Thurman Folder.

Bibliography

Books and Articles.

Abramson, Doris E., *Negro Playwrights in the American Theatre, 1925–1959* (New York & London: Columbia University Press, 1969).

Black World, November 1970.

Bone, Robert A., *The Negro Novel in America,* rev. ed., (New Haven & London: Yale University Press). 1965.

Fullinwider, S. P., *The Mind and Mood of Black America. 20th Century Thought* (Homewood, Illinois: The Dorsey Press, 1969).

Hughes, Langston, *The Big Sea. An Autobiography* (New York: Hill & Wang, American Century Series, 1963).

Thurman, Wallace, *The Blacker the Berry* (New York: Collier Books Edition, 1970).
———, *Infants of the Spring* (New York: The Macaulay Company, 1932).
———, *The Interne* (New York: The Macaulay Company, 1932).
The New Republic, August 31, 1927.
The Independent, September 24, 1927.

Unpublished Materials.

Yale University, James Weldon Johnson Collection, Wallace Thurman Folder.

CHAPTER 9
Notes

1. For another contemporary development of this theme, see Montgomery Gregory, "The Drama of Negro Life," in Alain Locke, ed., *The New Negro* (c. 1925, New York, 1969), pp. 159–60.
2. George Schuyler remembers that Theophilus Lewis was an avid reader of H. L. Mencken's *Smart Set,* which was probably a model for Lewis's own satire and wit; Lewis was the one who introduced *Smart Set* to Schuyler. George S. Schuyler, *Black and Conservative: The Autobiography of George S. Schuyler* (New Rochelle, N.Y., 1966), pp. 142–3; "The Reminiscences of George S. Schuyler," (Oral History Research Office, Columbia University, 1962), p. 131; interview, George S. Schuyler, October 16, 1970.
3. Interview, Theophilus Lewis, September 28, 1970; *Catholic World,* (May 1941), p. 239.
4. For a complete discussion of the magazine's role in the Renaissance, see the author's "The *Messenger* Magazine, 1917–28," unpublished Ph.D. dissertation (Yale University, 1971), chap. 3.
5. *Black and Conservative,* p. 142; "Reminiscences of George S. Schuyler," pp. 81–2, 129; Interview, Arna Bontemps (April 22, 1970). Thurman enjoyed a warm personal relationship with Lewis. In an undated letter to Harold Jackman, Thurman speaks of his pleasure in teaching piano to Lewis's son Theodore. (Carl Van Vechten Papers, James Weldon Johnson Collection, Yale University.) See also Langston Hughes's letter to the *Messenger* (May 1927, p. 171) praising Lewis.
6. Interview, Arna Bontemps (April 22, 1970). Even as late as the 1950s the theater page of most black newspapers was unlikely to be critical, and was usually simply laudatory of the performances of black actors. Interview, Theophilus Lewis.
7. *Messenger,* September 1923, pp. 818, 821.
8. *Ibid.,* December 1923, p. 923.
9. *Ibid.,* March 1924, p. 74.

10. *Ibid.,* June 1924, p. 182.
11. *Ibid.,* October 1924, p. 323.
12. *Ibid.,* January 1925, pp. 18, 62; James Weldon Johnson, *Black Manhattan* (c. 1930, New York, 1968), pp. 196–7, 199.
13. *Messenger,* June 1925, p. 230.
14. *Ibid.,* May 1926, p. 150.
15. *Ibid.,* March 1927, p. 85.
16. *Ibid.,* June 1927, pp. 193, 200.
17. *Ibid.,* February 1924, p. 43.
18. *Ibid.,* June 1924, p. 182.
19. *Ibid.,* May 1926, p. 150.
20. *Ibid.,* February 1925, p. 92.
21. *Black Manhattan,* p. 196, referring to "From Dixie to Broadway." A critic disputing Johnson's assertion was Montgomery Gregory, "The Drama of Negro Life," p. 156.
22. *Messenger,* October 1926, p. 302.
23. *Ibid.,* March 1924, pp. 73–4.
24. *Ibid.,* April 1924, pp. 109–10.
25. *Ibid.,* July 1924, pp. 223–4. A later writer, however, passed a harsher judgment. According to Loften Mitchell, "the critics disliked the work. They were many steps behind Negroes, who hated it." Mitchell, *Black Drama: The Story of the American Negro in the Theater* (New York, 1967), p. 83.
26. *Messenger,* March 1926, pp. 85–6.
27. *Ibid.,* May 1927, pp. 157, 169.
28. *Ibid.,* December 1923, 923–4.
29. *Ibid.,* July 1927, pp. 229, 243.
30. *Ibid.,* December 1924, p. 380.
31. *Ibid.,* April 1924, p. 110.
32. *Ibid.,* July 1926, pp. 214–5.
33. *Ibid.,* October 1926, p. 301.
34. *Ibid.,* September 1926, p. 278.
35. *Ibid.,* November 1924, pp. 342–3.
36. *Ibid.,* July 1925, pp. 268–9.
37. *Ibid.,* June 1926, pp. 182–3.
38. *Ibid.,* February 1927, pp. 61–2.
39. *Ibid.,* August 1926, p. 246.
40. *Ibid.,* December 1926, p. 362.
41. *Ibid.,* November 1926, pp. 334–5.
42. *Ibid.,* December 1923, p. 924; July 1927, pp. 229, 243.
43. *Ibid.,* September 1924, p. 291; January 1925, pp. 14–5. Bontemps remembers an absence of critical commentary on the black theater (interview, April 22, 1970). And Loften Mitchell feels that serious theater was a middle-class luxury which did not speak to the people "in terms of the truth of their daily lives." He was, of course, ex-

cluding the black musical revues from this indictment. *Black Drama,* p. 84.

44. Harold Cruse, *The Crisis of the Negro Intellectual* (New York, 1967), pp. 36–7.
45. *Messenger,* July 1926, p. 214.
46. *Ibid.,* June 1925, p. 230.
47. Interview, Arna Bontemps (April 22, 1970). Lewis's career after leaving the *Messenger* was a varied one. He continued to work for the post office until he was old enough to retire, for there was little prospect for a black theater critic making a living in that profession. He continued to be interested in the theater, however, and wrote occasional articles for such periodicals as *Catholic World, Commonweal,* and the Pittsburgh *Courier.* For the past twenty years he has been theater critic for the magazine *America.* In addition, he was one of the original members (in the 1950s) of New York City's Commission on Human Rights. Interview, Theophilus Lewis.

CHAPTER 10
Notes

1. ALS., Zora Neale Hurston to Harper & Brothers, in the Hurston Collection, University of Florida Library. Quoted by permission of the Hurston family, Mrs. Marjorie Silver, and the University of Florida Library.
2. Hurston variously gave her birthdate as January 7, 1900, 1901, 1902, and 1903; no contemporary records were kept, but the 1903 date is the one given in a 1936 affadavit by her brother John, and the one she most often cited.
3. Zora Neale Hurston, *Dust Tracks on a Road* (New York, 1942), p. 71.
4. *Ibid.,* p. 176.
5. ALS., Zora Neale Hurston to Constance Sheen, January 5, [1926], in the University of Florida Hurston collection. Quoted by permission of the Hurston family, the University of Florida Library, and Mrs. Marjorie Silver.
6. ALS., Zora Neale Hurston to Constance Sheen, February 2, [1926], in Florida's Hurston collection. Quoted by same permission as above.
7. All quotations in this paragraph from *Dust Tracks,* pp. 177–79.
8. *Ibid.,* pp. 182–83.
9. *Ibid.,* p. 182.
10. ALS., Zora Neale Hurston to Franz Boas, December 14, 1934. In The American Philosophical Society Library. Quoted by permission of the Hurston family and The American Philosophical Society.
11. *The Stylus* (Howard University), I, (May 1921), p. 42.

12. *Fire*'s only issue was published in either December 1926 or January 1927. Countee Cullen, writing in *Opportunity* of January 1927, welcomes it as the "outstanding birth" of the month.
13. XII (October 1927), pp. 648–63.
14. Zora Neale Hurston, "The Florida Expedition," 3 pp., typescript, signed, in The American Philosophical Society Library. Quoted by permission of the Hurston family and The American Philosophical Society.
15. ALS., Zora Neale Hurston to Franz Boas, October 20, 1929, in The American Philosophical Society Library. Quoted by permission of the Hurston family and The American Philosophical Society.
16. ALS., Zora Neale Hurston to Langston Hughes, April 12, 1928, in the James Weldon Johnson Memorial Collection of Yale University's Beinecke Library. Quoted by permission of the Hurston family and Yale.
17. *Ibid.* Quoted with same permissions as above.
18. ALS., Zora Neale Hurston to Langston Hughes, March 8, 1928, in James Weldon Johnson Memorial Collection of Yale University's Beinecke Library. Quoted by permission of the Hurston family and Yale.
19. XLIII (July–October 1930), pp. 294–312.
20. XLIV (October–December 1931), pp. 317–417.
21. ALS., Zora Neale Hurston to Langston Hughes, August 6, 1928, in James Weldon Johnson Memorial Collection at Yale University's Beinecke Library. Quoted by permission of the Hurston family and Yale.
22. Application for Rosenwald Fellowship, December 14, 1934, in Fisk University Library's Rosenwald Collection.
23. "Author Plans to Upbraid Own Race," *New York World Telegram*, February 6, 1935.

CHAPTER 11
Notes

* The idea that Charles S. Johnson was the chief promoter of the Harlem Renaissance was first suggested to the writer by Mr. Arna Bontemps. The term "entrepreneur" as an explanation of this promotion was suggested by Professor Dewey W. Grantham, Jr., of Vanderbilt University. In addition, Dr. Jessie Carney Smith, Librarian at Fisk University; Dr. Raleigh A. Wilson, Archivist; Mrs. Ann Allen Shockley, Associate Librarian and Head of Special Collections; Mrs. Sue P. Chandler, Assistant Librarian in Special Collections; and the entire Fisk Library faculty and staff have gone far beyond the "call of duty" to facilitate this research in the rich archives for black history contained in the Special Collections at Fisk University.

1. Langston Hughes, *The Big Sea: An Autobiography* (New York:

Alfred A. Knopf, 1940), p. 218. (Hereinafter cited as Hughes, *The Big Sea.*)

2. Arna Bontemps, *100 Years of Negro Freedom* (New York: Dodd, Mead & Company, 1961), p. 229. (Hereinafter cited as Bontemps, *100 Years of Negro Freedom.*)
3. For example, see Ralph L. Pearson, "Charles S. Johnson: The Urban League Years. A Study of Race Leadership" (unpublished Ph.D. dissertation, The Johns Hopkins University, 1970); and Nancy Joan Weiss, " 'Not Alms, But Opportunity': A History of the National Urban League, 1910–1940" (unpublished Ph.D. dissertation, Harvard University, 1969). (Hereinafter cited as Pearson, "Charles S. Johnson: The Urban League Years," and Weiss, "A History of the Urban League.") Two dissertations in progress at this writing, listed with the American Historical Association, are John H. Bracey, Jr., "A Critical Study of Black Sociology: The Work of W. E. B. Du Bois, E. Franklin Frazier, and Charles S. Johnson," and Patrick J. Gilpin, "Charles S. Johnson and Race Relations: The Entrepreneur in Race Relations with Special Emphasis upon the Years at Fisk University."
4. The following discussion is based upon Bontemps, *100 Years of Negro Freedom,* pp. 222–34; Edwin R. Embree, *13 Against the Odds* (New York: The Viking Press, 1946), pp. 47–70 (hereinafter cited as Embree, *13 Against the Odds*): and Charles S. Johnson, "A Spiritual Autobiography," n.d. [1947?], Charles S. Johnson Papers, Special Collection, Fisk University (Hereinafter cited as Johnson Papers.)
5. Charles S. Johnson, "A Spiritual Autobiography," n.d. [1947?], p. 1. Johnson Papers. (Hereinafter cited as Johnson, "A Spiritual Autobiography.")
6. *Ibid.,* pp. 4, 9.
7. Embree, *13 Against the Odds,* pp. 55–7.
8. "Legalized" jim crow came to Virginia in 1900.
9. Johnson, "A Spiritual Autobiography," pp. 3–4.
10. *Ibid.,* p. 3.
11. *Ibid.,* pp. 3–4.
12. Pearson, "Charles S. Johnson: The Urban League Years," p. 54.
13. *Ibid.,* pp. 55–57.
14. V. D. Johnston, Review of *The Negro in Chicago: A Study of Race Relations and a Race Riot,* Report by the Chicago Commission on Race Relations, in *Opportunity: A Journal of Negro Life,* Vol. I, No. 1 (January 1923), p. 27. (Hereinafter cited as *Opportunity.*)
15. *Ibid.*
16. Pearson, "Charles S. Johnson: The Urban League Years," p. 62.
17. "How It Began," *Opportunity,* Vol. XXV, No. 4 (Fall issue, October–December 1947), p. 184.
18. Weiss, "A History of the Urban League," p. 337.

19. *Ibid.*, p. 349.
20. *The Negro in Chicago: A Study of Race Relations and a Race Riot,* Report by the Chicago Commission on Race Relations (Chicago: The University of Chicago Press, 1922), p. 436.
21. *Ibid.*
22. *Ibid.*, p. 437.
23. E. K. Jones, " 'Cooperation' and 'Opportunity,' " *Opportunity,* Vol. I, No. 1 (January 1923), p. 5.
24. "Why We Are," *Opportunity,* Vol. I, No. 2 (February 1923), p. 3.
25. Charles S. Johnson, Radio Talk Script, WEVD, August 24, 1928, announcing Charles S. Johnson's resignation as editor of *Opportunity.*
26. Charles S. Johnson, "The Negro Renaissance and Its Significance," in "The Speeches of Charles Spurgeon Johnson: Papers and Addresses Read at Conferences, Institutes, Societies, Clubs, Etc.," Vol. V, No. 28 (April 22, 1955); assembled by Fisk University Library, January 1959 (13 vols.; unpublished), p. 9. (Hereinafter cited as Johnson, "The Negro Renaissance and Its Significance.")
27. By 1919 *Crisis* already had reached a circulation of 104,000. *Opportunity*'s peak circulation in 1927 and 1928 was only 11,000. See Weiss, "A History of the Urban League," pp. 364–65.
28. See Bontemps, *100 Years of Negro Freedom,* p. 229.
29. *Ibid.*
30. Charles S. Johnson, "The Rise of the Negro Magazine," *Journal of Negro History,* Vol. XIII, No. 1 (January 1928), p. 15. In this article Charles S. Johnson contended that in *Crisis* "there was more than a tinge of personal journalism, subtler aspects of the problem were attacked, the race was defended rather than explained, agitation was justified editorially, and the reporting of incidents was fraught with a cold irony."
31. Weiss, "A History of the Urban League," p. 354.
32. "The Debut of the Younger School of Negro Writers," *Opportunity,* Vol. II, No. 17 (May 1924), pp. 143–44.
33. Quoted in Ethel Ray Nance, "The New York Arts Renaissance, 1924–1926," *Negro History Bulletin,* Vol. XXXI, No. 4 (April 1968), p. 16.
34. Johnson, "The Negro Renaissance and Its Significance," p. 3.
35. "Opportunity's Literary Prize Contest Awards," *Opportunity,* Vol. II, No. 21 (September 1924), p. 277.
36. *Ibid.*
37. "An Opportunity for Negro Writers," *ibid.,* Vol. II, No. 21 (September 1924), p. 258.
38. Johnson, "The Negro Renaissance and Its Significance," pp. 10–11.
39. *Ibid.*, p. 11.
40. "Opportunity's Prize Contest," *Opportunity,* Vol. II, No. 22 (October 1924), p. 291.

41. "The Donor of the Contest Prizes," *ibid.,* Vol. III, No. 25 (January 1925), p. 3.
42. "The Contest," *ibid.,* Vol. III, No. 28 (April 1925), p. 100.
43. "Pot-Pourri," *ibid.,* Vol. III, No. 30 (June 1925), p. 187.
44. "Contest Awards," *ibid.,* Vol. III, No. 29 (May 1925), pp. 142–43.
45. In the first two contests, Johnson thought that the dramatic division was less than excellent. See "On the Need of Better Plays," *ibid.,* Vol. V, No. 1 (January 1927), 5–6.
46. "The Opportunity Dinner," *ibid.,* Vol. III, No. 30 (June 1925), p. 176.
47. "The Contest," *ibid.,* Vol. III, No. 29 (May 1925), p. 131.
48. "Pot-Pourri," *ibid.,* Vol. III, No. 30 (June 1925), p. 187.
49. The following discussion is taken from "The Opportunity Dinner," *ibid.,* Vol. III, No. 30 (June 1925), pp. 176–77.
50. It is interesting to note that Holstein, unlike Leach, was black. Fifteen years later, Langston Hughes wrote of Holstein that he was "a wealthy West Indian numbers banker who did good things with his money." Although Hughes observed that Holstein may not have been accepted in polite Washington society, he "was doing decent and helpful things that it hadn't occurred to lots of others to do. Certainly he was a great help to poor poets." Hughes, *The Big Sea,* pp. 214–15.
51. *Ibid.,* pp. 215–16; "The Opportunity Dinner," *Opportunity,* Vol. III, No. 30 (June 1925), pp. 176–77.
52. "The Contest," *ibid.,* Vol. III, No. 34 (October 1925), p. 291.
53. *Ibid.,* pp. 291–92.
54. "Opportunity's Literary Record for 1925," *ibid.,* Vol. IV, No. 38 (February 1926), p. 38.
55. The following discussion is taken from "Contest Awards," *ibid.,* Vol. IV, No. 41 (May 1926), pp. 156–57.
56. "The Awards Dinner," *ibid.,* Vol. IV, No. 42 (June 1926), p. 186.
57. "Contest Awards," *ibid.,* Vol. IV, No. 41 (May 1926), pp. 156–57; "A Contest Number," *ibid.,* Vol. IV, No. 42 (June 1926), p. 173.
58. "Stories and Poetry of 1926," *ibid.,* Vol. V, No. 1 (January 1927), p. 5.
59. "The Third Opportunity Contest," *ibid.,* Vol. IV, No. 46 (October 1926), p. 304.
60. "The Contest for Negro Writers," *ibid.,* Vol. V, No. 4 (April 1927), p. 107.
61. "The Contest," *ibid.,* Vol. V, No. 6 (June 1927) p. 159.
62. "The Contest Spotlight," *ibid.,* Vol. V, No. 7 (July 1927), pp. 204–05, 213.
63. "The Opportunity Contest," *ibid.,* Vol. V, No. 9 (September 1927), p. 254.
64. "The Van Vechten Award," *ibid.,* Vol. VI, No. 1 (January 1928), p. 5.

65. "Art Fellowships," *ibid.,* Vol. V, No. 11 (November 1927), p. 321.
66. Charles S. Johnson was always careful to acknowledge the important role that Locke played. See, for example, Johnson, "The Negro Renaissance and Its Significance," and "The Opportunity Dinner," *Opportunity,* Vol. III, No. 30 (June 1925), pp. 176–77. Nor did Johnson overlook the significance of James Weldon Johnson and Carl Van Vechten. At mid-century Charles S. Johnson said, "Undoubtedly the literary work of Johnson laid the ground for the upsurge of young writers and artists in the early twenties, referred to as the 'Negro Renaissance.' Here again the two names [Johnson and Van Vechten] . . . were among the sturdiest supporters of this movement." See Charles S. Johnson, "Literature and the Practice of Living," in "The Speeches of Charles Spurgeon Johnson: Addresses at Colleges and Universities, 1929–1950," Vol. I, No. 28 (January 7, 1950); assembled by Fisk University Library, January 1959 (13 vols.; unpublished).
67. Quoted by Arna Bontemps in his Introduction to Langston Hughes, *Not Without Laughter* (New York: Collier Books Edition, 1969).
68. "Out of the Shadow," *Opportunity,* Vol. III, No. 29 (May 1925), p. 131.
69. *Ibid.*
70. The following discussion is taken from "On Writing About Negroes," *ibid.,* Vol. III, No. 32 (August 1925), pp. 227–28.
71. The following discussion is taken from "Some Perils of the 'Renaissance,' " *ibid.,* Vol. V, No. 3 (March 1927), p. 68; and from "A Note on the New Literary Movement," *ibid.,* Vol. IV, No. 39 (March 1926), pp. 80–81.
72. The following discussion is taken from Charles S. Johnson's Introduction to *Ebony and Topaz: A Collectanea* (New York: National Urban League, 1927), pp. 11–13; and from Johnson, "The Negro Renaissance and Its Significance," *passim.*
73. Johnson, "The Negro Renaissance and Its Significance," p. 8.
74. Letter from Thomas Elsa Jones to Charles S. Johnson, May 25, 1927. Thomas Elsa Jones Papers, Special Collection, Fisk University. (Hereinafter cited as T. E. Jones Papers.)
75. Letter from Thomas Elsa Jones to Eugene Kinckle Jones, May 31, 1927. T. E. Jones Papers.
76. Letter from Eugene Kinckle Jones to Thomas Elsa Jones, June 15, 1927. T. E. Jones Papers.
77. For example, see letter from Charles S. Johnson to Thomas Elsa Jones, July 25, 1927. T. E. Jones Papers.
78. Letter from Thomas Elsa Jones to Charles S. Johnson, August 9, 1927. T. E. Jones Papers.
79. Letter from Charles S. Johnson to Thomas Elsa Jones, September 28, 1927. T. E. Jones Papers.

80. Letter from Charles S. Johnson to Thomas Elsa Jones, February 8, 1928. T. E. Jones Papers.
81. Letter from Charles S. Johnson to Thomas Elsa Jones, March 13, 1928. T. E. Jones Papers.
82. Weiss, "A History of the Urban League," p. 363.
83. *Ibid.*, pp. 337, 349.
84. *Ibid.*, pp. 337, 363.
85. *Ibid.*, pp. 363–64.
86. Pearson, "Charles S. Johnson: The Urban League Years," p. 28, n. 45.
87. *Ibid.*, p. 263, n. 83; quoted in Weiss, "A History of the Urban League," p. 362.
88. Weiss, "A History of the Urban League," p. 365.
89. *Ibid.*, pp. 365–67.
90. Hughes, *The Big Sea*, p. 334.
91. See Robert L. Allen, *Black Awakening in Capitalist America: An Analytic History* (Garden City, N.Y.: Doubleday & Company, Inc., 1969); Harold Cruse, *The Crisis of the Negro Intellectual* (New York: William Morrow & Company, Inc., 1967); and also Harold Cruse's *Rebellion or Revolution* (New York: William Morrow & Company, Inc., 1968).
92. John O. Killens, "Another Time When Black Was Beautiful," *Black World*, Vol. XX, No. 1 (November 1970), p. 25.

CHAPTER 12
Notes

1. *The Crisis*, 31(1925), pp. 12–13.
2. James Weldon Johnson, ed., *The Book of American Negro Poetry* (New York, 1922; revised, 1931).
3. Countee Cullen, ed., *Caroling Dusk* (New York and London, 1927).
4. Sterling Brown, *Negro Poetry and Drama* (Washington, D.C., 1937).
5. Langston Hughes and Arna Bontemps, eds., *The Poetry of the Negro, 1746–1949* (New York, 1949; revised, 1970).
6. Sterling Brown, "The New Negro in Literature (1925–1955)," in *The New Negro Thirty Years Afterwards* (Division of Social Sciences, Howard University Press, 1955).
7. See Vincent Harding's discussion of "significant, identifiable black responses to religion which often stormed beyond submissiveness to defiance" ("Religion and Resistance Among Antebellum Negroes, 1800–1860" in *The Making of Black America*, eds. August Meier and Elliott Rudwick, New York, 1969, Vol. I, pp. 179–97). See also Gary T. Marx, "Religion: Opiate or Inspiration of Civil Rights Militancy Among Negroes?" in Meier and Rudwick, Vol. II, pp. 362–75.
8. *The Crisis*, 72(1965), pp. 646–47.
9. *The Crisis*, 73(1966), p. 9.

10. *The Crisis,* 77(1970), pp. 403–04.
11. Quotations from poems that follow can be found in Hughes and Bontemps' *The Poetry of the Negro, 1746–1949* (New York, 1949; revised, 1970), Bontemps' *American Negro Poetry* (New York, 1963) and James Weldon Johnson's *The Book of American Negro Poetry* (New York 1922; revised 1931).

CHAPTER 13

Notes

1. Alain Locke, *New Negro* (New York, Atheneum, 1969), p. 14.
2. *Ibid.,* pp. 8–9.
3. *Ibid.,* p. 15.
4. *Ibid.,* p. 11.
5. *Ibid.,* p. 12.
6. *Ibid.,* p. 10.
7. *Ibid.,* p. 9.
8. Langston Hughes, "The Negro Artist and the Racial Mountain," *The Nation,* Vol. 122, (1926) pp. 692–94.
9. *Ibid.,* pp. 692–94.

Bibliography

Bone, Robert A., *The Negro Novel in America* (New Haven: Yale University Press, 1958).

Bontemps, Arna, "Harlem and Renaissance of the Twenties," *Black World* (November 1970).

Clarke, John Henrik, ed., *Harlem: A Community in Transition* (New York: Citadel Press, 1964).

Cruse, Harold, *The Crisis of the Negro Intellectual* (New York: Apollo Editions, 1968).

Locke, Alain, *The New Negro* (New York: Atheneum, 1969).

Meier, August, *Negro Thought in America 1880–1915* (Ann Arbor, Michigan: University of Michigan Press, 1963).

Index